COLUMBIA UNIVERSITY
STUDIES IN THE
SOCIAL SCIENCES

160

This Series was formerly known as
Studies in History, Economics and Public Law

THE BOXER REBELLION

A Political and Diplomatic Review

AMS PRESS
NEW YORK

STUDIES IN HISTORY, ECONOMICS AND PUBLIC LAW

EDITED BY THE FACULTY OF POLITICAL SCIENCE
OF COLUMBIA UNIVERSITY

Volume LXVI]   [Number 3

Whole Number 160

THE BOXER REBELLION

A Political and Diplomatic Review

BY

PAUL H. CLEMENTS

AMS Press, Inc.

New York

1967

Library of Congress Cataloging in Publication Data

Clements, Paul Henry, 1884-
    The Boxer rebellion.

    Reprint of the 1915 ed. published by Columbia Uni-
versity, New York, which was issued as v. 66, no. 3 of
Studies in istory, economics, and public law.
    Originally presented as the author's thesis, Columbia
University, 1915.
    Bibliography: p.
    Includes index.
    1. China—History—1900.   2. Boxers.   3. China—
Foreign relations.   I. Title.   II. Series: Columbia
studies in the social sciences; no. 160.
DS771.C6   1979   951.04   79-15870
ISBN 0-404-51160-0

Reprinted from the edition of 1915, New York.
First AMS edition published in 1967.
Second AMS printing: 1979.

Manufactured in the United States of America

AMS PRESS, INC.
NEW YORK, N.Y.

To

MY FATHER AND MOTHER

PREFACE

THE present volume comprises an examination into the causes of the Box Rebellion and its international complications, and a discussion of the Joint Note of 1900 and the Peace Protocol of 1901, whereby relations between China and the world were again established on an amicable basis. There need be no apology for contributing an additional work to the literature on this fascinating period of history. When the circumstances and results of this remarkable exhibition of wrath against the outside world are fully considered and appreciated, it can be realized how, at one stroke, entirely unforeseen by critics of the day, it shook China out of the sleep of centuries, revolutionized the history and politics of a race possessing great inherent possibilities, and formed the background, the cause, in fact, of momentous events which are taking place in the Far East to-day and the ultimate trend of which it is impossible to foretell. As the period of Chinese history under discussion, from 1895 to 1902, occupies a unique place in international politics and diplomacy, the author has carefully examined as source the invaluable British " Blue Books " dealing with the affairs of China; the reports and correspondence of the Department of State respecting the foreign relations of the United States, as well as numerous treaties, notes and declarations found elsewhere.

The author desires to acknowledge the invaluable assistance of Professor John Bassett Moore, who, at great sacrifice of time, went over the entire work with him; and to Professor Edwin R. A. Seligman for his instruction and advice in preparing the volume for the press. Acknowledgment is also due to Professors Ellery C. Stowell, Friedrich Hirth, and James Harvey Robinson for their many kindly criticisms and suggestions. It may be added that the studies of the author were first encouraged and directed into the Far Eastern field by his friend, Professor Amos S. Hershey, of Indiana University.   P. H. C.

COLUMBIA UNIVERSITY IN THE CITY OF NEW YORK, JULY, 1915.

CONTENTS

421]   9

PART II

THE INTERNATIONAL COMPLICATIONS OF THE BOXER REBELLION

PART III

THE RESTORATION OF ORDER AND THE PEACE PROTOCOL OF
SEPTEMBER 7, 1901

APPENDIX

PART I

CAUSES OF THE BOXER REBELLION

PART I

CAUSES OF THE REBELLION

THE Boxer Rebellion may be regarded as the culmination
of misunderstandings between China and the Powers in
every phase of international activity. It was the last, the
supreme, the most desperate effort of all to keep the Middle
Kingdom riveted to the standards of antiquity, and its failure, complete in every respect, even from the viewpoint of
the Chinese themselves, made possible and inevitable the
China of to-day.

A detailed examination of the causes, immediate and remote, of this final protest against western civilization would
demand an exhaustive review of Chinese institutions, character and customs entirely beyond the scope of this volume,
an examination leading back at least to the days of Confucius. A brief outline, however, may be given in passing.

showing how contributory events, one piled upon the other, at last brought about this racial cataclysm, with consequences so momentous and far-reaching that they could not be understood at the time, much less fully appreciated. In effect, the Boxer Rebellion, through the very completeness and humiliation of its failure, made possible the future position of China as a real member of the sisterhood of nations; this, however, at a heart-breaking cost, involving a shock to the national consciousness such as stands without parallel in history.

The Chinese had not always been isolated from the rest of mankind. Before the Manchu conquest in the XVIIth century there had been quite an extensive though spasmodic commercial intercourse with the west and a slight acquaintance with western culture. The products of China had been interchanged with those of the Roman Empire; Chinese engineers had been employed on the construction of public works in Persia; Buddhism had been introduced from India; a Chinese army had penetrated as far west as the Caspian region; Marco Polo and his two uncles had found a flattering welcome; the Jesuits had flourished at Peking; the Nestorian Tablet had been erected, a mute reminder to-day of what the current of history might have been; and the first embassies from Europe had been graciously received, provided they kowtowed. By such means a healthy curiosity toward the outside world had been occasionally stimulated. But, on the other hand, the Chinese had already developed to a great extent that exclusiveness characteristic of them up to the close of the last century. Nor is this to be wondered at, for such was the inevitable resultant of their past history, national ideals and environment.

Surrounded by tribes in a savage or semi-civilized state, which were greatly inferior from every point of view, it is not surprising that the Chinese should have looked upon these as barbarians, fitly to be designated by the radical for dog. Furthermore, a vast expanse of desert and mountain and sea made intercourse with the advanced parts of the world extremely hazardous and uncertain, all the more so when the favorite land routes were cut off by the fall of Constantinople and the ascendancy of the Seljuk Turks in western Asia. Moreover, the occasional exchanges of goods and ideas with European nations had been too small in volume appreciably to affect the Chinese race or to influence its development. Yet these little beginnings, if carefully fostered, might have led to greater things, and such undoubtedly would have been the case had it not been for the rigid policy of seclusion adopted by the alien Manchu monarchs, the greatest misfortune, considering that age of world expansion, which China could have suffered. Although in this the Manchus only copied the preceding Ming dynasty, yet the XVIIth century was not the century for the continuance of such a state policy, and therein lay the evil, to be accentuated all the more in the years to come.

The Manchurian conquerors of one of the most favored regions of the globe were not slow in realizing that, being relatively few in numbers, it was to their interest, as overlords of an intelligent and law-abiding though passive race constituting one-fourth of the human family, to close all avenues of approach from outside, to interdict all efforts at change, to seal the country so that a repetition of their own exploit, or disaffection with their own rule resulting from outside influences, would be impossible. In other words, it was the policy of the Manchu monarchs to keep the ideas of the country as they found them, *in statu quo*, and to prevent any expansion of these ideas either from without or from within. Thus the innate conservatism of the Chinese was immeasurably increased, thus antiquity was lauded as the only period of Chinese history worth while, thus the sages were exalted as the teachers of wisdom such as had never been heard since and never would be heard again by mortal man. Thus a careful watch was kept on all the frontiers; intercourse with Europe was practically prohibited, and humiliating concessions were demanded of the few embassies and traders who braved the discouraging conditions of entry. Thus by degrees the inherent prejudices of the Chinese were encouraged, generation after generation, through a monotonous repetition of this deadening policy, all the more successful as it emanated from the " Son of Heaven ", until was reached that stage of overweening national conceit and that dense, impenetrable ignorance of the outside world, unmoved by reason or fact or experience, which may be described as the antithesis of western progress and enlightenment.

Nor was the renewed contact with Europeans, from the XVIth century onward, at all likely to change the preconceived opinions of them on the part of the Chinese. Instead of being advance agents of a higher, or at least a more universal civilization, the early representatives from the Occident could not have been better chosen to harden in the Chinese mind all of the previous mistaken impressions. First in 1506 arrived the " Falanki " (Franks) at Canton, " and by their tremendously loud guns shook the place far and near ". About contemporaneously with these marauders came the Hollanders, who " inhabited a wild territory ", whose " feet were one cubit and two-tenths long ", and whose " strange appearance frightened the people ".[1] Next arrived the Portuguese in 1516, to ruin by their execrable conduct what promised to be a fair beginning. A like series of disreputable acts brought failure to the Spaniards, whose

---

[1] From a Chinese account, quoted by Douglas, *Europe and the Far East* (Cambridge, 1904; rev. ed., New York, 1913), p. 10.

outrages resulted in swift retaliation, twenty-three of their embassy suffering the " lingering death ". With the exception of the Russian missions of 1689 and after, and the British in 1793 and 1816, these determined efforts of Europe, exerted primarily, so it seemed, not for the establishment of friendly relations with China but for selfish purposes of gain by fair means or foul, were those of " pirates rather than peaceably disposed men ", whose methods of dealing with the Chinese, directly opposite to what they should have been, " went far to justify the Chinese Government in its policy of rigid seclusion from all associations with Europeans ".[1] Either, like the Dutch mission of 1656, they groveled for favors contemptuously doled out to them,[2] or they appeared in the faintly concealed guise of punitive expeditions, harrying the coast and committing every act of brigandage and uncivilized warfare, such as burning, killing, rapine and robbery, upon the defenceless inhabitants. That atavistic modes of thought were indelibly fixed in the minds of the Chinese by such a course of action on the part of European governments and people is not strange. Neither can the Chinese be blamed for condemning the whole world alike, for by these examples, each almost a repetition of the other, they were forced to place all nations in the same category. Thus, primarily the fault of Europe, all efforts to establish commercial relations with China proved futile until the country was partially opened by England in 1840, through the agency of the Opium war.[3]

[1] Holcomb, *China's Past and Future* (London, —), p. 108.

[2] For like Dutch experiences in Japan and at the Deshima " factory," see Foster, *American Diplomacy in the Orient* (Boston, 1903), pp. 12-16.

[3] For original sources on the early embassies preceding the Opium war, see Johan Nieuhof, *L'Ambassade de la Compagnie Orientale. des Provinces Unis vers l'Empereur de la Chine . . . fait par P. de Goyer*

Whatever may be said of the morality of England's act in waging this particular war, the fact remains that by such means, after diplomacy had completely failed,[1] China was at last forced into definite trade relations with the world, and that, through the sacrifice of British blood and treasure, other nations were enabled equally to participate in the advantages thus wrung from China. The Chinese, totally

et Jac de Keyser, trans. into French by J. de Carpentier (London, 1665), and an English trans. by John Ogilby (2d ed., London, 1673); Adam Brand, *Journal of the Embassy from Muscovy into China, 1693-'95*, trans. from High-Dutch by W. H. Ludolf (London, 1698); E. Y. Ides, *From Moscow Overland to China* (London, 1706); Æneas Anderson, *A Narrative of the British Embassy to China in the Years 1792, 1793 and 1794* (London, 1795); Houckgeest A. E. van Braam, *Authentic Account of the Embassy of the Dutch East India Company to China, 1794-'95*, trans. from the French of L. E. Moreau de Saint-Mery, 2 vol. (London, 1798); Sir. G. L. Staunton, *Authentic Account of the Embassy to the Emperor of China, undertaken by Order of the King of Great Britain* . . . *taken principally from the Papers of Earl Macartney* (London, 1797); Henry Ellis, *Journal of the Late Embassy to China* (*Amherst Mission*), 2 vol. (London, 1818); George Timkowski, *Travels of the Russian Mission through Mongolia to China and Residence in Peking in the Years 1820, 1821*, trans. into English by H. E. Lloyd, 2 vol. (London, 1827); Edmund Roberts, *Embassy to the Eastern Courts of Cochin-China, Siam and Muscat, in the U. S. Sloop-of-War Peacock, 1832-'34* (New York, 1837). See also Mrs. Helen Henrietta Robbins, *Our First Ambassador to China, an Account of the Life of George, Earl of Macartney, with Extracts from his Letters, and the Narrative of his Experiences, as told by himself* (London, 1908).

Other accounts of early embassies and dealings with China are found in Sir John Davis, *The Chinese* (New York, 1857); A. Delano, *Narrative of Voyages* (Boston, 1857); Sir Robert K. Douglas, *Europe and the Far East*; John W. Foster, *American Diplomacy in the Orient*; Charles Gutzlaff, *History of China*, 2 vol. (New York, 1834); Walter A. P. Martin, *Cycle of Cathay* (New York, 1906); S. Wells Williams, *The Middle Kingdom*, 2 vol., rev. ed. (New York, 1907).

[1] The imposing embassy under Lord Napier in 1834 was the last diplomatic effort of Great Britain before the Opium war to arrive at a peaceful understanding with the Peking Court. With its failure Great Britain resorted to military force as the last argument.

defeated, and unable further to stem the advance of international relations and commerce, concluded peace with
Great Britain under heavy penalties,[1] and later extended like
privileges of trade to the United States and France.[2]

[1] By the treaty of Nanking, August 19, 1842, concluding the Opium
war, China agreed to open five ports to foreign trade, these five original
"treaty ports" being Canton, Amoy, Foochow, Ningpo and Shanghai.
In addition the island of Hong Kong was ceded in perpetuity and a
war indemnity of $21,000,000 paid by China, which included within that
sum the damages for British opium destroyed at Canton in 1839 by the
famous Commissioner Lin. A regular tariff was established, and it
was agreed that henceforth all diplomatic intercourse between the two
nations was to be conducted on a basis of absolute equality.

[2] The United States was fortunate in securing probably the most
expert man in America for these negotiations, Caleb Cushing, a successful lawyer, later Attorney-General (his opinions while occupying
that office still being quoted as authority, especially as regards consuls),
a skilled diplomat and a brilliant personality readily adaptable to the
intricacies of dealing with the Oriental mind. As a result of his
talents, the American treaty contained sixteen more provisions than
the British treaty of two years previous, anl also a far clearer embodi-
ment of the principle of extra-territoriality.

It seems quite the fashion with some writers, when comparing
Cushing's treaty of Wang-hia with the treaty of Nanking, to disparage
the latter and unduly praise the former. In this regard it must be
remembered that England was dealing with a defeated enemy granting
concessions only at the sword's point; moreover, had it not been for
England's successful conduct of the war, Cushing's mission in all
probability would have been a total failure.

For President Tyler's comprehensive report on affairs with the Far
East at this time, which report was written by Webster in his capacity
as Secretary of State, see Richardson, *Messages and Papers of the
Presidents,* 10 vol. (Washington, 1896), vol. 4, pp. 213, 214. For the act
of Congress of March 3, 1842, appropriating $40,000 for the purpose
of establishing commercial relations between China and the United
States on a treaty basis, see 5 *U. S. Stat.,* 624; John Bassett Moore,
A Digest of International Law, 8 vol. (Washington, 1906), vol. 5,
p. 416. The full text of Webster's instructions to Cushing is found
in *Webster's Works,* vol. 6, p. 467, and in part in Moore's *Digest,* vol.
5, pp. 416, 417.

Tyler's unique letter to the Emperor of China is given in Foster,
op. cit., p. 82, and in United States 28th Congress, 2d Session, *Senate*

The Opium war begins a new epoch in the relations of China with the Powers, a period which may roughly be estimated as extending from 1840 to 1895, marked on one side by the unreasoning hostility of China to everything foreign and on the other side by constant aggressions of Europe, these aggressions, however, still tempered by a belief in and respect for China's latent military power and the prestige naturally accorded to so vast an empire.

But it was not to be expected that, through the defeats of a single war, China would or even could have reversed the policy and habits of centuries. In fact, there was little to show at the time that the war of 1840 had resulted in any material or moral benefit. The opening of the treaty ports was delayed, on the ground that they were " unsafe " for foreigners, and the same offensive tactics and thousand petty exactions were religiously adhered to by China as before the first international conflict. Only in the payment of the indemnity to England did China act with any degree of celerity, and then for the sole purpose of ridding certain Chinese territories of British troops, who were quartered upon the land until such payment was forthcoming. Government and people were united in the common cause of opposition to all demands of the foreign Powers. The Peking Court, following the customary practice of Oriental nations, pursued a policy of masterly inactivity coupled with a contemptuous disregard for treaty stipulations, although it must be admitted that China was as yet unacquainted with international law and the binding qualities of

Documents, no. 139. Another version, slightly differing in detail, is found in Williams' *Middle Kingdom,* vol. 2, pp. 565, 566. Says Williams concerning this letter, *op. cit.,* p. 565: " Caleb Cushing . . . brought a letter . . . which is inserted in full as an instance of the singular mixture of patronizing and deprecatory address then deemed suitable for the Grand Khan by western nations."

formal agreements. Especially was China unacquainted with agreements imposed through the agency of force. The great Taiping Rebellion, inspired by the disappointed scholar Hung Sui-tsuen, who had failed in his attempts at advance standing among the *literati*, furnished another element of uncertainty and disorder.[1] Trade was paralyzed, merchants complained; all was confusion. It was plain that further corrective punishment was necessary, and this finally came in 1857, indirectly through the accumulation of grievances and abuses ever since 1842, directly on account of the indignity to the supposedly British *lorcha* "Arrow".

France and Great Britain joined forces in the sharp and decisive struggle which followed. It was soon over, but again China misjudged the trend of international events. A supplementary punitive expedition in 1860, as the last argument of the exasperated Allies, struck at the very heart of the Chinese Government, burned the Summer Palace, drove the Court into hasty flight, and by these drastic measures gained that final step in diplomacy for which Europe had been laboring for centuries, namely, representation at Peking and recognition of equality.

A period of comparative international tranquility followed, one phase of which was the unique Burlingame mission in 1868 to the United States and Europe.[2] It seemed that China at last understood the impossibility of keeping foreigners out of the Middle Kingdom, and that the attempt

[1] The Taiping Rebellion is interesting from an international point of view as several times Europe was on the verge of recognizing the rebels. But sympathy for the movement soon changed to disgust at the lawless character and impossible claims of the revolutionary government, which finally collapsed through the victories of the Imperial troops led by Generals Ward and Gordon.

[2] For a sympathetic treatment of Burlingame and his career, see F. W. Williams, *Anson Burlingame and the First Chinese Mission to Foreign Powers* (New York, 1912).

to refuse all diplomatic and commercial intercourse with the rest of the world could be henceforth hardly more than a Utopian dream, a condition of the past never again to be realized. Therefore to all outward appearances China made the best of the unwelcome situation and, barring a desultory war with France over Tongking in 1885, remained on fairly good terms with the rest of mankind until 1894-95.

Nevertheless, the outbreak at the close of the last century revealed conclusively that ever since 1842, though outwardly acquiescent, China never forgave nor forgot, and that when the supreme moment should come, as it was judged to have come in 1900, in it would be expressed to the fullest measure the "concentrated wrath and hate of sixty years".[1] Defeated with monotonous regularity by Europe, forced at the cannon's mouth to conform to a mass of new and bewildering and in their eyes onerous treaty stipulations, none of which they desired, at no time had the Chinese met the Powers in a mutuality of interests. The Burlingame peace mission was an episode in itself, inspired by the idealism of one man, and may be regarded as entirely detached from the general current of Chinese politics. Though gifted with a vision of the future, Burlingame was fifty years ahead of his time, and his ideas regarding China's relations with the rest of the world were impossible of realization in his day as each country had to learn by bitter experience the lessons which culminated in the establishment of the Far Eastern Republic.

A further fact to be noted is, that by successfully weathering the great Taiping Rebellion, the Manchu monarchy gained a new lease on life, and, gradually increasing in power, by 1895 seemed strong enough to last indefinitely.

---

[1] Holcomb, *Outlook,* 1904, p. 407.

Consistent in its opposition to the foreigner and foreign relations, with the exception of the first two emperors of the dynasty, this recovery of power in the monarchy meant that the policy of closing the country would become stronger than ever, coupled as it was with the instincts of self-preservation; and that, once sure of its ground, the Peking Court would not hesitate to throw down the gauntlet to united Europe if necessary. It was the war with Japan that brought matters to a climax, revealed China's rottenness to the world, struck a blow at royalty comparable only to the disasters of 1860, and hastened the inevitable conflict with the Powers, a struggle which, considering all events, was bound to come sooner or later, and the surprise was that it so soon followed the humiliation of 1895.

Contrary to the general impression, the Chino-Japanese war cannot be called a national conflict in so far as China was concerned. Strictly speaking, it was regarded as an affair of the Manchu régime; its disasters were their disasters, its mistakes their mistakes. Also, the war was principally fought in a region foreign to the " Eighteen Provinces ", the invading Japanese for the most part entering, not China proper, but the dependency of Manchuria, the ancestral home of the reigning dynasty, and which the latter alone in duty were bound to defend. Therefore the Chinese considered themselves removed from all responsibility, and persisted in viewing the conflict as an incident of the Manchu foreign policy of no intimate concern to any but the Manchus. A like analogy to this somewhat curious reasoning was revealed a decade later when the Russian bureaucracy, not the Russian people, was supposed to have engaged Japan in this identical region. Of course, had both wars been successful instead of dismal failures, the train of reasoning in both instances would have been precisely the opposite in the case of all those affected. Thus the apparent lack of patriotism in both countries is afforded an easy and convenient explanation, as an unfortunate situation in which the governments were involved, but not the people. Granting the above weak argument, why should the Chinese have cared much about the unexpected turn of events? As a matter of fact, the mass of them did not care; they remained indifferent, aloof, almost neutral, one might say. It was not the war itself which in the main contributed to the cyclonic frenzy of a few years later. It was the consequences of that war, the revelation of the weakness of China to the world, the fastening of the stupendous indemnity, by which Japan realized a hundred per cent profit, upon the people at large, who thus had to pay a heavy price for Manchu folly; and, above all, the territorial loot of the Empire by Europe following the intervention at Chefoo. These staggering results in turn were among the causes of the catastrophe of 1900.

In order fully to understand the position of the European Powers in regard to the Far East at the time of the Boxer Rebellion, it will be necessary to sketch their territorial aggressions in China during the years immediately preceding the conflict. Of all immediate causes of this last upheaval of China against the Occident, these aggressions were the most important factor. Had they never occurred, it is doubtful whether there would have been a rebellion. To Europe's land-greed this sorry page of history is primarily due; and more than that, furnished the example and excuse for a series of recent events so effectively limiting China's sovereignty and integrity that even to-day the ultimate consequences cannot be foreseen.

After the intervention of Russia, France and Germany at Chefoo in 1895 on China's behalf, for which China well knew there would be a heavy reckoning in the near future, Russia was the first to show her hand. This, however, was done in a friendly manner and with perfect diplomacy, through the floating of a 4 percent loan of 400,000,000 francs at 94⅛ payable in thirty-six years, without security, the Czar himself guaranteeing the interest by royal ukase.[1] This unexampled generosity enabled China to liquidate half the war indemnity to Japan. The next step of Russia was to " facilitate the execution of the loan ", which was the ostensible purpose of founding the Russo-Chinese Bank with its thirty branches throughout Siberia and the Far East.[2] The bank proved of immense service to Russia as it was a desirable and necessary screen for demands on China, which demands, though seemingly obtained for this corporation, supposedly a private one, were in reality granted to the Imperial Russian Government through this convenient agency. The climax of early Russian concessions was revealed by the unauthorized publication of an agreement known as the Cassini Convention, the first part of which dealt primarily with railway and mining grants and the second with unusual privileges accorded Russia in Manchuria. Most significant of all was the provision that, as Russia " has never possessed a seaport in Asia which is free from ice and open the year around ", China was " willing " to lease the port of Kiaochau (Tsingtao) for fifteen years (Art. I). Russia was also to help fortify Port Arthur and Talienwan (Dalny, now called Dairen by the

[1] For the negotiations of M. Witte, Russian Minister of Finance, with Hottinguer and Co. and other French bankers, see Henri Cordier, *Histoire des Rélations de la Chine avec les Puissances Occidentales,* 3 vol. (Paris, 1902), vol. 3, pp. 304-308.

[2] See Kanichi Asakawa, *The Russo-Japanese Conflict* (New York, 1904), p. 85, from " Statutes of the Bank," published Dec. 8, 1896, in a Japanese source, the *Tokushu Joyaku,* pp. 642-660.

See W. W. Rockhill, *Treaties and Conventions with or concerning China and Korea, 1894-1904* (Washington, 1904), pp. 207-211, for " Charter of the Russo-Chinese Bank," Dec. 10, 1895, Engl. version.

Japanese), and was not to "permit any other foreign Power to encroach upon them", while China bound herself "never to cede them to another country " (Art. X).[1] But in obtaining these far-reaching concessions the Russian diplomats failed to take into account the tremendous uproar which Europe surely would raise and certainly did raise when the alleged Russian advantages appeared in the *North China Herald*. This convinced Russia that she had gone too far, and the existence of the Cassini Convention was flatly denied both by Russia and by China. By this simple expedient the agitation in Europe was quieted; and, Russian diplomacy having suffered a decided setback in the Far East, matters rested for a while, and Russia concerned herself only with building the Eastern Chinese Railway under an agreement obtained through the subsidiary Russo-Chinese Bank.

European spoliation of China was soon reopened, from an unexpected quarter, and it was Germany who gave Russia, and all the world for that matter, a practical illustration of how to deal with China regarding leases and concessions. Germany herself had looked longingly upon Kiaochau, and the reported leasing of that harbor to Russia through the Cassini Convention, though quickly repudiated, yet prompted Germany to action. An admirable pretext soon came in the murder of two German missionaries in the province of Shantung, where Kiaochau was located. Germany at once struck with the mailed fist. A naval expedition, despatched in all haste to Kiaochau, expelled the Chinese garrison, seized the port, and raised the

---

[1] The text of the Cassini Convention is given in Weale, *Re-Shaping of the Far East,* 2 vol. (London, 1905), vol. 2, p. 439, and Beveridge, *Russian Advance* (New York, 1904), p. 469. A French version is found in Cordier, *op. cit.,* vol. iii, pp. 343-347; also in *Revue Générale de Droit Internationale Public,* vol. xii, 1905, note to pp. 226-228.

German flag to the salute of twenty-one guns and three cheers for the Kaiser. Then began the tortuous negotiations with the Chinese Foreign Office, the Tsung-li Yamen, from the date when they first met " to consider this seizure of territory by a friendly Power ", to the time when China was forced to give way. Baron von Heyking, German Minister at Peking, finally announced to the world that Germany had received a lease of Kiaochau (city of Tsingtao and Kiaochau Bay) for ninety-nine years, preferential treatment in Shantung, railway and mining grants, and indemnity for the murdered missionaries. All this on account of the death of two priests of whom the German Government had never before heard.[1]

Russia in particular was much impressed [2] by the German action and immediately arranged to do likewise, but with far greater tact. Conceding Germany's right to Kiaochau, after an extensive correspondence between Berlin and St. Petersburg, Russia transferred her activities elsewhere, and soon had " permission " to winter her fleet at Port Arthur. To allay Japanese apprehensions, Russia

[1] The treaty for the lease of Kiaochau is given in British Parliamentary Papers, *China No. 1 (1899)*, Inclosure in no. 66, reprinted from the *Reichsanzeiger* of April 29, 1898; also in United States *For. Rel.*, 1898, Inclosure in no. 2884, pp. 187-190; Weale, *op. cit.*, vol. ii, pp. 455-459; Cordier, *op. cit.*, vol. iii, pp. 357-361; Alexis Krausse, *The Far East: Its History and its Question*, 2d ed. (London, 1903), pp. 344-346.

[2] So was Great Britain. Notice the following appreciation of the German action by the London *Times* of November 16, 1897:

" Instead of wasting time in making remonstrances at Peking, which would assuredly have been met as usual by the innumerable dilatory devices of Chinese diplomacy, the Germans have landed a force in Kiao-chou Bay, in order to bring to bear the only kind of influence that Chinamen seem able to understand . . . The experiment is one which we ourselves have tried on one or more occasions, with results so excellent as compared with any obtainable by diplomatic negotiation that there is reason to wonder why we do not always follow the more effectual method."

notified the Japanese Government that " Port Arthur had
been lent to Russia only temporarily as a winter anchor-
age ", and Japan replied that she " credited this assurance ".[1]   The British also were disinclined at first to oppose
Russian attempts to gain a satisfactory Far Eastern harbor,
doubtless as an added precaution at that time for Constantinople.   In fact, Mr. Balfour went so far as to say that
" we had always looked with favor upon the idea of Russia
obtaining an ice-free harbor on the Pacific ".[2]   It was not
that which alarmed England and later caused a sharp diplomatic struggle ending in British defeat, but, as the Marquis
of Salisbury expressed it: " The Russian Government had
now given a most unfortunate extension to this policy ",
by which Lord Salisbury meant the three Russian demands
which were being made on China, as follows:

I. The lease of Port Arthur.

II. The lease of Talienwan (Dalny).

III. The construction of a railroad to Port Arthur and
Talienwan, connecting either city with the Russian lines,
and thus making either one a terminus of the Great Siberian
Railway.

These demands were, of course, quite an elaboration of
the original innocent desire for an ice-free harbor.

Encouraged by England, China endeavored to persuade
Russia to consider the question of Port Arthur and Talienwan separately, but was peremptorily informed that the
lease of both places must be granted before March 27,
1898, " failing which, Russia would take hostile measures ".[3]   China delayed until the last day, then signed the

[1] *China No. 1* (*1898*), no. 29.

[2] *Ibid.,* no. 101.

[3] *Ibid.,* no. 126.

convention ceding Port Arthur and Talienwan, as well as the adjacent waters, " in usufruct " to Russia for twenty-five years, with the privilege of renewal if mutually agreeable.[1]   The Russian press, which means particularly the *Novoe Vremya,* was jubilant over this " new and undoubted diplomatic disaster to Lord Salisbury's Government ".[2]   In this the *Novoe Vremya* was quite right.   All that Great Britain had succeeded in accomplishing after a prolonged diplomatic struggle was to put her objections " on record ". Germany was silenced because of the Kiaochau affair ; France was Russia's ally, therefore her friend.   Japan received the disquieting news in ominous silence, which alone should have been enough to forewarn Russia.   All outward expressions of opposition to Russia in Japanese military and diplomatic circles remained practically unspoken, carefully concealed, to pour out in a resistless flood at the appointed time.

As the occupation of Port Arthur by Russia, not for commerce but as a fortified naval base, was held to " disturb the balance of power " in north China, the British began to press the Yamen for the lease of Weihaiwei, directly opposite from the Russian acquisition.   A short time before, Great Britain had declined the offer of this identical port on the praiseworthy ground that the Foreign Office aimed at " discouraging any alienation of Chinese territory ". This, however, with the reservation that the " existing position " would not be " materially altered by the action of

[1] U. S. *For. Rel.,* 1898, pp. 184, 186; " Précis " in *China No. 1 (1899),* no. 187, pp. 127-129; Asakawa, *op. cit.,* pp. 130, 131 ; Beveridge, *op. cit.,* pp. 118, 119 ; Cordier, *op. cit.,* vol. iii, pp. 362-364; Krausse, *op. cit.,* pp. 349, 350; Rockhill, *op. cit.,* pp. 50-52 ; Weale, *op. cit.,* vol. ii, pp. 459-462.

[2] *Novoe Vremya* of March 21 (April 2), 1898; trans. in *China No. 1 (1899),* Inclosure in no. 14.

other Powers ".[1]   Such an unusual attitude could not have been expected to last in Far Eastern diplomacy, and, as it was soon discovered that Russia had subjected the above " existing position " to a " rude shock ", Downing Street considered itself released from the above rather odd declaration.   But to palliate matters, Sir Claude MacDonald, British Minister at Peking, announced that England was at Weihaiwei solely to preserve the balance of power, and that England " would give it up to-morrow " if Russia would evacuate Port Arthur.   Little difficulty was experienced in persuading China beyond " wearisome discussions " over minor details, and as soon as the Japanese stepped out the British stepped in, on terms " similar to those granted to Russia for Port Arthur ".[2]

The Germans were not interested in England's new possession.   To them it was " a matter of indifference which flag floats over Weihaiwei ", but they pointed out that the British action " implies a change for the worse in the relations between Russia and England " (*Norddeutsche Zeitung*).[3]   This proved true, and Russia brought all possible pressure to bear upon China to prevent the port from falling into British hands, but was unsuccessful.   The Japanese, on their part, were only too glad to have a friendly power take their place and thus offer a welcome counterpart to Russian aggression.   It may be noted that, although

[1] *China No. 1 (1898)*, nos. 90, 91.

[2] U. S. *For. Rel.*, 1898, p. 190; *China No. 1 (1899)*, p. 199; Rockhill, *op. cit.*, pp. 60, 61. For Great Britain's " formal " declaration to Germany, " that in establishing herself at Wei-hai Wei, she has no intention of injuring or contesting the rights and interests of Germany in the province of Shantung, or of creating difficulties for her in that province," see Rockhill, *op. cit.*, p. 180; *China No. 1, (1899)*, pp. 27-31.

[3] *Norddeutsche Zeitung* of April 6, 1898. These comments first appeared in the *Kölnische Zeitung*, and were reproduced in the Berlin newspapers. See trans. in *China No. 1 (1899)*, no. 12 and Inc.

Weihaiwei was occupied on the pretext of preserving the balance of power, such " necessity " has long since passed; nevertheless, though the Russians have been driven out of Port Arthur, the British are still in possession of the town on the opposite mainland.

Through fear of French encroachments in the south, England found excuse for similar undertakings on the Chinese littoral directly across from Hong Kong, and demanded an extended territory upon the sudden discovery that the British colony lacked adequate protection. China was persuaded, we might rather say forced, to cede some two hundred square miles, " nothing more than was necessary ", before British apprehensions were relieved. Originally the British intention was to demand absolute cession, as with the island of Hong Kong in the Opium war, but this was by no means advisable, as both Germany and Russia had obtained their proprietory rights by leases of ninety-nine and twenty-five years respectively. In deciding between the two, England modestly chose the ninety-nine year lease, thus emulating Germany. One clause of the ensuing agreement referred to opium, both the high contracting parties engaging to unite in eradicating the evil as much as possible. Credit for this stipulation was due mainly to Sir Robert Hart.[1]

But England was not yet through with China. From having been the nation seemingly least disposed (always excepting the United States) to take advantage of China's helplessness she turned out to be one of the worst. Furthermore, China had earlier refused a British loan and this had greatly irritated Downing Street. To make the British position doubly secure in spite of the loan failure, now that

---

[1] See *China No. 1* (*1899*), no. 225 for a discussion of the Hong Kong Extension, and Inclosure in no. 225 for the *Convention*.

the partition of China seemed imminent, Great Britain in 1898 secured a pledge that the Yangtze Valley would never be alienated to another Power, thus arrogating the vast territories of central China and the richest provinces of the Empire as British sphere of influence.[1]   Then Japan judged it high time to act, and exacted a similar pledge from China as regarded the province of Fukien, and China, having again established the necessary precedent, again could not refuse.   Later the Japanese also negotiated for and received a settlement at Amoy.[2]

France, meanwhile, had been far from idle.   The year of the Chino-Japanese war saw the French already firmly established in Annam, Cambodia, Cochin-China and Tongking, embracing a territory of 315,250 square miles and a population of 18,000,000 souls.   And now while Russia, Germany and England were seizing provinces right and left France serenely appeared with similar demands, which apparently combined all that the former three had obtained. On April 11, 1898, the Yamen received an enumeration of what France expected, namely:

I. Kwangchouwan to be leased for ninety-nine years as a coaling station.

II. The right to construct a railway to Yunnanfu from the Tongking frontier.

III. The promise of China not to alienate to another Power the provinces of Kwangtung, Kwangsi and Yunnan, or the island of Hainan.

Like the Germans at Kiaochau, the French disembarked

---

[1] See *China No. 1* (*1899*).   Inclosures 2 and 3 in no. 20.

[2] *Ibid.*, nos. 41, 45, 164.   The United States for a time seemed interested in a settlement at Amoy as a Chinese base of supplies for the Philippines, but fortunately the idea was given up.   See U. S. *For. Rel.*, 1899, no. 132, p. 150; no. 42, p. 151; no. 169, p. 151; no. 211, p. 152; no. 290, p. 153.

an armed force at Kwangchouwan and raised the French flag with the same salutes and hurrahs. Even the inevitable proclamation to the inhabitants was not forgotten. But friction developed. It seemed that the Viceroy at Canton offered determined opposition to the French demands, which was very irritating, as he *"rendait toute entente impossible"*, a convenient and customary way at that time of deprecating the conduct of patriotic Chinese. Though the Viceroy was unsuccessful, the native population continued their resistance, with the result that two French sailors were set upon and beheaded. Of course this gave an excellent opportunity for further demands, and later came the welcome news of an additional murder, that of a French missionary. To such extent had good fortune thus come to France's aid that on June 9, 1898, M. Hanotaux, Minister of Foreign Affairs, was able to announce to his colleagues that the French demands had been met in full by China.[1]

Next, France raised quite an international disturbance when she suddenly demanded an extension of her settlement at Shanghai. That the ground to be incorporated was in part an old cemetery did not deter the French in the least. The difficulty lay not in the observance of the sacred customs and institutions of the Chinese, over which Europe rode roughshod at will, but in the fact that the English and Americans resident in Shanghai had property situated in the proposed extension. Consequently, France found the British Foreign Office and the American Department of State united in opposition. The usual diplomatic threats and parleys followed, until France either shaved down her demands or gave the necessary assurances. This ended all

[1] See Cordier, *op. cit.*, vol. iii, " Projet de Convention relatif a Kouang-tcheou Wan," pp. 370-372; U. S. *For. Rel.*, 1898, p. 191; Rockhill, *op. cit.*, pp. 55-57; France, *Documents Diplomatiques, Chine, 1898-1899*, pp. 2-4.

disputes, and everyone was highly pleased with the course affairs had taken, all but China, whose wishes, however, did not count.[1]

These leases and concessions marked the definite amount of territory actually placed under foreign administration, always with the saving clause that " China's rights were to be respected ", which rights were not respected at all. But actual cession of territory did not limit the extent of European aggression. The surrounding province or provinces were invariably designated by each Power as constituting a " sphere of influence ", wherein that individual Power considered itself entitled to dominate all others. Thus Germany, leasing Kiaochau, declared the entire province of Shantung as the German " sphere ". Russia, by virtue of the cession of Port Arthur and Dalny, claimed the Three Chinese Eastern Provinces (Manchuria). Japan, through a settlement at Amoy and a promise of non-alienation, claimed the province of Fukien. France claimed the territory bordering on Tongking; and England, through the " shadowy claim " over the Yangtze Valley, was supposed to have the first call upon the rich lands watered by that important tributary. In all there were eighteen provinces of the Chinese Empire, and of these eighteen thirteen were pre-empted by the Powers, the thirteen most populous, most wealthy, and most desirable, including within them all the important waterways, harbors, mines and economic centres that were possible of access to foreign commerce.

[1] For a complete review of the negotiations for the extension of the French settlement at Shanghai, see *China No. 1* (*1899*), nos. 319, 325, 359, 370, 384, 407, 409, 410, 416, 432, 437, 439, 440, 444, 448, 449, 452, 454, 455, 463; *China No. 1* (*1900*), nos. 24, 33, 44, 45, 51, 55, 119, 124, 127, 128, 131, 132, 182, 186, 197, 198, 200, 201, 204, 209, 233, 234, 235, 266, 388, 402, 413, 414, 444, 450, 458, 462; U. S. *For. Rel.*, 1899, nos. 129, 146, 168, 171, 183, 189, 203, 206, 228, 231, pp. 143-150; Cordier, *op. cit.*, vol. iii, pp. 438-446.

There were a few redeeming features of this sordid chapter of history, most prominent of which was the attitude taken by the United States. True to its time-honored policy, the American Government declined to participate in the territorial loot of the Empire. Instead, the moral support of the State Department, as directed by John Hay, was continually exercised for the benefit of China, protesting here and there against these unexampled aggressions, and in practical isolation standing aloof from the land-hunger of Europe. Finally, seeing that American commercial interests were being jeoparidized by the conflicting policies of the Powers, Secretary Hay submitted a Circular Note, September, 1899, in which he requested the adherence of every nation concerned to the following propositions:

I. Non-interference with any treaty port or vested interests of the " sphere " or leased territory of any Power.

II. Application of the Chinese treaty tariff, except in free ports, under Chinese control.

III. Equality of treatment as to harbor dues and railroad charges in the various " spheres ".[1]

This note was not political, as is popularly supposed, but economic, on the face of it merely to protect American and other commercial interests in China. Each Power was approached separately, consequently each Power was obliged to answer separately. By this diplomatic strategy Secretary Hay revealed diplomatic ability of a high order. The correspondence which followed with the governments of Europe and Japan was gratifying in results. Italy was un-

[1] See U. S. *For. Rel.*, 1899, no. 664, pp. 128, 129; no. 927, pp. 129-131; no. 205, pp. 131-136; no. 434, pp. 136-138; no. 263, pp. 138, 139; no. 82, pp. 140, 141; no. 761, p. 142; *China No. 1* (1900), nos. 345, 415, 422. See also Asakawa, *op. cit.*, ch. v, " Secretary Hay's Circular Note," pp. 135-139; Cordier, *op. cit.*, vol. iii, " La Porte Ouverte," pp. 446-448; Mahan, *The Interest of America in International Conditions* (Boston, 1910), ch. iv, " The Open Door," pp. 185-212.

qualified in her acceptance; Great Britain, France, Germany and Japan agreed, provided every Power did likewise. Russia, as was expected, gave the usual involved diplomatic reply, but practically acquiesced, and then closed with the beautiful sentiment that the Imperial Government attached the " highest value " to anything which would " consolidate the traditional relations of friendship existing between the two countries ",[1] which the State Department took for what it was worth.

Although no final agreement was made, Hay notified the American Ambassadors at London, Paris, Berlin, St. Petersburg and Rome, and the American Minister at Tokyo that he regarded these expressions of adherence as " final and definitive ". It is, of course, impossible to state the exact benefits of this note, inasmuch as these benefits were largely of a moral nature vastly greater than the mere acceptance of the commercial principles therein stated. However, by this skillful stroke of diplomacy, the territorial entity of China was doubly assured, for so long as a " sphere " was not alienated to another Power exclusively, there was little danger of it passing entirely into that Power's hands. Secretary Hay well knew that exclusive economic domination is the invariable forerunner of political absorption; therefore, by insisting upon an equality of commercial treatment and economic opportunity for all nations, he was able to prevent that final step towards complete political control.

But the Hay note could not do the impossible; it could not reconcile the great mass of Chinese, who were unaware of the note, with existing conditions as brought about largely by the extraordinary political policies of Europe, the effects of which upon China in the year 1899 were most unfortunate. The Chinese, unable to help themselves, and

[1] U. S. For. Rel., 1899, no. 761, p. 142.

seeing city after city leased out to foreign Powers and entire provinces dominated by foreign influence, grew extremely suspicious of every move made by Europe, and many of them, not understanding the policy of the American Government, placed the United States in the same category. The Powers, in their mad scramble for land, did not take into account the rights of the Chinese, but arranged among themselves where their particular " spheres " and leases should be located, and not until the disastrous year of the Boxer Rebellion did they realize and reluctantly concede that China, after all, possessed remarkable innate vigor and was far less decrepit than had been imagined; that she was, in fact, capable of something more than mere retaliation by mob violence and riots. In 1899, however, the united opinion of Europe was that China would soon disappear as a sovereign entity, dismembered and divided. Everything then pointed that way, partly because China had not yet shown any determined resistance to European aggression, and also because the European demands had been comparatively easy of realization. Besides acquisitions of territory, there were numberless other demands too tedious to mention, consisting mainly of religious and commercial concessions, railway grants, and heavy indemnities for every conceivable item that could possibly be called an injury. Europe seemed under the impression that China was an immense golden harvest to be reaped by the first comer, and in the pursuit of this agreeable task little thought was given to international law and still less to international comity and ethics.

Now to return to the internal situation of the Empire as it affected the Government and the reigning dynasty, upon whom fell the brunt of criticism and blame for this disastrous condition of affairs.

Because of the crushing defeats which overtook the Court

in its personal quarrel, as the non-Manchu part of the Empire viewed it, with Japan, the Manchu monarchy " lost face " with its subject Chinese; and of those who felt the weight of responsibility and humiliation heaviest upon them the Emperor was the foremost. Kuang Hsu will live in history as the instigator of reform in China, even though the sum total of his efforts, with the exception of the University of Peking, was doomed to failure. Frail, in delicate health, with a sensitive, almost feminine face; subject at times to melancholia, but again to violent outbursts of temper; a dreamer, of a poetic, philosophical cast of mind, Kuang Hsu was a well-intentioned man; but he lacked that firmness of character, that deliberate disregard of consequences, that ruthless pursuit of a fixed policy necessary to make of himself another Peter the Great, who had, one might say, the like mission to perform. Although he had been chosen by the Empress Dowager on the death of the preceding Emperor Tung Chih mainly on account of his minority and the negligible qualities which he possessed and apparently would retain, yet for a while he seemed capable of great things. As it was, he astonished the world for a brief period, but it was only a momentary flash. His physical disabilities, his indecision, his fears, his lack of princely attributes, his negative training in governmental affairs during his years of preparation, due to the enervating surroundings into which a corrupt Court had deliberately thrust him, made of this pathetic descendant of the wise Kang Hi another Louis XVI, and like that unfortunate monarch, though filled with ambition to ameliorate the condition of his people and to rehabilitate the nation, he lacked those essentials of greatness, that knowledge of individual character and ability, that Napoleonic trait of correctly estimating current events, that prophetic insight into the future and moulding the future to his particular desires which were indispensable to the institution of permanent reforms such as he attempted. Considering the extreme difficulty of his situation, it was the complete absence of every one of these characteristics essential for success which makes the life of the well-meaning Kuang Hsu a tragedy in history. He was unequal to his appointed task, and, lacking genius, was crushed by obstacles which at that time only a superman could have overcome.

As early as December, 1890, and again in June of the following year Kuang Hsu had endeared himself to the foreign element in China by decrees in which he pointed out to his subjects that Christianity was protected by existing treaties with the Powers and by instructions to officials issued from the Court. Said he:

The doctrines of the western religion have for their purpose the teaching of men to be good, and although our people become converts they do not cease to be subjects of China, and are amenable to the local authorities. There is no reason why peace and quiet should not prevail between the people and the adherents of the new religion.

Officials in the cities and provinces were admonished to protect Christians and foreigners, and punishment was to follow in case of disobedience or negligence.

But Kuang Hsu at that early date had not yet found himself. Lacking a commanding intellect and personality, he needed some strong support to lean upon, some spirit bolder than his to blaze the way, to inspire him to action. As has been noted, the defeats of the Chino-Japanese war had been most keenly felt by him, and these disasters in themselves made him more than ever susceptible to schemes for retrieving the face of China by a glorious return to ancient prosperity and power, this on a new basis, however.

Always an omnivorous reader, especially interested in

foreign books, among which missionaries place the Bible, the Emperor soon became imbued with foreign ideas of culture and progress, as contrasted with the ultra-conservative tenets of the Chinese sages. Some credit is due the Imperial tutor, Weng Tung-ho, associated with the Emperor since the latter's childhood, for not having hampered the Imperial desires. Weng was a man of considerable force of character in his way; in fact, he was the leader of the Southern or Chinese party at the Court, as opposed to the Northern or Manchu, composed mainly of the Empress Dowager, her satellites, and the Imperial Court. An enlightened Chinese scholar of the old school, but not wholly lacking modern tendencies, Weng deserves praise for having allowed his pupil free rein; possibly he contributed to a certain extent to the brief but momentous era of reform, the " Hundred Days " as this melancholy bit of history has aptly been described.[1] His curt dismissal on June 15, 1898, through the general shake-up following the death of Prince Kung, came as a surprise to the Court circle and to the Diplomatic Corps at Peking. No doubt the Imperial pupil found his master too cautious, for, although Weng has been favorably viewed by some writers,[2] yet Sir Claude MacDonald, British Minister at Peking, found him " extremely obstructive, notably during the Burmah frontier and West River negotiations ". MacDonald acknowledged, however, that Weng was " prepossessing, courteous, and scholarly—an excellent type of the Conservative Chinese statesman ".[3]

[1] Albert Maybon, La Politique Chinoise: Etude sur les Doctrines des Partis en Chine (Paris, 1908), title to ch. iii of pt. ii.

[2] For a good critical estimate of Weng Tung-ho, see J. O. Bland and Edward Backhouse, China under the Empress Dowager (Philadelphia, 1910), pp. 234, 235.

[3] China No. 1 (1899), no. 268.

Weng was dismissed because another had found more favor in the Emperor's eyes. The Chinese destined to be the right-hand man of Kuang Hsu in this initial progressive movement was one Kang Yu-wei, native of a small village near Canton and author of a work on the development of Japan which the Emperor had read and appreciated. In January, 1898, Kang Yu-wei had obtained an interview with the Tsung-li Yamen and in a three hours' harangue had expounded his political theories to them. The Yamen, though composed entirely of the old order, with rare impartiality advised him to memorialize the Throne. The result of this suggestion was a meeting of Kang Yu-wei with the Emperor. A partnership was struck between the two which lasted throughout the reform period and ended only with

Following is the holograph decree dismissing Weng, *Ibid.*, Inc. 1 in no. 268:

An Imperial Mandate

Weng Tung-ho, Assistant Grand Secretary and President of the Board of Revenue, has of late made many errors in the conduct of business, and has forfeited all confidence; on several occasions he has been impeached to the Throne.

At his private audiences with the Emperor he has replied to His Majesty's questions with no regard for anything except his own personal feeling and opinion, and he has made no attempt to conceal his pleasure or displeasure either in his speech or in his countenance. It has gradually become clear that his ambition and rebellious feeling have led him to arrogate to himself an attempt to dictate to the Emperor. It is impossible to permit him to remain in the responsible position of a Grand Councillor. In former days a strict inquiry would have been held, and his crime punished with the utmost rigor of the law. Taking into consideration, however, his long service as tutor to the Emperor, His Majesty cannot bring himself to meet out to him such a severe penalty.

Let Weng Tung-ho vacate his posts, and retire into private life, as a warning that he is preserved (from a worse fate).

Kuang Hsu, 24th year, 4th moon, 27th day.
(June 15, 1898).

the *Coup d'Etat,* when the Empress Dowager destroyed everything by a single blow.

The reform movement consisted in all of some twenty-seven decrees. Three of them were promulgated while Weng Tung-ho was still in office, but a veritable deluge followed the appointment of Kang Yu-wei. The first revolutionary decree, published to the world in the official Peking *Gazette* of June 11, 1898, is noteworthy in that it clearly states what the Emperor was trying to do and what abuses he would endeavor to correct.[1] In fact, it is the outline of the Emperor's policy throughout the reform period. It is also a fine example of Chinese literary effort. The decree reads as follows:

For a long time past the condition of Imperial affairs has been a subject of discussion among the officials of the Empire, both metropolitan and provincial, with a view to bring about changes necessary for improvement. Decrees have been frequently issued by the Emperor, for a special system of examinations, for doing away with the surplus soldiery, for the alteration of the military examinations and for the institution of colleges.

In spite of the fact that these things have been so often carefully thought out, and so many plans have been formed, there is no general consensus of opinion, and discussion is still rife as to which plans are best. There are some among the older officials who affirm that the old ways are best and need no alteration, and that the new plans are not required. Such babblings are vain and useless.

The Emperor puts the question before you thus: In the present condition of Imperial affairs, with an untrained army,

[1] Said MacDonald rather cynically in forwarding the first two decrees to Lord Salisbury: "They show that a real need for radical reform is thoroughly recognized by the Court at last, but there is little reason to hope that the Imperial admonitions will move the Chinese bureaucracy deeply." *China No. 1 (1899),* no. 266.

with limited funds, with ignorant " literati," and with artisans untaught because they have no fit teachers, is there any difficulty in deciding, when China is compared with foreign nations, who is the strong and who is the weak? It is easy to distinguish between the rich and the poor. How can a man armed with a wooden stick smite his foe encased in a coat of mail?

The Emperor sees that the affairs of the Empire are in an unsettled condition, and that his various decrees have availed nothing. Diversity of opinion, each unlike another as fire differs from water, is responsible for the spread of the existing evil. It is the same evil as that which existed in the Sung and Ming Dynasties (*circa* A. D. 1000 and 1500). Our present system is not of the slightest use. We cannot in these modern days adhere to the ways of the Five Kings (*circa* B. C. 2500); even they did not continue exactly after the manner of their respective predecessors. It is like wearing thick clothes in summer and thin ones in winter.

Now, therefore, the Emperor orders all officials, metropolitan and provincial, from prince down to " literati," to give their whole minds to a real effort at improvement. With perseverance, like that of the saints of old, do your utmost to discover which foreign country has the best system in any branch of learning and learn that one. Your great fault is the falseness of your present knowledge. Make a special effort and determine to learn the best of everything. Do not merely learn the outside covers of the books of knowledge, and do not make a loud boast of your own attainments. The Emperor's wish is to change what is now useless into something useful, so that proficiency may be attained and handed on to posterity.

The Metropolitan College will be the chief one, and must be instituted at once. The Emperor orders that the Grand Councillors consult with the Tsung-li Yamen on the subject, and to come to a decision as soon as possible, and then to memorialize the Throne.

Any of the compilers and graduates of the Hanlin College,

the secretaries of the Boards, the officers of the Palace Guards, expectant Intendants, Prefects, district magistrates and subordinate officials, sons and brothers of officials, the hereditary officials of the Eight Banners, and the sons of the military officials of the Empire, can enter the College who wish to do so. By this means knowledge will be handed down from one generation to another. It will be strictly forbidden to members of the College to be careless or dilatory in their studies, or to introduce as students any of their friends without regard for the latter's capabilities; for such things would frustrate the benefit of this excellent plan of His Imperial Majesty.

Kuang Hsu, 24th year, 4th moon, 23d day,
(June 11, 1898).[1]

On the heels of this momentous decree followed another designated for the " Viceroys and Governors of the Empire ", who were commanded to " select from all grades of their subordinate officials such men as are to their knowledge of good reputation in everyday life, and who are honest, and have some knowledge of modern things, and have no grave faults". These candidates were to be further examined by the Tsung-li Yamen and the successful ones recommended to the Emperor for special posts in the official service.[2]

So far so good; nothing startling had as yet appeared to frighten the conservative gentry. The next day, however, a decree was announced containing two distinct parts, one of which related to commerce and foreign intercourse. " Commercial matters are of the highest importance and the suggestion (for the appointment of special Ministers of Commerce) is one which deserves to be acted upon. . . . It is to be hoped that strict conformity to these regulations (the establishment of Commercial Bureaus) will lead to a

[1] *China No. 1 (1899)*, Inc. in no. 266.
[2] *Ibid.*, Inc. 2 in no. 266.

daily improvement in trade ". Therefore, officials and merchants were exhorted " to consult together for the most speedy and satisfactory arrangement of commercial matters. . . . We must not adhere blindly to our old customs"; and provincial officers were advised to memorialize the Throne in order to inform the Emperor how things were progressing.

The other half of the decree contained a " suggestion " from some one (it might have been Weng Tung-ho, and probably the rock upon which his fortunes were wrecked) which recommended that " members of the Imperial Family should go abroad ". The decree rightly commented upon this as " a new departure ", but " quite in accordance with modern custom ". Therefore, the Court of the Imperial clan was ordered " to select from the Princes of the first three ranks any who were well versed in modern affairs and ideas, and who are on the side of modern improvement ". These were to await the Emperor's instructions.[1]

In the opinion of the Court, the above " startling innovation "[2] was carrying matters too far, and even those Princes designated as " well versed in modern affairs and ideas ", if there were any such, failed to greet the Emperor's plan with any degree of enthusiasm, favoring as it did a radical change in their hitherto circumscribed political activities as regulated by the Empress Dowager. Weng's dismissal followed as a matter of course, largely through Palace intrigue, and Kang Yu-wei became the man of the hour, soon to emerge into world prominence by fathering a mass of reforms which, because of their very magnitude and rapidity of appearance, nullified their purpose and whatever utility they might have possessed.

[1] *China No. 1* (*1899*), Inc. in no. 267.
[2] As characterized by Sir Claude MacDonald in *Ibid.*, no. 267.

The results of Kang Yu-wei's association with the Emperor were amazing. First of all came the definite abolition of the old examination system. In the future, instead of solely embracing literary efforts and caligraphy, the candidate's ability was to be tested mainly by practical questions, in other words by western learning. The *Pa-ku* or literary essay, the nation's pride from time immemorial and heretofore the *pièce de résistance* of all Chinese scholars and prospective *Chin-shih's,* was to be relegated to an inferior position.[1]   By this far-reaching decree the entire system of education in China was for the time being overthrown, and the *literati,* discredited, reduced in rank and practically useless, almost became a public charge. Then followed the reorganization of the army, particularly of the eight Manchu " Banners ", at one time a fine lot of medieval soldiery but in 1899 as scandalous a rabble as ever existed; the founding of institutions of learning in the provinces as " feeders " to the new Peking University; the establishment of official Gazettes throughout the Empire; the right of any and all Chinese to memorialize the Throne;[2] the proposed creation of a new navy; the installation of central mining, agricultural and railway bureaus at the capital;

[1] The British Minister considered this decree "probably the most important ordinance." He continued: "A species of essay, of which the composition is governed by highly artificial rules, has hitherto been one of the most prominent features of these examinations. For this is now to be substituted a form of essay of a more practical character. The effect of this reform may be compared with the change that would be brought about if in England an absolute mastery of Sanscrit verse had been obligatory on all public servants, and were now dispensed with. In other words, the large army of students in the Empire will save some years of almost useless study. The change has been made with such suddenness that injustice is done to those who have been preparing for the examination under present conditions, and considerable discontent must be aroused, but the future effect cannot be otherwise than good." *China No. 1 (1899)*, no. 297.

[2] Hitherto restricted to high officials, if the documents were sealed.

and, what caused the most consternation of all, the abolition of many of the sinecures and fat allowances that had been enjoyed as perquisites by the Manchus for generations, thus reducing a number of the useless horde to penury.[1]   Further measures designed to secure for China a budget like those of the European Powers, defined the mode of subscription to the Chinese Internal Loan, abolished some of the Grain and Salt offices and their attendant grafts;[2] founded the " Chinese Progress Magazine "; provided for a railway from Peking to Hankow;[3] protected the Christian religion and relations with the foreigner; converted many of the temples into schools; planned a total revenue of 70,000,000 taels annually;[4] and offered liberal rewards or official employment, if capable, to those who introduced " new books ",[5] or established colleges, or arsenals for the manufacture of rifles and cannon, or opened up mines, or invented something useful, or improved agriculture. Criticism and suggestion concerning the policy of the Government was to be freely allowed in the official newspapers.

In the decree of September 5th, a rather pathetic commentary on this ill-starred movement, the Emperor realized that all was not plain sailing, and that it was " one thing to issue a reform edict and another to get it obeyed ".[6]   Speak-

---

[1] One of the very last decrees gave the Manchus permission to settle in the provinces if they wished to " earn their living." Bland and Backhouse, *op. cit.*, p. 198.

[2] Those abolished were " all Comptrollers of the Grain Tax in provinces where there is no grain transport, and Comptrollers of the Salt Revenue in provinces where no salt is produced." *China No. 1* (*1899*), no. 362.

[3] Cordier, *op. cit.*, vol. iii, p. 405.

[4] Douglas, *op. cit.*, p. 326.

[5] " Presumably books that show originality of thought." *China No. 1* (*1899*), no. 362.

[6] *Ibid.*, no. 371.

ing of the difficulties of his task, and the opposition which
he had aroused, Kuang Hsu thus addressed his subjects:

In promoting reforms, we have adopted certain European
methods, because, while China and Europe are both alike in
holding that the first object of good government should be the
welfare of the people, Europe has travelled further on this
road than we have, so that, by the introduction of European
methods, we simply make good China's deficiencies. But our
statesmen and scholars are so ignorant of what lies beyond our
borders that they look upon Europe as possessing no civilization. They are all unaware of those numerous branches of
western knowledge whose object is to enlighten the mind and
increase the national prosperity of the people. Physical well-
being and increased longevity of the race are hereby secured for
the masses.

Is it possible that I, the Emperor, am to be regarded as a
mere follower after new and strange ideas because of my
thirst for reform? My love for the people, my children,
springs from the feeling that God has confided them to me
and that to my care they have been given in trust by my illus-
trious ancestors. I shall never feel that my duty as sovereign
is fulfilled until I have raised them all to a condition of peaceful prosperity. Moreover, do not the foreign Powers surround
our Empire, committing frequent acts of aggression? Unless
we learn and adopt the sources of their strength, our plight
cannot be remedied. The cause of my anxiety is not fully
appreciated by my people, because the reactionary element deliberately misrepresents my objects, spreading the while base-
less rumors so as to disturb the minds of men. When I reflect
how deep is the ignorance of the masses of the dwellers in the
innermost parts of the Empire on the subject of my proposed
reforms, my heart is filled with care and grief. Therefore do
I hereby now proclaim my intentions so that the whole Empire
may know and believe that their sovereign is to be trusted and
that the people may coöperate with me in working for reform
and the strengthening of the country. This is my earnest hope.

I command that the whole of my reform decrees be printed on yellow paper and distributed for the information of all men. The district magistrates are henceforward privileged to submit memorials to me through the provincial viceroys, so that I may learn the real needs of the people. Let this decree be exhibited in the front hall of every public office in the Empire so that all men may see it.[1]

From July 11th to September 20th, the Emperor and his advisers, first Weng Tung-ho, then Kang Yu-wei, had their own way with little or no interference from the Empress Dowager who, true to her word, seemed to have gone into complete retirement. Filial piety, however, was one of the predominant traits in the composition of Kuang Hsu's character, and at first he had unconsciously bowed to his Imperial aunt's former absolutism by commanding that equal honors and presents be conferred upon Tzu Hsi as if she were still jointly associated with him in authority.[2] The alliance with Kang Yu-wei altered the situation. With all his flights of imagination and inability to forecast the future, Kang had wit enough to appreciate the fact that the real power still lay with the Empress Dowager, whom he hated and feared with the intensity born of a presentiment of impending disaster. Knowing that she repaid his antagonism with interest, he strove with all his energy to eliminate the " Old Buddha " from Chinese politics by driving from the Emperor's mind all emotions of gratitude to the one who had placed him upon the throne. It being impossible for Kang, in the nature of things, to keep his designs secret, the knowledge of his active hostility towards Tzu Hsi soon became public property in the Palace. The good-humored tolerance with which she had previously regarded

[1] As reprinted by Bland and Backhouse, *op. cit.*, pp. 199, 200.

[2] Imperial decree of June 11. *China No. 1 (1899)*, Inc. 2 in no. 268.

the reform movement then gave place to a realization of its perils, which might even result in her being forcibly assisted on the road to Heaven. Though fully cognizant of the drift of events, each succeeding day more unfavorable, she bided her time, holding her impatient satellites in check until the danger to herself and to her party became overwhelming. Then her inactivity, which the Emperor had assured himself meant indecision and a sense of security, was transformed into one of those lightning-like acts of which she alone in all China seemed capable. As by a bolt from the blue, the shell of reform was crushed by a single blow, well directed and dealt with astonishing rapidity.

The Emperor had severely crippled the existing official system by abolishing six of the Government Boards and apportioning their duties among the remainder,[1] thus turning loose a large staff of dispossessed office-holders to swell the ranks of the malcontents against reform. But worse was to follow. A secretary of the Board of Rites, Wang Chao, had the misplaced courage to submit a memorial which easily outdistanced even the grandiose schemes of Kang Yu-wei. This document contained the astonishing recommendations that the queue be abolished, that Christianity be established as the state religion, that a national parliament be assembled, and that the Empress Dowager and the Emperor make a journey of observation to Japan and Europe, to witness with their own eyes the contrast in civilization and progress with China and to profit thereby. It can be imagined how these proposals amazed the ultra-Confucian

[1] These six Boards were abolished "on the score of economy," as their duties were "largely nominal." Thereby, however, 160 officials were dismissed. The Emperor had also resolved that "the horde of expectant officials at the various provincial capitals" should be likewise "carefully weeded out." *China No. 1* (*1899*), no. 362. See also no. 371.

members of the Board. In an interview with Wang, they begged him to reconsider. He had the temerity to refuse, and insisted that the memorial be sent as it was to the Emperor. That was accordingly done, but the Board attached as a rider a counter-communication denouncing Wang as a visionary and praying that his recommendations be interpreted as impracticable and absurd. An unlooked-for result, the Emperor was furious at this attempt, as he chose to regard it, of the Board to dictate his actions and to aid the Imperial mind with advice, no matter how humbly given. It seemed that Kuang Hsu was not as open to conviction by arguments from outside as his edicts had proclaimed him. In a fit of anger of the martinet variety, such as he frequently displayed, with a stroke of the vermillion pencil he dismissed in disgrace the two Presidents of the Board (one a Chinese and the other a Manchu) and four Vice-Presidents [1] for having dared to offer suggestions, and further for having broken the seal of Wang's memorial, instead of submitting it unopened. The injudicious author of the communication was himself rewarded by a position as Judge in one of the provinces.[2] That was the last important act of Kuang Hsu in his brief but not inglorious career as reform dictator. The cashiered officials of the Board of Rites, together with their Manchu and Chinese sympathizers, proceeded in a body to the palace of the Empress Dowager where, *en retraite,* the amiable old lady was enjoying herself among her flowers and satisfy-

[1] The Imperial wrath also fell upon Li Hung-chang, who was dismissed, September 7, from the Tsung-li Yamen, an act which gave great pleasure to Englishmen in China, as they feared Li's pronounced Russian proclivities. " He has recently shown himself markedly antagonistic to our interests." MacDonald to Salisbury, *China No 1 (1899),* no. 321.

[2] Wang was not able to enjoy his reward, as the reform movement collapsed shortly afterwards.

ing her passion for theatricals. On their knees the humiliated bureaucrats besought her to resume the reins of government, and Tzu Hsi, feminine to the last by dismissing them without indicating her mind, perceived that the psychological moment had arrived for a return to that power which she coveted.[1]

Kang Yu-wei and the Emperor sensed the danger and resolved to act before the Empress Dowager could have her plans perfected. Kuang Hsu, completely under the influence of his adviser, at last was willing to seize Tsu Hsi and hold her a prisoner, thus to prevent her from doing any further mischief to reform. To accomplish this, it was necessary first of all that Jung Lu, Viceroy of Chihli and commander of the northern military and naval forces, should be disposed of, as he was the main reliance and support of Tzu Hsi and next to her the chief obstacle to the new régime. The commission to make an end of Jung Lu fell upon Yuan Shih-kai, protegé of Li Hung-chang and later governor of Shantung, who had assembled through his own initiative and energy the best and only foreign-drilled troops in China at that time, some seven thousand in all.[2] His instructions were to repair immediately to Tientsin, arrest Jung Lu, summarily behead him and return in all haste to Peking, surround the palace of the Empress Dowager and take her captive. Unfortunately for the Emperor, Yuan Shih-kai, although a modern Chinese, elected to do otherwise. Of liberal nature and tendencies, the most popular native official with the foreigners, yet he feared, and rightly so, that the reform movement was but a creation of the mist, doomed to failure through the inability of his

[1] Bland and Backhouse, *op. cit.*, p. 197; Douglas, *op. cit.*, pp. 328-330; Sergeant, *op. cit.*, p. 178; Smith, *China in Convulsion*, vol. i, pp. 145, 146.

[2] Drilled by the German von Hanneken. See Cordier, *op. cit.*, vol. iii, p. 408.

country to grasp it; and that the future of China, instead of brightening, was in reality getting darker. As might have been expected, far from decapitating his blood-brother Jung Lu, Yuan, in a scene of Shakespearian intensity,[1] merely informed him of the sentence, and together they hurried back to Peking and laid bare the plot to the Empress Dowager, who already had more than an inkling of it. Immediately, this energetic old woman, accompanied solely by an escort of eunuchs picked up on the spur of the moment, hastened to the palace where the Emperor was living in solitary grandeur, and taking him utterly by surprise, overwhelmed him with her wrath and contempt. " You are after all but an unsophisticated child. Return at once to your inner apartments! It is evident that I must resume control to save the Empire, which you, in your extreme unwisdom and foolishness, seem to be doing your best to drive to perdition ".[2] Her swift action, so characteristic of her conduct in every one of the many crises of her life, completely unnerved the mild-mannered Kuang Hsu. Without opposition either by word or deed he surrendered the great seal and his authority with it. But he managed to warn Kang Yu-wei in advance. " My heart is filled with very great sorrow, which pen and ink cannot describe. You must go abroad at once, and without a moment's delay devise some means of saving me ".[3]

The decree of September 21st, in name only from the Emperor, marked his fall from power and the ruin of his party:

[1] For interesting accounts, differing in detail, of the meeting between Yuan Shih-kai and Jung Lu, see Bland and Backhouse, *op. cit.*, p. 206; Cordier, *op. cit.*, vol. iii, p. 408.

[2] As reprinted in Douglas, *op. cit.*, p. 331.

[3] As reprinted in Sergeant, *op. cit.*, p. 185.

The affairs of the nation are at present in a difficult position, and everything awaits reform. I, the Emperor, am working day and night with all my powers, and every day arrange a multitude of affairs. But, despite my careful toil, I constantly fear to be overwhelmed by the press of work.

I reverently recall that Her Majesty the Empress Dowager has on two occasions since the reign of Tung Chih (1861) assumed the reins of Government with great success in critical periods. In all she did Her Majesty showed perfection.

Moved by a deep regard for the welfare of the nation, I have repeatedly implored Her Majesty to be graciously pleased to advise me in government, and have received her assent.

This is an assurance of prosperity to the whole nation, officials and people.

Her Majesty will commence to transact business from today in the side Hall.

On the 23rd of September I, the Emperor, will lead my princes and high officials to make obeisance in the Chih Chang Hall. Let the proper officials reverently and carefully prepare the fitting programme of the ceremony.[1]

Such was the *Coup d'Etat,* in itself a bloodless revolution and the end of reform. The reasons for the failure of the " New China " are easily understandable. In attempting too much, the reformers accomplished practically nothing at all. Their ideal structure was top-heavy, and, built upon no foundation worth speaking of, was crushed by its own weight. Their mistakes were many; one blunder followed another; no adjustment was offered to harmonize existing conditions. Old China was completely discarded in this craze for the modern order, and institutions and customs which heretofore had been the backbone of the na-

---

[1] *China No. 1 (1899),* Inc. in no. 386. Also reprinted in Bland and Backhouse, *op. cit.,* p. 208; Sergeant, *op. cit.,* p. 186; *U. S. For. Rel.,* 1898, Inc. in no. 49, p. 218. A French version is given in Cordier, *op. cit.,* vol. iii, p. 408.

tional existence, were henceforth to be regarded, if not as entirely useless, at least as of secondary importance. Undoubtedly the main reason why the movement collapsed was the poor judgment displayed by Kang Yu-wei and the Emperor. In their zeal for innovation and change, they struck too deeply at the root of " things Chinese ", at institutions conservative to a fault and the most difficult in the world to modify or change. The edicts, covering as they did a great variety of subjects, military, political, educational, social and civil, were presented to the nation in helter-skelter fashion, in head-long haste, and their acceptance and observance could have been possible only through a complete revolution in Chinese life, manners and thought, a breakaway in two months from the civilization of two thousand years. No attempt was made to placate opposition or to allay prejudices; the reformers rode rough-shod over many, in fact almost all, of those cherished ideals which had become atavisms with the Chinese centuries ago. They entirely forgot time and place, and exhibited throughout that unconsciousness of existing conditions to be met and overcome before success is assured which seems typical of most idealists when placed in a position of authority. It was as impossible for the China of 1898 to swallow the indigestible remedies which the reformers proposed as to be governed by the Republic of Plato, and as far as the ability of the masses was concerned at that time to understand and assimilate what was being offered them, Plato would have done as well as Kang Yu-wei.

The reformers, through their lack of foresight and of ability to strike the happy medium, had the misfortune to antagonize everyone in the Empire not of their own party, both Manchus and Chinese, from the highest to the lowest. First, the *literati,* the pride of the people, symbolic to them of the heights of human attainment, were thrust aside with scarcely an effort made to incorporate them into the new order, their labors discredited, their honors automatically removed, themselves reduced to failures. Thus at the outset the innate conservatism of the Chinese received an unexpected shock, and the most powerful, the most numerous, the most revered leaders among the masses, these *literati* to be found in every village, hamlet and wayside inn, became the most insistent opponents of the new régime. In addition, the Manchus were practically unanimous against the movement, for they understood that were it to succeed, its triumph would mean their annihilation, existing as they did solely on sufferance; by bribery, corruption, and the disinclination of the subject race to a violent change of any kind. They were not alone in their whole-hearted opposition to the abolition of official sinecures and grafts; the attempt to eliminate the " squeeze " likewise alienated the thousands of petty Chinese magistrates in the provinces, who, without these illegal perquisites, could not exist on their miserably inadequate salaries. By the conversion of temples into schools for " western learning ", the religious sensibilities of the people were outraged, and those sensibilities were still further inflamed by the multitude of priests who feared the apparent favoritism of the edicts towards Christianity. Still more distasteful were the actions of a certain proportion of the " Young China ", whose display of egotistical ignorance of the fundamentals of human nature produced exactly the opposite effect to that which they desired.[1] A goodly number of them ridiculed the *literati,* made light of filial piety, scorned the national heroes, thus holding up to contempt the most sacred traditions of China, ingrained ages ago in the Chinese character, and among its

[1] " I consider that the cause of true reform in China has been much injured by the injudicious conduct of Kang Yu-Wei and his friends." MacDonald to Salisbury, *China No. 1 (1899)*, no. 401.

finest attributes. Thus the reform was discredited mainly through its own violence and lack of ability to appreciate the past, to conciliate the present and to interpret the future. The movement is analogous to many of the purist and religious waves of unrest which sweep every once in a while over the United States, such as the abolitionist fanaticism which brought on the Civil War, and the perennial " revivals " which spring up here and there. Like each of these the reform movement was at cross-purposes with humanity at large, and like each of these must either destroy the opposition *in toto* or fail in the attempt, either everything or nothing.

It may seem rather curious on first thought that the Powers should have been so indifferent to this struggle for the rehabilitation of China, and that no encouragement was received by the reform party from the foreign representatives at Peking. The fault for this, however, lies with the reformers themselves. They made no attempt to enlist foreign sympathy or foreign co-operation, and the only information that the Ministers received of the movement was when each successive edict was published in the official Peking *Gazette* As to the purposes of Kang Yu-wei and his ultimate plans, the foreign representatives were as much in the dark concerning these as the rest of China, and each new surprising innovation startled them as much as it did the outside world. Neither the Emperor nor any of his advisers had any diplomatic ability, and the capable and experienced Li Hung-chang, as has been noted, was in the opposite camp. Kang's knowledge of world politics was small; the term embraced a sphere which lay outside his special line of activities. To quote a British critic:

It must be remembered . . . that his knowledge of China's relations with foreign Powers and of negotiations with them is very slight; he appears to have been absorbed in questions of internal reform and to have paid little or no attention to matters of foreign policy. He speaks generally of the desirability of an Anglo-American alliance for the protection of China, and the danger to the world of Russian control of the masses of Chinese, but only as a man repeating what he has read in the way of wide political speculation.[1]

In fact, the reformers underrated the value of foreign sympathy for the cause and the benefits which might have accrued to them from foreign diplomatic aid. They seemed content only with the internal aspects of the situation, which was a serious mistake. Consequently, it is small wonder that the British consular and diplomatic corps should have termed the *Coup d'Etat* a " Palace revolution ",[2] understanding thereby merely the triumph of one Court faction over the other.[3]

Although the *Coup d'Etat* itself was accomplished without loss of life, succeeding events revealed choice instances of that brutish hate and persecution generally found in Oriental despotisms. The arch-conspirator Kang Yu-wei escaped,[4] much to the chagrin of the Empress Dowager, who doubtless had reserved for him the most exquisite tortures at her command. We learn with surprise that Kang "formed a party for his own selfish purposes; therefore his offense is very grave ". Such was Tzu Hsi's denunciation of her

[1] Henry Cockburn, *Memorandum* of conversation with Kang Yu-wei on Voyage from Shanghai to Hong Kong, September 27-29, 1898, in *China No. 1 (1899)*, Inc. 2 in no. 401.

[2] Acting Consul-General Brenan (Shanghai) to Lord Salisbury, *ibid.*, no. 337. The term is used extensively in the cited volume of the *Parliamentary Papers*.

[3] For a criticism of the inactivity of the Powers see Smith, *China in Convulsion*, vol. i, p. 150.

[4] With the help of British sympathizers. See *China No. 1 (1899)*, nos. 343, 379 and Inc., 386, 387, 401 and Inc.

greatest enemy. Nor was that all. The decree of September 29th is an illuminating document not alone for its misrepresentation of Kang's reform program, which, in spite of its many glaring errors, was attempted with the highest and most laudable motives possible, but also as illustrating how, in times of national hate, fear or distress, history and current events are often deliberately distorted by educated and uneducated alike in the blind effort to justify or condemn the action in question. In presenting the other side of the lantern, a wholly false view by the way, Tzu Hsi said:

Whereas the present times and affairs are full of difficulties, the Court has diligently planned for the Government, seeking reforms for its prosperity according to the plans for the welfare of the people as handed down by our ancestors. The Emperor has labored night and day with unwearied diligence, but unexpectedly there appeared a manager of affairs, Kang Yu-wei, a leader of false doctrines, a deceiver of the age, a slanderer of men, who led a crowd of low followers and took advantage of the attempt at reforms to impose his own rebellious conduct. . . . It is also reported that his murderous band had formed a society to preserve China, but not the Manchu dynasty. This rebellious conduct is certainly to be detested. My great filial affection for the Empress Dowager (the edict is Tzu Hsi's, and in name only from the Emperor) must be known to foreigners and Chinese. Kang Yu-wei's learning is crafty and false. Those books which he constantly made were opposed to the classics, misleading and destructive of the sages and laws. Because of his constant advocacy of reforms he was appointed to a post in the Foreign Office, and we (meaning Kuang Hsu) appointed him to immediately repair to Shanghai to take charge of the Government press (the reform *Gazette*), but he lingered in the capital to stir up strife and practice his dark designs. Unless the protection of our ancestors had enabled us to clearly see his schemes before-

hand, there is no telling what would have happened. Kang
Yu-wei, the chief of rebels, has now absconded; therefore let
all the provincials strenuously seek him out and arrest him for
severest punishment.[1]

Unfortunately, Kang's brother was captured, together
with five other young men, all of these of good family, well
educated, and of high standing in Chinese social life. These,
brave to the last, were publicly decapitated without a
moment's delay for their share in the late movement. But
the Empress Dowager proceeded no further than with the
pursuit of the sponsors of reform. It was deemed good
policy to let their misguided followers alone. " Besides the
persons arrested, there is no guaranteeing that among officials and *literati* there may not be others who were seduced
by him (Kang Yu-wei) ; but the Court will act with great
forbearance, and will not probe deeply, in order to make
known our caution in inflicting punishments." [2]

One of the most prominent of those who fell under suspicion was Chang In-huan, who was one of the two members
of the first Chinese Peace Commission to Japan in 1895.
Although it was satisfactorily proved that Chang " did not
belong to Kang Yu-wei's party ", yet " his reputation is a
bad one " (decree of September 26th). The " reprehen-
sible " Chang was further stigmatized (decree of September 29th) as " very clever at imposing on people ", and it
further developed that " his actions were deceitful, myster-
ious, and fickle, and he sought after the rich and powerful".

The truth of the matter was that Chang had the misfortune to be an enemy of Li Hung-chang, who was now returning to power with the Empress Dowager. September
25th it was rumored in Peking that Chang was to be exe-

[1] U. S. *For. Rel.*, 1898, Inc. in no. 54, p. 221.
[2] Decree of September 26, in *China No. 1 (1899)*, Inc. 4 in no. 386.

cuted, " the same evening or next morning ". Sir Claude MacDonald, the British Minister, immediately bestirred himself " to make an appeal on his (Chang's) behalf for at least due consideration of any charge brought against him". MacDonald continues :

The report reached me late in the afternoon, and it was therefore necessary to take prompt measures. It was supposed that Li Hung-chang had been consulted by the Empress Dowager in the matter. I accordingly addressed a letter to his Excellency pointing out the horror with which such sudden executions were regarded by all western nations, and the bad effect the secret and hasty condemnation of an official of Chang's rank, who was so well known in Europe, would produce, and begged his Excellency to use whatever influence he possessed to prevent such hurried action. I concluded my letter by saying that I appealed to him, Li, because he was the only statesman now in Peking who was conversant with European methods, and would, therefore, thoroughly realize the disastrous impression which such a summary execution would produce throughout the western world.

Thanks to the British Minister's efficient aid, Chang was saved from probable death, but was detained in prison and later banished to the frontier of Chinese Turkestan.[1]

As a concession to Europe and to the foreigners in China, doubtless to allay foreign apprehension and avert diplomatic interference, the Empress Dowager announced that " we shall endeavor to arrive at a happy medium, and not simply follow our own inclinations. Therefore all officials, great and small, ought to sympathize with us, and earnestly strive to aid us in the administration of the Government and to proclaim the truth ". But the effect of

[1] *China No. 1* (*1899*), nos. 339, 343, 386, 387; U. S. *For. Rel.*, 1898, Inc. 3 and 5 in no. 54, pp. 220, 221.

these fine words was diminished by the repressive measures against reform. Tzu Hsi reasoned correctly that the object of the Emperor in abolishing the six Government Boards in Peking and many other sinecures had been " to sift out and reduce the number of supernumeraries " and " all necessary duties ". However, Tzu Hsi discovered that the " provincial officials did not investigate the matter ", with the result that " numerous memorials recommending great changes " poured in upon the Government. In reasoning on these memorials, said an edict:

Falsehoods have been propagated. What will be the end? If the truth is not made known there is reason to fear that the people will become excited by this random talk, and tranquility will cease to prevail, and all our efforts for the prosperity of the Empire will avail nothing.

As an easy solution of the difficulty and to her own satisfaction and that of the entire Manchu tribe, the Empress Dowager ordered the six Boards to be " restored and conduct their affairs as usual ".[1] As regards the Emperor's dismissals of useless officials in the provinces, these orders were declared void. Also, the task of deciding which of the "official posts and officers in the various provinces ought to be abolished ", and which " unemployed officials " should be " dispensed with " was left to the discretion of the "Governors and Governors-General ", who, understanding perfectly the present state of affairs at Court, naturally enough did nothing.

The permission given by Kuang Hsu allowing anyone to

[1] These six Boards, of no use whatever to the efficient administration of the Government, were (1) the Imperial Supervisorate of Instruction, (2) the Office of Transmission, (3) the Grand Court of Revision, (4) the Court of Imperial Entertainments, (5) the Court of the Imperial Stud, (6) the Court of Imperial Ceremonial.

memorialize the Government, so that " we should see with the eyes and hear with the ears of everybody " was taken away. The result was that only high officials, as heretofore, could present sealed communications. But these officers were instructed " to say what they have to say in fitting language ". The Empress Dowager had been pained to find that the reform edicts were " full of frivolous statements; some even touch on the extravagant ", and all were " much wanting in order ". It was the last error which was above all a deadly sin with the *literati*. The *Chinese Progress Magazine* was declared " of no benefit to good government and will vainly distract men's minds ", therefore Tzu Hsi recommended that it " be abolished at once ". The Imperial (Peking) University was allowed to stand, as it was " for the culture of the people ". As for the new education in the provinces, " let the local officials in all prefectures and districts where it is proposed to establish minor colleges consider the local conditions and the convenience of the people ", which meant, as the people at large did not concern themselves about colleges, that nothing would be done. Regarding temples, these " shall continue as formerly " and " need not be converted into schools " as the reformers had planned. This order was for the reason " that the people may not be offended " in their religious, or rather their Confucian and Taoist, susceptibilities. Regarding trade, agriculture, the reorganization of the army, and the development of revenue, all of these " are of undoubted consequence to the State ", but " *must imperatively be introduced gradually* ",[1] in other words, not at all. Furthermore, "all business must be deliberated upon with the greatest care in order to decide what should be introduced and what rejected, so that the good may be retained and not a single

---

[1] The *italics* are the author's.

flaw remain ". What " good " would thus be " retained ", as far as new ideas were concerned, may be judged by the admonition that " all obey the teachings ", which meant Confucius and the ancient system only, with no modern hybrid. This ended reform, and China, with hardly a dissenting voice, contentedly slid back into the old groove.[1]

Two phases immediately connected with the Empress Dowager's return to power demand comment. One of these was the reception given to the wives of the foreign representatives. Report has it that Prince Henry of Prussia, the first " barbarian " to meet Her August Majesty face to face, had solicited the interview at the instigation of Lady Mac-Donald. Whatever may have been the determining cause, the meeting itself was probably no more than a clever bit of diplomacy on the part of Tzu Hsi to make herself agreeable to anyone of influence, so as to gloss over as much as possible her practical usurpation of the throne. As for the reception, it was a distinct success. Lady MacDonald made a brief address in which she expressed the " feelings of respect and pleasure " of the ladies at this permission " to offer personally our congratulations upon the 64th birthday of Your Imperial Majesty ", and concluded with the hope that now " the peoples of the East and West will continue to draw nearer to each other in social intercourse ", which was hoping a great deal at that time. To which Tzu Hsi, through Prince Ching, replied that Lady MacDonald's words were " propitious and pleased me greatly ". In fact, Her Majesty almost overacted. Each of the visiting ladies was embraced and given a pearl ring, and later Tzu Hsi sent each a portrait painted by herself, which must have been a fair copy, as she was quite a skillful artist. She also drank a " loving cup of tea " with an individual sip for

[1] *China No. 1 (1899)*, Inc. 3 in no. 386; U. S. *For. Rel.*, 1898, Inc. 2 and 6 in no. 54, pp. 219-221.

each guest, to give weight to her reiterated phrase of all being in " one family ".[1] It was confidently believed at the time, however, that at last the barriers were down and that a new era was to begin. Minister Conger gave the opinion that the reception might " inspire within the Imperial Palace a desire to see and know more of western people and western things; and that when it is once known by the Chinese people generally that the Empress Dowager is herself willing to see and entertain foreigners, some of their antipathy will be allayed ". But events proved otherwise, and by the irony of fate these same ladies with their distinguished husbands, who no doubt had been included by Tzu Hsi in her transient friendship, were trapped in their own Legations, the one place sacred the world over by international law and immemorial custom, fighting for their lives with the energy of despair.[2]

The other phase dealt with the health of the unfortunate Kuang Hsu. Never of robust constitution, always inclined towards illness and melancholia, it is small wonder, considering the terrific strain of the last few weeks on his sensitive nature, together with his present close confinement, that mind and body should have suffered a serious relapse. As early as September 25th, but two days after the Empress Dowager assumed full powers, an Imperial edict announced:

[1] "At the instance of the foreign ladies of the Legations, this touching interview was repeated at the beginning of the year 1900, under like conditions. Five months later Her Majesty was issuing Edicts which ordered her troops, in large numbers and constantly recruited with fresh men, to throw Krupp shells and fire Mauser and Männlicher bullets into the dwelling-places of these same ladies from the West, with a view of their speedy extinction, thus leaving only the Chinese (and Manchu) contingent of the " one family " surviving. Smith, *China in Convulsion*, vol. i, p. 28. See also Sergeant, *op. cit.*, pp. 198-202.

[2] See U. S. *For. Rel.*, 1898, no. 114 and Inc. 1 and 2 in no. 114, pp. 223-225; *China No. 1 (1899)*, no. 426; *China No. 1 (1900)*, no. 22.

Ever since the fourth moon we have constantly been indisposed, and although for a long time have been under treatment there has been no improvement. Therefore, if there is any person who is skilled in the science of medicine, let him be recommended immediately by any official in the Empire, and if he is now residing in some other province, let him come to Peking speedily and without delay.[1]

No competent Chinese physician, even with foreign training, seems to have appeared, and some three weeks later the subject was voluntarily broached to the British Minister by Prince Ching and the Tsung-li Yamen. In the interview which followed, the Chinese Foreign Office intimated that " the rumors with regard to the Emperor's health and designs upon his life were well known to them", by which they referred to the persistent talk going the rounds in Peking that Kuang Hsu would soon " ascend on High " through the instrumentality of his august aunt. Prince Ching took advantage of the occasion to act as apologist for the Empress Dowager, stating that she was " not wholly opposed to reform, but China was not prepared for such sweeping reforms as those recently laid before the Emperor ", which was probably the truth. In conclusion, the Prince " confidentially " asked the British Minister " how the present unrest could best be calmed down ", and MacDonald suggested the happy expedient that a foreign physician be called upon to give " a certificate as to the Emperor's health ", which would have " a very reassuring effect ". The advice of MacDonald was received " with every sign of approval", although he was quite sure it would be disregarded. Some days later, October 18th, a pleasant surprise was given him when he learned that his suggestion had been acted upon

[1] U. S. *For. Rel.*, 1898, Inc. 1 in no. 54, p. 219.

and that Dr. Detheve of the French Legation was commissioned to examine the Emperor and " certify as to his condition ". The Doctor's diagnosis showed that Kuang Hsu was suffering from Bright's disease, but was in no immediate danger. The part of this incident which seems to have rankled in Tzu Hsi's mind was not the consultation with the foreign physician but the " semi-official " warning of MacDonald to the Yamen in which he expressed his " firm conviction that should the Emperor die at this juncture of affairs, the effect produced among western nations would be most disastrous to China ". The British Minister's timely protest, falling little short of diplomatic interference, may have saved the Emperor's life, but no doubt it also carried with it a further addition to that legacy of hate and retaliation which the Manchu Court was storing up against Europe, to be settled at the first convenient opportunity.[1]

The resumption of the regency by the Empress Dowager was most unfortunate for China and the world, and its disastrous consequences were exceeded only by the territorial aggressions of the Powers. Together with the land-greed of Europe it was the determining cause of the Boxer Rebellion, at least it greatly accelerated the conflict. It provided the excuse by which the revolt against outside civilization and intercourse, growing steadily ever since 1840, could be brought to a head and expressed, as it were, in a nationalistic way. The interpretation given in the length and breadth of China to the overthrow of reform, crushed as it had been by those now highest in authority, could mean nothing else to the overwhelming mass of Chinese than that' a recurrence to the old order would quickly result, that everything at variance with their own mode of life and affairs, such as Europe willed and not as they wished, would

[1] *China No. 1* (*1899*), nos. 358, 363, 373, 401.

be repudiated; and that a united, a supreme effort, would be made to free the land once for all from that "unceasing stream", the hated foreigner and his work. The Boxer Rebellion was that effort, and it had for prelude a score of spasmodic attacks on foreigners and missionaries, varying in intensity but gradually growing worse, all of which, it is significant to note, occurred after the *Coup d'Etat,* and in spirit and inception are directly traceable to that event.

There were other immediate causes. The burden of the Japanese indemnity has already been touched upon and was misfortune enough in itself. To make the financial situation worse, agrarian and taxation troubles brought on acute distress in the congested districts of certain provinces. With two years of bad weather and bad crops and the always sensitive economic balance was disturbed, as even in normal times the line of demarcation between sufficiency and starvation in some parts of China is very thinly drawn. This reduced thousands to a give-and-take existence; robber bands increased as never since the Taiping Rebellion; brigandage and piracy flourished,[1] and the ranks of the

[1] Constant complaints from the British in Hong Kong and south China "of the disgraceful prevalence of piracy in the Cantonese waters, both on the rivers and along the coast," aroused the British Minister, especially as the Governor of Canton was adjudged "singularly helpless in the matter," and as the pirates had become a "serious scandal and hindrance to trade." The British authorities sent a small gunboat, the "Sandpiper," to patrol the West River, which action irritated Viceroy Tan, who announced that "hereafter, should a British man-of-war come into conflict with pirates on the inland waters and people be wounded in the encounter, China cannot be held responsible, nor can China be blamed if, owing to remissness, the British war-ship is not able to protect itself. . . . If British men-of-war cease to come (up the West River), China will afford protection as before." But the Chinese authorities seemed unable to cope with the situation. British Consul Mansfield at Canton wrote, July 27, 1899, that, "at the present moment there is a feeling of uncertainty in regard to both life and property, which is unprecedented. Robberies on land and by water are of daily occurrence. Blackmailing

" Fists of Righteous Harmony " Society were swelled by
the discontented and the famishing. Naturally all of these
difficulties reacted against the foreigners. The Yellow
River, appropriately termed " China's sorrow ", overflowed
again,[1] covering immense areas, destroying villages, and
driving a multitude from home and kindred to subsist on
charity, on anything whatever to keep body and soul together. Superstition, the popular and dreaded *fung-shui,*
held the foreigner accountable for the disaster. The *likin*

and the abduction of persons go on with practical impunity. The
robbers and pirates are driving a flourishing trade, and their successes,
coupled with the almost certain immunity from any sort of punishment, add continually to their numbers, which are now said to aggre-
gate several thousands." Accordingly, another vessel was dispatched,
H. M. S. " Tweed," assisted by a torpedo boat as tender. Admiral
Seymour of the China Station was of the opinion that the three
British ships would have only a " very partial effect," and that, " if
China is to be relieved of the responsibility of policing these rivers,
and it is undertaken by Great Britain," it was essential that a " numer-
ous flotilla of shallow draft vessels " be sent. Then came the Boxer
Rebellion, and the piracy question was left to the local authorities
to deal with as best they could, while England, along with the other
Powers, busied herself to relieve Peking.

China No. 1 (1900), no. 74 and Inc. in no. 74, no. 83 and Inc. 1 and
2 in no. 83, nos. 96, 99, 102, 113, 120, 156 and Inc. 1, 2 and 3 in nos.
156, 258 and Inc. in nos. 258, 274-276, 287 and Inc. 1, 2, 3, 4 and 5 in nos.
287, 301 and Inc. in nos. 301, 302-305, 320 and Inc. 1, 2 and 3 in nos.
320, 323 and Inc. in nos. 323, 325 and Inc. 1 and 2 in nos. 325, 341 and
Inc. 1, 2 and 3 in nos. 341, 343 and Inc. in nos. 343, 350 and Inc. 1, 2,
3 and 4 in nos. 350, 361 and Inc. 1 and 2 in nos. 361, 362, 365, 372 and
Inc. in nos. 372, 374 and Inc. 1, 2 and 3 in nos. 374, 377 and Inc. 1 and
2 in nos. 377, 382 and Inc. 1 and 2 in nos. 382, 389, 403 and Inc. in nos.
403, 405, 411, 416, 418.

[1] Li Hung-chang was ordered by Imperial decree to confer with the
Controller-General of the Yellow River and the Governor of Shantung
as to schemes to prevent future floods. As MacDonald said, Li's
task was " an arduous one." The Yamen also asked the British Minister whether English engineers were available as advisers. Great
Britain offered to send three competent engineers from India, but again
the Boxer Rebellion intervened and cut negotiations short. *China No.
1 (1899),* nos. 388, 390, 403, 424, 434, 461.

question,[1] always a bone of contention between China and
Europe, came into prominence at the worst possible time
and added its share to the prevailing discontent. The evils
of the contraband trade in opium, severely felt because of
the general lack of prosperity, became acute, and here without doubt the foreigner was to blame.

It soon developed that the antipathy of the native population to the missionaries was as strong as in the preceding
generation. The propagator of the Gospel was regarded as
the advance-agent of his particular Government, sent to
China not for religion's sake but in a political capacity thus
disguised. Nor does it seem possible how the Chinese could
have reasoned otherwise when the Catholic clergy, openly
aided by France, actually demanded and obtained mandarin
rank for their bishops and a sliding-scale of lesser dignities
for the lower priesthood, with singular foresight providing
even for the ceremonial cannon-shot.[2]   It is to be regretted

[1] Serious rioting, especially at Hankow, followed the transfer of the
likin and salt taxes to the Imperial Maritime Customs, where they were
to be hypothecated for the Anglo-German loan.

Ibid., nos. 100, 103, 111, 145, 147 and Inc. in nos. 147, 185, 212 and
Inc. in nos. 212, 218, 460 and Inc. 1, 2, 3 and 4 in nos. 460, 468;
China No. 1 (*1900*), no. 75 and Inc. in no. 75, no. 107 and Inc. in no. 107.

[2] An excellent discussion of the question of rites is given in Cordier,
op. cit., vol. iii, pp. 478-495, a review of the entire period of Catholic
activities in China. See also *China No. 1* (*1900*), no. 176 and Inc.,
188, the memorial of March 15, 1899, for the above political status to
Catholics. "The same day the Imperial assent was given" (Inc. in
no. 176).

Speaking of these ceremonies, says Cordier, *op. cit.*, vol. iii, p. 478:
" Il faut bien reconnaître que le chiffre de 720,866 Chrétiens (Cordier's
work was published in 1902) pour toute la Chine est médiocre; il fut
plus élevé au XVIIe siècle; si l'on recherche les causes de cet in-
succès des missionaires catholiques dans l'Empire du Milieu, on
trouvera que la *Question des Rites* a été la pierre d'achoppement sur
laquelle est venue se heurter l'Église romaine, grâce aux intrigues qui
se sont nouées autour des Souverains Pontifes ignorants des choses de
Chine et ne les entrevoyant que par les yeux de conseillers souvent de
mauvaise foi."

that no criticism on this attitude of the Chinese can be advanced, as argument would be too much confounded by fact. Fortunately, the Protestants declined like political ostentation, although their magnanimity to China was overlooked by the Boxers in the catastrophe which followed. Equally exasperating were the difficulties experienced with the mixed courts (extra-territoriality) and with the administration of the law in general, and here both Protestants and Catholics were equally culpable. It was claimed and in many instances proved that the Christian convert, too many times a " rice-Christian ", was unduly favored, that with either missionary, priestly or consular intervention at his call he would escape scot-free or with a light sentence, while the orthodox Chinese was punished as the letter of the law demanded. Also, considering the nature of missionary activities, it was inevitable that among the representatives of the Christian religion there would be some who were unfit for their extremely difficult calling, who were narrow-minded, prejudiced, intolerant, viewing the totally different conditions and standards of life in the Chinese community through the distorted vision of the average New England village. Tolerance for and a sympathetic understanding of the faults and failures of mankind, together with a correct understanding of mankind itself, is always difficult for the idealist and the reformer. Especially is it hard for him to realize that a code of conduct and morals of great success, apparently, in one part of the world, may be a total failure when transplanted to another part, due to the different environment, to racial atavisms, and to the variability of human nature, which can never successfully be bound down to one philosophy applying to all alike. Thus it was that the native convert was weaned from filial piety, which the majority of his Christian advisers confused with ancestor worship, through a lack of knowledge of Chinese social conditions. For a time, although this policy is now happily reversed, he was taught to reject the teachings of his native literature, the moral guide of the race for centuries and imperishably linked with it, for the spiritual benefits of the Scriptures. He was led to expect that the judges, through foreign pressure, would treat him with partiality. He was instructed to refuse his tithe for the humble village festivals, parades and theatricals, the only pleasures, besides a fight or an accident, which relieve the fearfully monotonous existence of the laboring classes, this because he was made to understand that such innocent amusements were sinful according to the Bible, or to whatever religious sect the particular missionary happened to belong. Even in those fields wherein the missionaries did a truly wonderful service for China and the Chinese, for which they deserved and have received unstinted praise, such as increasing the comforts of life and raising the standard of living, introducing sanitation, hospitals, medical attendance, and spreading general education, their work was either ignored or misunderstood, because of its obvious correlation with the religion of Europe. The fault lies largely with Christianity. It has the misfortune in every alien land of running counter to almost all the cherished local institutions. It offends everyone, it antagonizes every creed, it mingles with none, because its fundamental tenets deny the co-existence of any other faith or standard of morality. In China, Christianity encountered further opposition. This was the predilection of the vast majority of Chinese, especially the educated classes, for their own code of life and morals, which leaves little to be desired as it is eminently practical and earthly, with no speculations on divinity and the hereafter. Probably China never will become Christianized, for the Chinese mind does not lend itself to theological dogma. It would indeed be a misfortune if the Far

East, in emulating the development of Europe, had yet to undergo that course of instruction in Christianity which marked its path even in modern history, such as the Revolt of the Netherlands, the Thirty Years' war, the Inquisition, the Edict of Faith, the fires of Smithfield, or, granting these lamentable aftermaths of the " religion of peace " as impossible to-day, to suffer intestine persecution, political discrimination, Catholic disabilities, the *Kulturkampf,* the warfare between science and theology, and the factional differences of our score of antagonistic denominations. Better Stygian darkness, of course according to *our* view, than light at such a cost. The Chinese have never had a religious war; in that they have been thrice blessed.

But what above all was an impenetrable mystery to the Chinese at this time was the fact that Christian Powers, instead of themselves being guided by the doctrine of "peace on earth and good will to men ", to which they gave such constant lip-service through their clerical representatives, should have followed the diametrically opposite policy that " might makes right ", that whatever could not be obtained by fair means should be acquired by a resort to blood and iron. It was the European code of political morals, essentially Machiavellian, which counteracted every good result obtained by the missionary, which predestined reform to failure, and which fittingly wound up with the greatest disaster of all, the Boxer Rebellion. The mistakes of the time were largely Europe's mistakes, even to that final blunder, the bombardment of the Taku forts, which instantly united all the rebellious and anti-foreign elements against western aggression. An enumeration of the immediate determining causes of the Boxer Rebellion is more to be found in diplomatic archives than in a study of any other sources. Leases, commercial servitudes, the loss of sovereignty over the finest harbors, the hypothecation of *likin* and salt revenues, the contracts to promoters and concessions to missionaries forced at the cannon's mouth, the talk of partition, the diplomatic wrangles over " spheres of influence " and " balance of power ", the exaction of the last possible farthing as indemnity for acts for which neither Europe nor the United States would have granted indemnity or apology— the answer of the Chinese to all these national humiliations was the outbreak of 1900. In fact, from the day of the German seizure of Kiaochau, which there introduced the sorry argument of the mailed fist in Chinese politics, the Boxer Rebellion was a foregone conclusion, and apology and blame for succeeding events should primarily be laid at Europe's door, not at China's.

Naturally, the Chinese population of the foreign " spheres ", in their fear over what seemed then the certain dissolution of the Empire, wreaked their vengeance first upon the missionaries, as these were nearest at hand and in the imagination of the people symbolized the presence of the Powers in China and could not be dissociated from them. It seems rather appropriate that the province of Shantung, the scene of the initial European aggression and of the German *Hinterland,* should likewise have cradled the Boxer movement [1] and furnished the first concerted opposition to Europe. It so happened that three American missionaries in this locality were roughly handled. Without going too much into detail over this particular affair, it may be noted that the missionaries submitted a correspond-

---

[1] For accounts of the organization of the Boxer movement and its preliminary stages, see Cordier, *op. cit.,* vol. iii, ch. xxiv, "Les Boxeurs," pp. 451-462; Smith, vol. i, ch. x, " Genesis of the Boxer Movement," pp. 152-174; ch. xi, " Gathering of the Storm," pp. 175-195; ch. xii, " Spread of the Rising," pp. 196-217; Bland and Backhouse, *op. cit.,* ch. xvi, " The Genesis of the Boxer Movement," pp. 247-250; Rev. F. L. Hawks Pott, *The Outbreak in China* (New York, 1900), pp. 79-91.

ence later sent to the American Minister at Peking, giving the following conclusions, which are valuable as they typify the situation in the early months of the Rebellion:

1. It (their particular affair in Shantung province) is clearly not an isolated case, but one of several simultaneous occurrences, showing a widespread and violent antiforeign feeling.

2. The present outbreak is directly connected with the *Coup d'Etat* at Peking. The people are led to believe that the reaction against the Reform Government, of which they have vaguely heard, involves the expulsion of the foreigners.

3. Vigorous measures must at once be taken in the way of stringent instructions to local officials, and plain-spoken proclamations, backed up by the necessary force, if this antiforeign feeling is to be subdued before worse things happen.

4. We have no complaint to make of the civil authorities, with whom we have had to deal. The Prefect Ting Cheng and the hsien or county official of I-chou-fu, Chen Kung Liang, certainly did all in their power to answer the appeal of the ladies for help.

The action of the Chu Chou official, as related above, was prompt and effective. The prefect for six days travelled literally day and night.

None of these named was responsible for the trouble, as they made every exertion to rescue us and the German priest. It would be a great injustice if they were made to suffer in the premises.

5. We can not say as much for the military authorities of I-chou-fu. The hsieh tai, or resident colonel in command of the *regular troops* [1] of the prefecture, is a Mahomedan named Li Ying. When the ladies appealed to him he refused to do anything, on the absurd ground that the country of Ji Chao is the territory of his subordinate, the tu ssu, commandant of Ngan Tung Wei, on the seacoast. Colonel Li has, it is true, very few soldiers under his command, but that lack is in itself

---

[1] The *italics* are the author's.

a just cause for complaint, and besides he did not use any of the few men he has, as he might well have done. Still more culpable is the case of Brig. Gen. Tai Shou Li, who was sent down from Chinan-fu in the spring under pressure from you (Consul Fowler),[1] as he himself admitted, for the express purpose of protecting the foreigner. He is supposed to command a liang (500) of troops, but at present has here in the city (I-chou-fu) only about 80 or 100 men. When the ladies appealed to him on this occasion for soldiers to go to our rescue he said that he could not comply without an order from the governor. In response to this we have simply to say that if it be true that every time an emergency arises he must wait for orders from Chinan-fu, 640 li away, he is not of much use here, and the sooner he gets the necessary authority the better for the foreigner.

6. If the Ho Chia Lou[1] people carry out their promise to make full restitution for the damage done by them, we are not disposed to prosecute them for their flagrant lawlessness. That would probably be a wise step, if only to bring home to them the gravity of their crime. We should feel disposed, however, in view of our compact made with them, to intercede with the authorities for them at the proper time.

7. We agreed to a settlement upon the basis of their simply making good the damage, because :

(1). Although we were ourselves placed by them in undoubted peril of our property, if not of our lives, we were not actually attacked ;

(2). We recognize the fact that the people of Ho Chia Lou, while inexcusably in the wrong themselves, had a certain amount of real grievance against some of our Christians (meaning the native converts), which, while not enough to justify their resort to lawless violence,

[1] American consul at Chefoo.

[2] One of the neighboring villages.

must still be taken into account in judging their conduct.[1]

Such was the situation as early as November, 1898. Minister Conger acted with vigor and promptitude to have the above case adjudicated by indemnity and punishment. After months of weary negotiations with the Yamen, he was able to report in October, 1899, that a " satisfactory indemnity " had been paid, and thus, although the American Minister failed to secure the punishment of the rioters,[2]

[1] Report by Messrs. Killie, Faris and Chalfant, in U. S. *For. Rel.*, 1899, Inc. 1 in no. 142, pp. 154-157.

These three able missionaries later, December 26, 1898, sent a second report to Consul Fowler (*Ibid.*, Inc. 6 in no. 142, pp. 159, 160), saying in part:

" It should be added that the attacks upon the Christians (still meaning the native converts) are of a most vindictive character. . . . The affair (in the same vicinity) has not yet assumed the proportions of an organized rebellion, but is rapidly drifting in that direction."

They were also of the opinion that:

" 1. The present outbreak shows conclusively that the military force in this prefecture is not adequate enough to police the territory.

" 2. The country south of us is in a constant state of disturbance, owing to the local banditti who come and go over the border lines between Shantung and Kiangsu.

" 3. There is now a state of famine in northern Kiangsu and lawless outbreaks are occurring there and in the extreme southern parts of this province.

" 4. It is quite likely that some of the German syndicates who are visiting our city from time to time may attempt to buy lands and open mines here in the spring, a proceeding which, however commendable in itself, is almost sure to give rise to local disturbances."

[2] " Upon this showing (an enumeration of what Conger had accomplished) the Department (of State) is disposed to think that, while the procedure suggested by you may operate to bring about a settlement of this particular case satisfactory to the immediate sufferers, you have foregone a convenient opportunity for insisting upon the responsibility of the local authorities of I Chou-fu, whose punishment you might have continued to urge on the lines of the policy laid down in the instructions heretofore sent to the legation in analogous cases, such

this particular incident was regarded as closed.[1]

Germany meanwhile received a welcome opportunity to display her military organization. A punitive expedition of 125 soldiers, " for the purpose of enforcing order and peace ", penetrated inland to within fifteen miles of the Ichoufu disturbances, and with characteristic German thoroughness burned two small villages because the inhabitants had attacked a German lieutenant and engineer. Another detachment 120 strong marched to Jihchao where a German Catholic priest had been maltreated, and quickly restored order, carrying away, it was reported, a number of the local officials and gentry to be held as hostages until the inevitable indemnity had been satisfactorily arranged.

While such was the melancholy prelude, far worse disturbances characterized the closing months of 1899 in this same region. The lawlessness was now distinctly of Boxer character, the combination between the Fists of Righteous Harmony and the Big Sword Societies producing a new crop of riots, looting and massacres. It seemed that the officials made hardly an effort to quell the disorders; in fact, if not actually encouraging or assisting, they sympathetically delayed or ignored the prosecution of the prominent

punishment being in complete accord with Chinese ideas, and being, moreover, apparently the only recognized method of preventing the recurrence of such inquiries. There is ground for apprehension lest an omission, the appropriate case arising, to strongly bring to the knowledge of the Tsung-li Yamen the purpose of this Government to insist upon the punishment of the local officials may tend to weaken any representations you may hereafter be called upon to make in that sense under standing instructions."

Act.—Sec. A. A. Adee to Min. Conger, U. S. *For. Rel.*, 1899, no. 203, p. 176.

[1] *Ibid.,* no. 142 and Inc. 1, 2, 3 and Subinclosure, 4, 5, 6, 7, 8, 9, 10, 11 and 12, no. 148 and Inc. 1 and 2, nos. 151, 160, 181 and Inc. 1 and 2, no. 186 and Inc., nos. 191, 196, 211 and Inc. 1, 2 and 3, no. 215 and Inc. 1 and Subinclosure, no. 232 and Inc. 1, 2, 3, 4 and Subinclosure, 5, 6 and 7, no. 265 and Inc. and Subinclosure.

malefactors. The indignation of the Diplomatic Corps at this open favoritism to the Boxers in Shantung and elsewhere reached such a pitch that the Peking Court judged it expedient to remove the Governor, Yu Hsien, who was called to the capital " on consultation ", and though relieved of his duties in the turbulent province, was decorated with the character *Fu,* signifying happiness, " because of his failure to protect the Christians and their property".[1] As a further mark of favor, he was transferred as Governor to Shansi. To square itself with the aroused diplomats, the Court appointed Yuan Shih-kai Governor of Shantung, the best selection possible, whom the American Minister pronounced an " able, brave, courageous man ", and who " has mingled much with foreigners, and it is believed that if the right kind of orders are given him from the Throne, the rioting will be stopped and order restored ".[2]   But such orders were not given, and the new Governor was too shrewd a statesman to work his individual will against a movement which apparently had the good wishes of the Imperial Government. Had he been unhampered by advice from Peking, and allowed to use his great natural abilities and his foreign-drilled army against the undisciplined hordes opposing all authority, the Rebellion would have been nipped in the bud. Possibly, however, Yuan Shih-kai arrived too late. Shortly after his appearance upon the scene in Shantung the murder of the British missionary Brooks vastly complicated the situation,[3] and although the courageous Governor did all in the limited power allowed him to undo the work of his predecessor, the riots had already reached that stage (January, 1900) which clearly

[1] Minister Conger, in U. S. *For. Rel.,* 1900, no. 316, pp. 93, 94.

[2] *Ibid.,* no. 289.

[3] *China No. 3 (1900),* nos. 1-5, 9, 10, 18, 22, 26, 30, 31.

foreshadowed the international catastrophe of the same year.[1]

Meanwhile, like disturbances were taking place in other parts of the Empire, separate though sympathetic movements which, growing rapidly worse in volume and intensity of hatred to Christianity and the foreigner, finally coalesced through their affinity of purpose in the tragedy we know as the Boxer Rebellion. There was the riot at Shashih, directed against the British and Japanese, in which " nothing was spared " : the Custom House, Haikwan Bank, Commissioner of Custom's house, China Merchants' property, Jardine, Matheson and Co.'s property (one of the great English trading companies in China), and the Japanese Consulate—all were destroyed.[2] There were the riot in Chihli,[3] the anti-foreign and anti-Christian disturbances in central Szechwan,[4] the Kwangsi insurrection,[5] the antimissionary riot at Foochow,[6] the trouble in Yunnanfu,[7] the terrible outbreaks in Paotingfu,[8] the Kienning riots,[9] the murder of the British missionary Fleming,[10] of Robinson

[1] On the Shantung disturbances, see *China No. 1* (*1899*), no. 446; *China No. 1* (*1900*), no. 401; *China No. 3* (*1900*), nos. 8, 9, 11, 16; U. S. *For. Rel.*, 1900, nos. 223, 228, 234, 246, 249, 252, 289, 307, 312, 316, 332, 338, 339, 345, 356, 368.

[2] *China No. 1* (*1900*), nos. 83, 170, 223, 269, 270, 346, 364, 411, 415, 417, 419, 453, 458.

[3] *China No. 3* (*1900*), nos. 11, 19, 21.

[4] *China No. 1* (*1899*), nos. 330, 341; *China No. 1* (*1900*), no. 194. For the riots in Szechwan in 1895, see U. S. *For. Rel.*, 1895, nos. 87-172.

[5] *China No. 1* (*1899*), nos. 230, 247, 298, 305, 315; *China No. 1* (*1900*), no. 222.

[6] *China No. 1* (*1900*), no. 181.   [7] *China No. 3* (*1900*), no. 40.

[8] *China No. 3* (*1900*), nos. 37, 62.

[9] *China No. 1* (*1900*), nos. 202, 205, 206, 210, 213, 214, 293, 313, 318, 347, 355, 364, 384, 439.

[10] *China No. 1* (*1899*), nos. 393, 431, 466, 471; *China No. 1* (*1900*), nos. 5, 10, 49, 108, 118, 157, 170, 180, 193, 199, 207, 215, 216, 218, 219, 237, 241, 249, 256, 265, 269, 326, 334, 338, 393, 407.

and of Norman.[1] These calamities were all contributory to those in Shantung, inspired by the same motives, producing the same results, and directed towards the same ends.

Serious trouble in Peking itself gave the foreign representatives their first unmistakable hint of coming misfortunes. As early as September, 1898, the temper of the rabble in the capital, reinforced as they were by 10,000 Kangsu troops temporarily quartered there, revealed itself as a conclusive index to the future. At the annual mid-autumn festivals the trouble began, simultaneously in four different places. To quote M. Cologan, Dean of the Diplomatic Corps:

It is not necessary to mention them (the attacks) in detail. It is sufficient to state that the father of a member of the Legation of the United States was severely wounded, and that a member of the British Legation and an English lady, a French citizen, and two Japanese subjects were wounded or attacked or insulted—all while proceeding from the railroad station.[2]

The British Minister observed:

There were a large number of bad characters in the streets, which, to a certain extent, accounted for this behavior on the part of the mob, but there has been, since the so-called *Coup d'Etat*, a very considerable amount of unrest in the city, more especially since the execution of six of the reform party. These men were supposed by the common people to have been put to death by order of the Empress Dowager because they had dealings with foreigners. It was, therefore, considered safe to insult foreigners in every possible way.[3]

Sir Claude MacDonald further remarked that the inci-

---

[1] *China No. 3* (*1900*), nos. 66, 70, 71, 75.

[2] U. S. *For. Rel.*, 1898, Inc. in no. 81, p. 233.

[3] *China No. 1* (*1899*), no. 399.

dents referred to were due not to individual feeling against the persons concerned but to the fact that they were Europeans, Americans, and Japanese; in other words, that they represented the races which, as the populace believed, would soon be driven out of China forever. Of course the Yamen expressed regret, and later even punished those responsible for the outrages. What makes this particularly notable is the welcome opportunity it gave the Ministers of objecting to the presence of the Kangsu troops in the capital and also of demanding Legation guards. As these two factors may be considered the beginning of international complications with China, they will be treated in the next part.

In closing, it is pertinent to observe how singularly the Europe of 1899 misread events. None looked for an organized resistance of the Chinese people, much less of the Chinese Government, and the possibilities of any opposition to the wishes or acts of the Powers were then as lightly entertained as later they were tremendously overestimated. The journals of Europe saw in the approaching storm only incipient riots against Christianity, to be regarded merely as the usual pot-luck attending the fortunes of missionaries in the Far East. The deep, underlying cause of this international misunderstanding, immensely greater than the missionary or religious question, to wit, the recent territorial aggressions of the Powers, in fact, the conduct of Europe ever since 1840, entirely escaped notice. Referring to the fears of the British, who alone seemed to have an inkling of what was coming, the *Ost Asiatisches Lloyd* (reproduced by the Berlin *Post* of March 20, 1900), in protesting against the " attitude of certain organs of the English and Chinese press that have circulated the most incredible rumors about events in China of a nature to make people in Europe believe that China is either on the threshold of a revolution or of a general collapse of her system of government ", said :

One could heartily laugh over the whole affair, were it not that the question has undoubtedly a most serious side to it. The reports which even the most respectable papers have published during the last few weeks have made a deep impression which will not be easily removed upon the Chinese population, and more especially among traders, who naturally know little about the dynastic and political conditions of their country, but who place implicit confidence in the statements of Europeans.

The wild tales that are telegraphed to Europe and America must influence the value of Chinese stock, but more especially the confidence of the home market in Chinese affairs.

Do the English press organs realize the result of their attitude?

Thus English newspapers recently announced to the world the sensational news of the dethronement of Huang-fu (Kuang Hsu), a report which the world endeavored to better by adding that perhaps the Emperor had committed suicide. Confidence in the stability of the present state of things in China is naturally seriously shaken by such rumors, the effect of which is already making itself sufficiently felt in the Far East.[1]

Equally was the Chinese character misunderstood. Europe, wholly influenced by the superficial estimate gathered from the results of the Chino-Japanese war and the ease with which territory had been filched from the Empire, was unable to entertain a contrary opinion, and not until the siege of the Legations and the difficulties of the Allies in reaching Peking (a curious resemblance, by the way, to Lord Wolseley's advance on Khartoum), was it believed that such a display of patriotism and resolution on the part of the alien race would ever have been possible, and not till then were certain capabilities of the Chinese character critically regarded, if not with admiration, at least with respect.

[1] *China No. 3 (1900)*, no. 25.

PART II

THE INTERNATIONAL COMPLICATIONS OF THE BOXER REBELLION

PART II

THE INTERNATIONAL COMPLICATIONS OF THE BOXER REBELLION

Question of the Kangsu Troops—First Legation Guards—Second Legation Guards — Attitude of Chinese Government towards the Boxers—Imperial Decrees concerning Boxers—Distinction between "Good and Bad" Societies—Instructions to Viceroys—Arrival of Foreign Warships at Taku—Dynastic Succession—Attitude of the Yangtse Viceroys—Policy of United States—Bombardment of Taku —A State of War existing? — Seymour Expedition — Capture of Tientsin—Second Allied Army—Capture of Peking.

FROM an international standpoint the Boxer Rebellion consists of four parts:

    I. Preliminary diplomatic affairs.

    II. Siege of the Legations.

    III. Efforts of the Allies to reach Peking.

    IV. The punishment inflicted upon China.

After the assault upon Mr. Campbell, Assistant Chinese Secretary of the British Legation, while visiting the railway bridge in course of construction at Lukouchiao, by a party of the Kangsu troops then encamped in the Imperial Hunting Park at Peking, the British Minister addressed a note to the Tsung-li Yamen "protesting against the presence of these uniformed brigands near Peking and the railway lines", and, "in view of their well-known anti-foreign professions", he demanded "their removal without loss of time to a safe distance". He insisted further "on a thorough investigation and punishment of the offenders". The same afternoon he repeated his demands.

The Yamen was "very apologetic" and seemingly showed every disposition to conciliate Minister MacDonald. They informed him that a decree had already been issued to inquire into the affair, and they promised "that steps would be taken to pen the whole army (between 10,000 to 15,000 men) temporarily in the Hunting Park, and keep them out of mischief until they were drafted gradually to more distant stations". As MacDonald added to Lord Salisbury: "There can also be little doubt that the Chinese Government are themselves (in addition to the Legations) afraid of these Mahommedan brigands—for they cannot be called soldiers".

That was on October 24, 1898. The matter was brought up at a meeting of the Diplomatic Corps, October 27th, advising the Yamen, for the sake of peace and prevention of further outrages, to have the troops removed at once.[1] To this collective note the Yamen replied substantially as to the British Minister, agreeing that if the troops were left in Peking, "grave disorders might ensue". Therefore, "it had been decided to send these troops elsewhere soon". In the opinion of the Diplomatic Body, the Yamen's reply was "not entirely satisfactory", and "further and more energetic steps" must be taken by the united Ministers to force immediate action.

Two of the soldiers concerned in the previous attacks were punished by the authorities quickly enough. But, as the Chinese Government "had, as far as could be ascertained, taken no steps whatever for the removal of the Kangsu troops" it was "unanimously decided" to address

[1] In conclusion M. Cologan, the *Doyen*, said: "En prévenant le Yamên à temps, le Corps Diplomatique accomplit un acte amical et il s'efforce de mettre fin à une situation anormale, qui au lieu de s'apaiser, semble devenir chaque jour plus délicate et critique." *China No. 1 (1899)*, Inc. 1 in no. 422.

another note to the Yamen of a more peremptory character, adding that " the Kangsu troops should quit the Province of Pechili not later than the 15th of November, and
further that the place to which they were going should be
stated ".[1] The representatives of the Powers were united
in this demand. The Japanese Minister, M. Fumio Yano,
informed the Diplomatic Corps that, should China refuse
to accede to the above stipulations, " Japan would join with
the other Powers in compelling them (the Yamen) to
do so ".

In answer the Yamen pointed out, following a further
note of November 11th, that " it has now been settled that
these troops are to leave in detachments, beginning on the
15th or 16th instant, until they have been withdrawn. The
troops are to go to the west of Chichow and to be stationed
along the mountains ".[2] The Diplomatic Body answered
that this arrangement, although " inspired by a desire to
put an end to the difficulties which have arisen, does not
completely satisfy them ", as, " contrary to one of the demands made, the Kangsu troops will not leave the Province

---

[1] M. Cologan, *Doyen* of the Diplomatic Body, to the Tsung-li Yamen:
" En s'inspirant de ces idees, le Corps Diplomatique me charge
d'écrire cette note au Yamên pour demander :
" 1. Que ces troupes aient au plus tard le 15 November quitte la
Province du Péchihli.
" 2. Que la destination qui leur sera donnée soit indiquée.
" 3. Si ces décisions n'étaient pas prises et notifiées au Corps Diplomatique, ce serait pour les Gouvernements étrangers le cas d'aviser aux
mesures nécessaires pour garantir la sûreté des étrangers et pour as-
surer la circulation sur les chemins de fer et la liberté des communications télégraphiques." *China No. 1 (1899)*, Inc. 1 in no. 443.

[2] "Although they (the troops) will not be outside the territory of
Chih-li, they will be very far from the railway, and we can certainly
assure you that the movements of the officials and merchants who
travel by the railway will in future not be interfered with in any way."
The Tsung-li Yamen to the *Doyen* of the Diplomatic Body, *China No. 1
(1899)*, Inc. 1 in no. 462.

of Chihli immediately ". Therefore, at the end of their patience, they considered it " their duty to refer the matter to their Governments ", leaving it to the latter to decide what should be done. Then Prince Ching and the Yamen likewise considered it their duty " to explain this matter ". It was made clear to the Diplomatic Corps that "the Kangsu troops came here (Peking) to be reviewed. They are more than 10,000 in number, and were sent into camp at Nanyuan. A great many carts are required for the march, and the troops must leave gradually in detachments. It is therefore difficult to act quickly ". But it was resolved that, " when the day for their departure is fixed we will inform your Excellency (the *Doyen*) immediately ". With the question of these " uniformed bandits " thus disposed of in a half-way satisfactory manner,[1] the attention of the diplomats was taken up with the urgent need for Legation guards, which was equally serious.

The necessary precedent for armed protection of the Legations had already been established by a similar situation of insecurity during the Chino-Japanese war. Therefore the Ministers were confident that without undue pressure brought upon the Chinese Government their request would be amicably granted. This matter had been carefully reasoned out by the American State Department in 1895. In response at that time to Minister Denby's statement that " the question of the right of the Legations to have escorts here (Peking) is abstract and independent of the probability of its exercise ", Secretary of State Gresham replied: " I do not find in any of the treaties with China provisions authorizing the protection of the Legations by foreign troops ". But the Secretary equally ob-

---

[1] U. S. *For. Rel.*, 1898, Telegram p. 225, Telegram p. 226, no. 56 and Inc. 1 and 2, no. 81 and Inc. 1, 2, 3, 4, 5, 6; *China No. 1 (1899)*, nos. 421, 422, 435, 442, 443, 450, 462; *China No. 1 (1900)*, nos. 20, 28.

served that " China, like any other Government, is bound
to offer adequate protection ", and if this were not forthcoming, " there is no reason why the Legation should court
danger " by remaining defenceless.   Therefore he authorized a military guard to be sent to Peking " under similar
conditions " as those of other Powers, in accordance with
the most-favored-nation clause of the American treaties.[1]

As Legation guards were again an urgent necessity, a
meeting was held by the Diplomatic Corps, October 4, 1898,
in which it was decided by unanimous vote " to notify the
Chinese Government of the proposed departure from Tientsin for Peking to-morrow of bodies of British, German,
and Russian marines, and to ask that all facilities, including a special train, should be extended to them by the
Chinese authorities ".   It was also intimated that the
French, American, Japanese, and Italian marines were " to
come straight on to Peking on their arrival at Tientsin ".
Of course China objected, and the Chinese Minister at London denounced the contemplated move as " a slur upon the
Chinese Government ".   The Tsung-li Yamen, in answer
to the note of October 4th, replied :

We hope that your Excellency (Cologan) will ask your colleagues to be kind enough not to bring their soldiers for pro-

[1] " The President sees no reason why the Legation should court
danger by remaining at Peking in the face of imminent or threatening
peril; and you have the right to an adequate escort to assist you in
avoiding it by removal to a place of safety where you would be under
the immediate and legitimate protection of your own flag.   Nevertheless, in view of your telegram of the 18th instant, reporting that other
Legations are bringing military guards to Peking with the consent of
the Chinese Government, I telegraphed the 19th instant, as follows :
" You say troops have arrived with China's consent to protect other
Legations.   In coöperation with Carpenter you are authorized to bring
up marines under similar conditions."
U. S. *For. Rel.*, 1895, vol. i, pp. 198, 199; Moore's *Digest*, vol. v, p. 626.

tection. This for the purpose of preventing the spirit of the people from being excited, the circulation of false rumors, and provoking, we fear, other troubles.

Later followed an interview with the British Minister, in which Prince Ching begged MacDonald to reconsider his decision, assuming that his consent " would be sufficient to stop the arrival of the guard of all the Legations ". In answer, MacDonald advised the Prince and the Ministers of the Yamen " to accept the inevitable, and to accept it gracefully ". Then he promised them that, " by taking stringent measures to insure good order, they might hope to shorten the stay of the guards in Peking ", but remarked that " opposition, while it would be futile, would certainly increase the number of the guards and lengthen their stay in Peking". After a two-hour discussion, Prince Ching decided to " accept the inevitable ", moreover, did it " gracefully " as requested, for arrangements were made to supply a train in which to convey the foreign detachments.

The British guard reached Tientsin first, and consisted of an officer, 25 men, and a machine gun. On October 4th the Russians arrived, 30 mounted Cossacks and 38 marines, with a small field-gun. The Germans disembarked the following day, with 30 marines. It was the intention of these three divisions to leave immediately for Peking, but they were forbidden to do so by the Viceroy of Chihli until he had orders from the Yamen to that effect. When they did reach Peking, further trouble developed, as witnessed by the communication of the Yamen to the *Doyen* of the Diplomatic Body:

PEKING, OCTOBER 7, 1898.

From an official communication, it was stated in your Excellency's note of October 5, instant, that the number of soldiers composing each of the escorts (Russian, English, and German) was about thirty. But the detachments arrived today, the Germans had thirty, the English less than thirty, and the Russians alone had sixty-six.

This is not in accordance with the note which your Excellency sent us.

We request, therefore, that your Excellency will be kind enough to reply immediately and explain to us the cause of it.

This is important.

M. Cologan got out of the difficulty by replying that he had given approximate figures only to facilitate " the composition of the train " which the Chinese Government was to furnish. However, although the matter was dropped, a decidedly unpleasant feeling had been aroused, and the Ministers of the Yamen again felt that they had been tricked.

A short while after, the American contingent arrived, " 18 well-armed marines and a gatling-gun ". They also rode in a special train.[1] When these various troops arrived, the " demeanor of the crowd was quiet and respectful ", for the sufficient reason that no other attitude was possible. As it was, the Diplomatic Body held the Yamen responsible for the whole affair, particularly because at the meeting on the evening of the 4th of October, a despatch from the Yamen was read in which the assaults on foreigners were treated " very lightly ", and neither in this despatch nor in a *Red Letter* which accompanied it was there the least expression of regret for what had occurred. This decided the foreign representatives to summon their guards at once from Tientsin. However, MacDonald was of the opinion, " should no untoward event occur, and matters remain quiet ", that the guards could be withdrawn in three weeks, with the reservation that it was impossible to predict the future with any degree of accuracy.

[1] See U. S. *For. Rel.*, 1898, vol. i, Inc. 10 and 11 in no. 81.

As a matter of fact, the troops stayed much longer. The Imperial Government, becoming impatient, early in December requested the diplomats " to decide as to the date on which the guards can with safety be withdrawn ", but this request " received no encouragement ". It is amusing how naive the diplomacy of China and the Powers was every once in a while at this time, not alone on the side of the Peking Court but on that of the foreign Ministers as well. Far from letting the question rest, the Chinese representatives at the European capitals and at Washington continued insistent in their demands that the objectionable troops be removed. Finally, after these had spent a quiet winter in Peking, conditions were adjudged such that their presence was no longer necessary, and in early spring, 1900, comparative order and security having been restored, these initial defenders of the Legations evacuated their respective compounds and marched away to the coast.[1]

But the situation in China, though for a brief period quiescent, except here and there an explosion of wrath against the foreigner and his proselytism, came to take a decided turn for the worse. The cloud of the Boxer Rebellion, at first a mere speck upon the horizon, spread slowly but surely, gaining momentum and magnitude with every fresh outbreak of unbridled fury and misguided patriotism. From Shantung, where the energetic Yuan Shih-kai had enforced a sort of armed tranquility, the activities of the Boxers spread to the neighboring provinces, leaving death and destruction in their wake, and setting the country around, even to the gates of Peking, in a turmoil. The foreign Ministers were not blind to what was going on, but hoped that the Central Government would eventually suppress the

[1] *China No. 1* (*1899*), nos. 345, 348-350, 355, 357, 400, 402, 405, 406, 414, 425; *China No. 1* (*1900*), nos. 12, 145; U. S. *For. Rel.*, 1898, pp. 228-232, 235-244.

unexampled lawlessness growing daily more unrestrained. In this the authorities failed absolutely, and the publication of ineffective decrees, the disinclination to denounce the Boxers, and the laxity of the Imperial troops and officials in punishing or even in apprehending the rioters convinced the diplomats that, after an absence of guards for over a year, it was again imperative to have the security of the Legations insured by the presence of their own nationals.

Their decision came quickly, through the force of immediate events. As Conger reported to the Department of State:

To the consternation of all, on Monday the 28th (of May, 1900), word came that the railroad was attacked, two bridges and two stations burned on the Paoting-fu line, and that all the foreigners connected with the line had fled to Tientsin, or were besieged in their homes. Later in the day it was learned that Fengtai, the second station on the Tientsin line, only 10 miles from Peking, and where are located the railroad machine shops, was being burned, no trains were running between Tientsin and Peking, and the Boxers were reported marching on Peking.[1]

This disastrous news stirred the Diplomatic Body to instant action.

A hurried meeting was called, in which " it was decided to bring the Legation guards to the city without delay ". The following letter was addressed to the Tsung-li Yamen:

PEKING, MAY 28, 1900.
Your Highness and Your Excellencies:
I have the honor to inform your Highness (Prince Ching) and your Excellencies that the representatives of Germany, England, Austria-Hungary, United States, France, Italy, Japan, and Russia have decided at a meeting of the Diplomatic Corps to bring immediately some detachments of troops to Peking.

[1] U. S. *For. Rel.*, 1900, no. 383, pp. 132, 133.

I am instructed to request of you, in the name of my colleagues, to give the necessary instructions, that the detachments, whose arrival is expected at once, may find at Tangku the trains to bring them to this capital.

It goes without saying, that this decision of the Ministers does not authorize the Chinese Government to avoid taking the measures, which the Ministers have demanded for so long a time, necessary to put an end to the rebellion for which it is responsible and the continuance of which can only aggravate the present situation in China.

Accept, etc.,   COLOGAN, *Doyen.*[1]

In reply the Tsung-li Yamen called the attention of the diplomats to the fact that the Chinese Government " had already sent troops to investigate and take the necessary action ". But this communication lost all its force by their admission that these troops were recruited from the *Hou Chen Ying,* the camp commanded by the violent reactionary Prince Tuan, and from the *Wu Wei Kun,* the army of Jung Lu. As both of these armies and also Prince Tuan were notoriously pro-Boxer and anti-foreign, all hope was eliminated from that quarter. But the Yamen did beg the Ministers to delay their requisitions for guards at least three or four days, by which time the measures of the Imperial Government would be " crowned with success ". The Ministers waited two days, with no change for the better in the situation. Then followed an interview in person with the Yamen,[2] in which Sir Claude MacDonald, opening the meeting, asked " that permission be granted and facilities be offered to transport guards to Peking for the purpose of protecting the Legations ". He assured the members of

[1] U. S. *For. Rel.,* 1900, Inc. 8 in no. 383, p. 137; *China No. 4 (1900),* Inc. 5 and Trans. in no. 1.

[2] The Ministers of Great Britain, Russia, France and the United States were present.

the Yamen present [1] that it was a " friendly request ", but, should it be refused, " the guards would come up without permission and, no doubt, in larger numbers than at present intended ". The interview terminated with the threat of the Ministers that they would have their guards " permission or no permission ". On the first of June the Yamen gave their official consent, but begged to state that there was " really no necessity " for such action, " but if the foreign representatives insist on this step the Yamen will on their part interpose no obstacles ". It was stipulated, however, that " each Legation should have twenty to thirty men on an average, and no more ", the same as eighteen months previous.

The Ministers lost no time in communicating with Tientsin, and the first train-load of guards, instead of the regulation 20 to 30 as permitted by the Yamen, brought 75 Russians, 75 British, 75 French, 50 Americans, 40 Italians and 25 Japanese. The German and Austrian contingent arrived the following day. In all there was at Peking during the siege a total of 21 officers and 429 men.[2] It was fortu-

[1] Hsu Yung-i, Hsu Ching-cheng, Yuan Chang, Liao Shou-heng, and Lien Yuan.

[2] Total of guards present, by nationality:

	Officers	Men
American	3	53
Austrian	5	30
British	3	79
French	3	45
German	1	50
Italian	1	28
Japanese	1	24
Russian	2	79
Total	19	388
French	1	30
Italian	1	11
Grand total	21	429

U. S. *For. Rel.*, 1900, Inc. 2 in no. 399, p. 190.

nate for every nation concerned, equally including China, that these troops were at Tientsin awaiting the order to advance. Had they not arrived at Peking to take part in the International Episode which began a few days later, no relief of the Legations would have been necessary, as the Legations would have ceased to exist.[1]

Now as to the attitude of the Chinese Government towards the outbreaks, first against the native Christians and later including the foreigners. To begin with, the Empress Dowager had no particular antipathy against the west, but was forced to ally herself with the reactionaries in order to crush Kang Yu-wei and the reform party, whose program necessarily demanded her complete retirement from Chinese politics. Her activities against the Emperor and his friends were thus inspired by purely personal motives, ambition being her motive at all times and not hatred of Europe. When the disturbances in Shantung began, she was undoubtedly in favor of stamping out the riots, in fact, started out by instructing the Government and people by Imperial decrees to that effect. But the inefficient methods of the army and the administration, and the halfhearted manner in which punishment was meted out, and then only when such action was absolutely necessary, convinced the shrewd Tzu Hsi that the sympathies of the population lay with the disturbers of the peace and not with the restoration of order or the imposition of penalties such as Europe demanded. A skillful prognosticator of current events, she was more than anxious at this period to conciliate her subjects and to meet their desires because of the telling blows which had been dealt the Manchu monarchy by the Chino-Japanese war, the signing-away of territorial

[1] For review see *China No. 3* (*1900*), nos. 50, 53-56, 58-60, 65, 69, 72; *China No. 4* (*1900*), no. 1 and Inc. 5 and 6 in no. 1; U. S. *For. Rel.,* 1900, pp. 129, 131-133, 137-139, 142, 144, 190.

and economic concessions, and the overturning of prece-
dents and other acts which had offended custom and tradi-
tion. For the sake of the Throne, the wishes of the majority of the people, whatever they were, must be upheld,
for Her Majesty was well versed in the history of the preceding dynasties. Also, the Manchu family quarrel had
ended with the elevation of Prince Tuan, bitterly anti-foreign, as spokesman for the Government, ably assisted by a
host of the old-fashioned. The result was a complete re-
versal, helped, of course, by contemporary incidents, of the
policy of the Court during the Rebellion. At the beginning
of the disorders it was deemed best, for the sake of a good
understanding with the Powers, to proceed energetically
against the rioters, in words if not in deeds. But the rebels,
far from dispersing, increased in numbers. As the Rebellion changed at different periods, gradually acquiring national character, it finally reached that point where the
Chinese Government could not have subdued it even if they
had so wished, and with this increase of the Rebellion in
magnitude and power the policy of the Court was altered
until at last, instead of suppressing, the authorities were
actually organizing, financing, and directing the war against
the world.[1]

However, judging by appearances, the first decrees
seemed entirely satisfactory. Regarding the initial disorders in Shantung the edict of October 6, 1898, declared:

Ever since foreign nations have had commercial relations

---

[1] Minister Conger to Secretary Hay, September 3, 1900: "That the
Throne indorsed and encouraged the Boxers in their attacks against
foreigners, organized them, placed princes and ministers in command
of them, paid them, exhorted them, extolled them, and made common
cause with them is abundantly confirmed by the Imperial decrees
transmitted in my dispatch no. 305 of August 17, and is therefore responsible for the whole movement and its results."
U. S. *For. Rel.*, 1900, no. 400, p. 190.

with China there has been no difference in their treatment. The local officials have been repeatedly instructed to protect all missionaries in China.   Both officials and gentry in all the provinces should respect the desire of the Court to treat all alike. They should exhibit sincerity and honesty and be without doubt and suspicion, in order that there may be continual and mutual peace, etc.[1]

Somewhat later appeared a more explicit decree:

The customs and government orders of western nations are different from those in China.   Although these differences exist, yet the adoption of western methods in military affairs, agriculture and commerce have proved really beneficial. Therefore, if what is good is selected and carried out in order, the benefits will increase daily, etc.

Western people have come from afar and across many oceans to China for the special purpose of exhorting people to do right.   Therefore they (meaning the missionaries) should be protected, according to treaty, in order that friendly relations may be preserved.   Moreover, it is to be feared that ignorant and foolish persons will make false conjectures which will prove misleading.   They surely do not bear in mind that the Empress Dowager is at all times earnestly striving to prosper her country, and so she is kind to the people from distant lands, and her treatment of foreigners and Chinese is the same.

The people and missionaries of this province (Shantung) have lived together amicably for a long time.   The saying " do not forget to entertain strangers " should be considered, and more than this, strangers should be treated with great courtesy.   Moreover, Christians and natives, who live in the same village and drink from the same well, are friends.   Who, with heaven over their head and earth beneath their feet are not the sons of the Court?   How much more even should they be mutual friends and not cherish any enmity or suspicion!

[1] U. S. *For. Rel.*, 1899, p. 158.

In addition to instructing the local authorities to exhort the people, proclamations have been issued for their enlightenment.

This proclamation has been issued for the purpose that all the soldiers and people of this province may understand that hereafter they must obey the decrees which have frequently been promulgated in order that the missionaries and native Christians may all be treated as friends. Moreover, if any dare disobey and spread rumors and cause trouble by inciting the populace, they must be immediately apprehended and severely punished, and will not be shown any leniency.

Beware! [1]

Judged by a strict literal interpretation, the above edicts left little to be desired. They expressed in forcible terms clearly set forth and admitting of no cavil the Government's disapproval of the revolutionary movement, and the apparently sincere efforts of the Court to enforce a settlement. But it must be borne in mind that these were Oriental decrees, not the proclamations of western Powers, and addressed to an Oriental audience, not to a European. [2] Too often they were to be construed in a sense directly opposite to the wording of the text. Again, even if intended to the letter, they had to contend with the maladministration and corruption of the Government, with the sympathy of the ruling Manchus for the disturbing masses, with the covert hostility of almost every one at this time, from the highest to the lowest, to Europe and Europe's ways. True, had Yuan Shih-kai been allowed to play his part alone, he would have ended the Boxer Rebellion only a little while after it began, but he was hampered by secret instructions from the Court and the Yamen, by orders in direct contradiction to those intended for publication. Consequently,

---

[1] U. S. *For. Rel.*, 1890, p. 158.

[2] See Smith's fine criticism of the decrees in *China in Convulsion*, vol. i, pp. 188, 189.

when the ablest Governor failed, it goes without saying that others failed likewise in crushing the revolt. Moreover, these edicts seemed primarily to be designed for the purpose of satisfying the demands of the Diplomatic Body, of throwing dust in their eyes, a plan which, though excellently in accord with Manchu statescraft, did not work very successfully. The tone of the foreign representatives towards these ineffective efforts to restore order soon became decidedly pessimistic, due to long and continued association with the tortuous methods of the Chinese governmental and diplomatic policy.

It will be remembered that Italy had applied in 1899 for a lease of Sanmen Bay and had been refused, to the wonder of the world. Italy did not press her demand, preferring to let the matter drop, but the consequent effect of this slight diplomatic victory on the Peking Court was immense, and was magnified out of all proportion to its real importance, which was after all very slight. Italy, had she wished, could have made short shrift of Chinese opposition, but not caring much either way, had been counseled to refrain from all attempts at force and thus save annoyance and possible embarrassment to the Triple Alliance. The result was unfortunate for China because of the false estimate of having beaten Europe at its own game. Notice the tone of the following edict:

As the Italians have not had their ambition gratified in respect to the cession of Sanmen Bay to them, it is apprehended that they may try to seek opportunity for seizing other portions of the coast. Moreover the arbitrary and aggressive methods of the French at Kuang-chouan, where they are stirring up disturbances in order to obtain pretexts for demanding further concessions from the Imperial Government, may lead to actual hostilities between China and France. It behooves us, therefore, to exercise the utmost vigilance and watchfulness to guard against sudden aggression and to be always prepared to resist an enemy. . . . This Yamen has received the special commands of Her Imperial Majesty the Empress Dowager and His Imperial Majesty the Emperor to *grant you full power and liberty to resist by force of arms* all aggressions upon your several jurisdictions, *proclaiming a state of war, if necessary, without first asking for instructions from Peking*,[1] for this loss of time may be fatal to your security and enable the enemy to make good his footing against your forces, etc.[2]

Before commenting on this decree, it may be advisable to add the secret edict issued November 21, 1899, to the Viceroys, Governors, Tatar Generals and provincial commanders, a communication even more significant than the above:

Our Empire is now laboring under great difficulties, which are becoming daily more serious. The various Powers cast upon us looks of tiger-like voracity, hustling each other in their endeavors to be the first to seize upon our innermost territories. They think that China, having neither money nor troops, would never venture to go to war with them. They fail to understand, however, that there are certain things which this Empire can never consent to, and that, if hardly pressed upon, we have no alternative but to rely upon the justice of our cause, the knowledge of which in our breasts strengthens our resolves and steels us to present a united front against our aggressors. No one can guarantee under such circumstances who will be the victor and who the conquered in the end. But there is an evil habit which has become almost a custom among our Viceroys and Governors which, however, must be eradicated at all costs. For instance, whenever these high officials have had on their hands cases of international dis-

---

[1] The *italics* are the author's.

[2] *Circular dispatch* from the Tsung-li Yamen to the Viceroys and Governors of the Maritime and Yangtse provinces. U. S. *For. Rel.*, 1900, p. 85.

pute all their actions seem to be guided by the belief in their breasts that such cases would eventually be " amicably arranged." These words seem never to be out of their thoughts; hence when matters do come to a crisis, they of course find themselves utterly unprepared to resist any hostile aggressions on the part of the foreigner. We, indeed, consider this the most serious failure in the duty which the high provincial authorities owe to the Throne, and we now find it incumbent upon ourselves to censure such conduct in the most severe terms.

It is our special command, therefore, that should any high official find himself *so hard pressed by circumstances that nothing short of war would settle matters, he is expected to set himself resolutely to work out his duty to this end.* Or perhaps it would be that war has already actually been declared; under such circumstances there is no possible chance of the Imperial Government consenting to an immediate conference for the restoration of peace. It behooves, therefore, that our Viceroys, Governors, and Commanders-in-Chief throughout the whole Empire unite forces and act together without the distinction of particularizing of jurisdictions so as to present a combined front to the enemy, exhorting and encouraging their officers and soldiers in person to *fight for the preservation of their homes and native soil from the encroaching footstep of the foreign aggressor.* Never should the word " peace " fall from the mouths of our high officials, nor should they even allow it to rest for a moment within their breasts. With such a country as ours, with her vast areas stretching out several tens of thousands of *li*, her immense natural resources, and her hundreds of millions of inhabitants, if only each and all of you would prove his loyalty to his Emperor and love of country, what, indeed, is there to fear from any invader? *Let no one think of making peace, but let each strive to preserve from destruction and spoliation his ancestral home and graves from the ruthless hands of the invader.*[1] Let these our words be made known to each and all within our domain.[2]

[1] The *italics* are the author's.

[2] U. S. *For. Rel.*, 1900, pp. 85, 86.

The foreign diplomats were not aware of these two decrees until the beginning of 1900, over a month after they had been issued to the Viceroys.   On the second of January, Conger, the American Minister, transmitted them to the Department of State.   Although they had, he said, " only just come to light ", yet it seems that they should have given the Diplomatic Body fair and sufficient warning of the coming catastrophe, appearing as they did almost half a year before the Legations were finally in a state of siege.

With such unmistakable indications of the disasters rapidly approaching, why were the second Legation guards not ordered until the end of May?   Why was there not sufficient discernment to have these troops in Peking by the new year, thus taking time by the forelock, producing the " salutary effect " so much desired, and sparing China her international disgrace?   However, there is nothing so easy as to prophesy the future when it is already past history. The whole world at that time, diplomats, travelers, scholars, merchants, saw only the China of the Japanese war, the " China in decay ", the " break-up of China ", the "disappearing Empire "; and the other China, the one that was soon to oppose the united energies of Europe, was not thought of by even the boldest imagination.   The reason was that China had as yet shown herself incapable of resistance in an organized and national way to the despoilers from over the seas.   It was believed that such resistance was not only improbable but actually impossible.   As a refutation of this fallacious theory the Boxer Rebellion is alone noteworthy, for it revealed to mankind the then astonishing and partly unwelcome fact that China as a political entity was destined to endure the same as racially; that the period from 1840 to 1900 could never be repeated by either side; that the Boxer outbreak, failure though it was when judged by material advantages, yet again gained for

China that respect due a sovereign power which had been denied to the Empire during the preceding few years. Opinions of the Far East in 1901 were in many ways the antithesis of those not only firmly believed in but put into practice in 1900 and before. China, unwittingly enough, had gained a moral victory, in which was concealed the foundation for future greatness.

One cannot help admiring in the above decree the effective manner in which the grandiloquent style aptly characterized the recent activities of Europe. No better criticism of European territorial aggression has been expressed than this, where the Powers, amusingly enough, are represented as casting upon the defenceless Empire looks of "tiger-like voracity", and the accusation that they were "hustling each other" to gather in the harvest of leases and concessions was equally and painfully true.

The most discussed decree of all, which aroused most anger and comment among the diplomats and foreigners, was the one which discriminated between "good and bad societies", which ordered that certain organizations, meaning the two essentially composing the Boxer union,[1] must not be confounded in the public mind along with the banditti and other outlaws. The style of this edict was particularly ambiguous, more than typically Oriental, and was expressly designed to defeat what seemed at first glance to be its ostensible purpose. By reading between the lines of this extraordinary communication, or having it carefully explained to them by the *literati,* well versed in such governmental hypocrasies, the Boxers naturally were charmed with its contents, as it effectively encouraged them in future acts of bloodshed and pillage and offered them immunity from that punishment which heretofore had dampened their

[1] The "Fists of Righteous Harmony" and the "Great Knife" societies.

enthusiasm and spoiled the thoroughness of their work. Said the edict in part:

It must be borne in mind, however, that a discrimination should be made in the nature or object of leagues or societies. There are reckless and worthless fellows who associate themselves together and become joined in sworn brotherhood and, relying on their numbers, create trouble and make disturbances.

If law-abiding and loyal people, attending to their proper duties of life, should combine together to study and practice the skill of experts in any art of science (of militia) for the purpose of serving their own protection, or where villagers band together for the mutual protection and guarding of their villages and hamlets, this is moreover nothing more or less than carrying out the duty of keeping watch and rendering mutual help.

Should the local officers, when cases occur, not exercise extra care in making a due discrimination between them, and carelessly listen to rumors, and regard all societies as being composed of evil doers and punish men recklessly with death, this would result in there being no discrimination made between the good and the bad. The people's minds would therefore be in fear and doubt, as the good and the bad would be treated alike. Not only would the temper of the people be disquieted, but the action of the officials would be bad and improper, etc.[1]

The natural result followed. The Boxers, immune from punishment by their Imperial protection, became bolder and before long appeared in the vicinity of the capital itself. However, as it was necessary for the Government to save its face with the Diplomatic Corps and the world at large, admonitions exhorting the officials to act against the disturbers continued to be issued. But these had no effect whatever, and instead of alleviating the situation, in reality

---

[1] U. S. *For. Rel.*, 1900, pp. 88, 89.

made it worse. The decree of May 17, 1900, though stringent enough in tone, was absolutely useless, as the preceding edict had already informed the Boxers that any command against them was but a dead letter and need not be feared nor obeyed. Said the edict:

The society called the "Fists of Righteous Harmony" having spread to Peking, we some time ago issued our instructions direct from the Palace to the office of the gendarmerie to take action in good earnest to prohibit its operation.

We have now learned that wicked and malicious persons, under the name of the Society of Boxers, have posted placards [1] containing false statements everywhere in the inner and outer cities of Peking, the object being to create suspicion and disturb the minds of the people, which it is greatly to be feared will result in stirring up trouble.

Let the office of the commandant of the gendarmerie, the Governor of Peking, and the police censors of the *Wu Cheng* (the five divisions of the city and suburbs of Peking) confer together as to the best manner of taking protective measures to search out and prohibit this society and to decide upon some satisfactory rules to be put into operation at once. The result of their deliberations, however, must first be submitted to us in a memorial.

Let Yu Lu (Viceroy of Chihli) in like manner take action to stringently prohibit this society.[2]

Again, on May 29, the Court expressed itself as follows:

Lately, in the vicinity and neighborhood of our Court, the villagers and rustics have been practicing boxing and their physical strength. There are the good and the evil-minded scattered together, and as we entertained great fear that trouble would happen, we issued our commands repeatedly to the vari-

[1] For books and proclamations against foreigners and Christianity, see U. S. *For. Rel.*, 1900, pp. 123-125.

[2] *Ibid.*, p. 134.

ous Yamens, both inside and outside of Peking, to strictly prohibit them from practicing.

We have now learned that the Boxers are very numerous, and that there are traces of disbanded soldiers and rebels being among them; that they have recklessly created disturbances and brought about disorder; and they have even extended their outrageous acts to killing a military officer, burning and destroying the telegraph poles and railway. We are grieved that they do not obey the law. And what is the difference between them and the rebels? etc.[1]

Again, on June 8, came a plainly-worded decree:

On account of the Boxers having created trouble in the neighborhood of the capital, and the minds of the people having become excited, and a feeling of unrest prevailing, we repeatedly issued our commands that stringent measures be taken to investigate and deal with the matter. But of late there are vagabonds and rowdies armed with swords and weapons who roam about the streets and market places in gangs of from three to five persons. They assemble together and disperse at uncertain times, and if they are not at once stringently prohibited a state of disorder will certainly prevail. The gendarmerie, the Governor of Peking, and the police censors of the five cities are charged with and responsible for the arrest of outlaws and patrolling and guarding the place. How is it that this class of persons are allowed to band together at the very gates of our Court and cause excitement in the minds of the people? etc.[2]

It is not necessary to quote further. As affairs in China approached a climax the Empress Dowager, partly from necessity and partly from choice, came more and more under the influence of Prince Tuan and the reactionaries and anti-foreigners. The Boxers, at first discouraged, then

[1] U. S. *For. Rel.*, 1900, p. 134.
[2] *Ibid.*, p. 147.

secretly countenanced, finally were openly aided by the Court, and by June 20th, less than a fortnight after the appearance of the preceding decree, we find them actually paid and provisioned by the Imperial Government. Said an edict in this regard:

Whereas the Boxers have now assembled together in Peking, the Prince and Ministers (of the Tsung-li Yamen) are collecting contributions of silver and rice in order to enable them to accomplish the loyal and patriotic object they have in view, and render it convenient for them to attack and exterminate (the foreigners and Christians). The Prince and Ministers have recently heard, however, that there are persons who have no sense of shame, who impersonate others and fraudulently solicit contributions with the avowed purpose of seeking their own profit. This practice is certainly detrimental to the interests of the Boxers, etc.[1]

As if that was not enough, telegraphic instructions were sent out a week later from the station at Paotingfu to the Viceroys and Governors in south and central China, as follows:

Whereas open war has now broken out between China and the foreign Powers, and the Boxer Society around Tientsin, and throughout Chihli, coöperating with the Imperial troops have been victorious,—we have already issued decrees praising their bravery. These loyal people are to be found throughout the Empire, and all Governors and Viceroys, if they can raise forces from their number, can rely on them to oppose insolence of the foreigners with greatest success. The higher provincial authorities shall, therefore, memorialize immediately regarding their plans of campaign. The Viceroys of the Yangtse and coast provinces are hereby commanded to use their most strenuous endeavors to put these instructions into effect.[2]

[1] U. S. *For. Rel.*, 1900, p. 192.
[2] *China No. 3* (1900), no. 240.

Meanwhile, what was the attitude of the foreign diplomats in regard to the " Fists of Righteous Harmony "? [1] Their interview with the Yamen soon convinced them that little help towards a mutual understanding was to be expected from that quarter, as the Chinese Foreign Office had stubbornly refused at first to publish decrees against the Boxer society, and when finally forced by diplomatic pressure to comply, had responded with the ineffectual documents cited above. There seemed little else for the diplomats to do than to suggest a naval demonstration of the Powers, in order to bring the Peking Court to its senses. But to such action the Russian Minister, M. de Giers, was strongly opposed, as at the least it was an extreme step and might " give rise to unknown eventualities ".[2] Therefore it was decided to bring guards to the capital instead, in the hope that this would have the like " salutary effect ". However, to make doubly sure, Vice-Admiral Seymour of the China Station telegraphed to the Admiralty that, as affairs at Peking were " becoming more serious ", he was proceeding to Taku with the warships *Centurion* and *Whiting*, while the *Fame* and *Endymion* would shortly follow. On June 6th, a further addition, the *Phoenix* and *Aurora*, arrived from Weihaiwei. A meeting of the Allied commanders of the warships in the harbor was held on board the *Centurion*, in order " to discuss (the) situation and arrange concerted action if necessary ". But to any " concerted action " of a hostile nature the American commander, Admiral Kempff, was of opinion contrary to the rest of the Allied officers. This was because of the rather anomalous attitude of the United States towards China,

---

[1] In the opinion of the British Minister, the term "League of Patriotic Union" was "the nearest equivalent of the later Chinese designation of the Boxers." *China No. 4 (1900)*, no. 2, p. 21.

[2] *China No. 3 (1900)*, no. 43.

resulting from its traditional friendship for that country and its disinclination to become embroiled with Europe in Far Eastern hostilities. This attitude of the American Admiral, which was not his personal view, as he was simply following the dictates of the Department of State, later subjected him in particular, and the United States in general, to much adverse criticism. At present it is acknowledged that the stand of the United States was the correct one at the time under discussion, before the attack on the Taku Forts. Admiral Seymour was unhampered by instructions, the British Government telegraphing him as follows: " The situation is difficult, and your discretion must be quite unfettered. You may take precisely what measures you think expedient ". An identical message was sent the same day, June 7, 1900, to Sir Claude MacDonald at Peking.[1]

As the time had now arrived when coming events were casting their shadows before, the foreign representatives at the Chinese capital acted with energy and decision. As a final effort to come to a definite understanding before it was too late, MacDonald proposed that the Diplomatic Corps demand an audience with the Emperor and the Empress Dowager. There was no longer any doubt how matters stood at Court. The unfortunate Kuang Hsu was at last reduced to a complete nonentity. In an Imperial decree of January 24, 1900, conveniently labeled "by the Emperor's own pen ", he had been forced to declare that, " since last year we have suffered from ill health ", with the result that " affairs of State have increased in magnitude and perplexity, and we have lived in constant dread of going wrong ". For this reason, " we therefore implored the Empress Dowager to aid us in the Government. This was more than a

---

[1] *China No. 3 (1900)*, nos. 82 and Inc., 84.

year ago, but we have never been restored to health, and we have not the strength to perform in person the great sacrifices at the altar of Heaven and in the temples of the spirits of the land ". With affairs in this melancholy state, according to the judgment of the Old Buddha and her crowd, it was discovered that " we (the Emperor) suffer from an incurable disease ". Therefore, " it is impossible for us to beget a son ", which meant that " the Emperor Mu Tsung Yi (the preceding Emperor Tung Chih) has no posterity ", and, as a result, " the consequences to the lines of succession are of the utmost gravity ". After " sorrowfully thinking on this ", in addition to being browbeaten into submission, the puppet Emperor " humbly implored Her Sacred Majesty carefully to select from among the near branches of our family a good and worthy member ", the same to be the Heir Apparent. And so, " after repeated entreaties ", Tzu Hsi " deigned to grant her consent that Pu Chun, son of Tsai Yi, Prince Tuan, should be adopted as the son of the late Emperor Mu Tsung Yi ".[1] The immediate effect of this declaration was to eliminate Kuang Hsu entirely from Chinese politics, and, as if that was not enough, the reign of China's reform Emperor was further passed over and ignored as if he had never existed. Typical Oriental despotism here, where, for the sake of personal ambition, the interests of the country and the welfare of the people were lost sight of through Palace intrigues, by the sordid gains and aggrandizements of the few at the cost of the many. Had the Empress Dowager really been actuated by sincere patriotism this act might be forgiven because of existing conditions, but such was not the case. Instead of choosing a virile, able successor, for instance like Prince Pu

[1] *China No. 3* (*1900*), nos. 28, 29; U. S. *For. Rel.*, 1900, pp. 91-93. Pu Chun was deposed as Heir Apparent by a decree of Nov. 30, 1900, on the ground that he was lacking in respect for Her Majesty.

Lun, she merely took care that the Heir Apparent should be one of tender years, so that her own continuance in power as long as she was destined to live would not be endangered.

By this arrangement of the dynastic succession the Court committed itself to the Boxer cause, and this meant that sooner or later collusion with the enemies of western civilization was unavoidable. Indications of an abrupt change in the attitude of the Chinese Government were soon manifest. On June 8th the situation had become so threatening that the foreign diplomats petitioned the Yamen for permission to increase their guards. Their request met with a peremptory refusal. The next day the Court deliberately allied itself with the revolutionary movement by appointing four new members to the Tsung-li Yamen, Prince Tuan as President to succeed the able Prince Ching, and three new Ministers, Chi Hsiu, Pu Hsing, and Na Tung, all reactionaries of the extreme type. With Prince Tuan as head of the Foreign Office there was no doubt that harmony with the Throne would be assured, but, as Conger remarked, his appointment as virtual Premier of China was " extremely unfortunate ". The American Minister at this early stage (June 11th) drew a correct portrait of the Prince:

He is known to be malignantly antiforeign, a patron of the Boxers, and has many of them in his division of the army. His policy toward them cannot, therefore, be expected to be a repressive one, but must mean continual persecution and attacks upon missionaries and their followers, destruction of their property, hindrance of trade, and constant menace and danger to all foreigners and foreign interests.[1]

[1] See *China No. 3* (*1900*), nos. 61, 186, 222, 225; U. S. *For. Rel.*, 1900, pp. 145, 154.

Within a month Prince Tuan was in practical control of the capital, for the time being reducing even the Empress Dowager to a secondary position.

Of course that ended all hopes of an Imperial audience of the Diplomatic Corps. But a temporary concession was granted the foreign representatives when three Ministers of the Yamen paid a visit to Conger in the already barricaded American Legation. In the interview which followed, Conger reproached the Government as being directly responsible for the outbreak. He wanted to know "why the Chinese troops did not fire upon the Boxers instead of trifling with them; nothing but killing them could ever bring about order". The Ministers acknowledged that the "native troops were practically useless", and Conger retorted in a burst of pardonable pride that with one thousand American soldiers he could kill every Boxer in Peking. It seemed about all that the Chinese Ministers wanted was information concerning the first relief expedition to Peking; but in this they were not enlightened. That was the last personal interview;[2] even by that time (June 17th) the diplomats and their families were "completely besieged" in their various Legation compounds, "with the entire city in possession of a rioting, murdering mob", and "with no visible effort being made by the Government in any way to restrain it".[1] This report was not received by the Department of State until September 25th, for by June 13th the curtain had practically been rung down on affairs in Peking.

The incidents of the siege of the Legations and of their

[1] See *Memorandum* of interview in U. S. *For. Rel.*, 1900, pp. 152, 153.

[2] *Ibid.*, no. 392, p. 154. Conger reports, June 15, that, "we are simply trying to quietly defend ourselves until reinforcements arrive, but nearly 100 Boxers have already been killed by the various Legation guards."

relief have been told by enough writers,[1] so that it would be superfluous to add to the mass of already available material. In conclusion we will note some of the instances which demand comment in a work of this kind.

Efforts were made from the first to restrict the field of operations to Peking and Tientsin, and instrumental in bringing about this position was the Consular Body in central and south China. At Shanghai the Consuls issued a proclamation to the wavering inhabitants which was written in Chinese and designed as much as possible to conform to the Oriental mode of expression and thought. Such action was imperative as all trade had stopped because of the fighting in the north, and because, with eight foreign warships in the harbor, with steamboat service discontinued, and with cotton mills idle, conditions were peculiarly those which incite the ignorant and lawless of the population to mob violence and looting. Therefore, to reassure the timid and to persuade them to remain, after thousands already had left the city, the Consular Body published the following:

[1] A graphic description of the siege of the Legations is found in Smith's *China in Convulsion.* Thomson, *China and the Powers: A Narrative of the Outbreak of 1900* (London, 1902), gives a detailed account of the attack on the Taku Forts, the siege of Tientsin and the two expeditions. See also Allen, *The Siege of the Peking Legations* (London, 1901); Hooker, *Behind the Scenes in Peking, being Experiences during the Siege of the Legations* (London, 1910); Landor, *China and the Allies,* 2 vol. (New York, 1901); Martin, *The Siege in Peking: China against the World, by an Eye-Witness* (New York, 1900); Oliphant, *Diary of the Siege of the Legations in Peking during the Summer of 1900* (London, 1901); Russel, *Story of the Siege of Peking* (London, 1901); Simpson, B. L. (Putnam-Weale), *Indiscreet Letters from Peking; being the Notes of an Eye-Witness* (New York, 1911); Viaud, L. M. J. (Pierre Loti), *The Last Days of Peking,* trans. from the French (Boston, 1902). For sources see MacDonald's *Correspondence* of the Siege in Peking, *China No. 4 (1900).* See also *China No. 3 (1901); China No. 4 (1901);* U. S. *For. Rel.,* 1900, *passim;* Cordier, *op. cit.,* vol. iii, pp. 516-537.

Owing to the troubles in the north, many rumors have been circulated in Shanghai which have unsettled the minds of the people. In their ignorance of the true state of affairs they have frightened themselves and each other, and in fleeing homeward from Shanghai have in many cases fallen a prey to robbers.

We, the Consular Body at Shanghai, have consulted with the Chinese authorities regarding the protection of life and property in this neighborhood, and have agreed to act in coöperation in putting down any disturbances that may occur. The municipal council holds the volunteer corps in readiness for the protection of the (foreign) Settlement, and our warships have taken up their positions in the river for the same purpose, and for that alone.

With such precautions, both on shore and afloat, and with the cordial coöperation of the Chinese authorities, there is no reason why the troubles in the north need spread into these parts. There is no cause for alarm, and we hereby give notice to all that the presence of foreign men-of-war in the river is only a measure of precaution for the protection of the Settlement, and that there is no foundation of truth in the idle rumors with which many persons are now exciting themselves.

Joaquim Maria Travassos Valdez,
Consul-General for Portugal and Senior Consul.[1]

It was necessary above all to obtain the assistance of the leading Viceroys, Governors and *taotais* if peace in the south was to be preserved. Fortunately for China and the world, it so happened that some of the greatest Chinese statesmen were then serving in provincial administrative capacities, among them Li Hung-chang as Acting Viceroy of the Two Kwangs (Kwangtung and Kwangsi provinces); Liu Kun-yi as Viceroy of Kiangsu, Kiangsi and Anhwei; Chang Chih-tung, Viceroy of Hunan and Hupeh; Yuan

---

[1] U. S. *For. Rel.*, 1900, p. 250.

Shih-kai as Governor of Shantung, Wang Chih-chun as Governor of Anhwei, and Yu Lien-san as Governor of Hunan. The Viceroy of Chekiang was undecided at first, as he had already published Prince Tuan's edict to the people calling for active participation against the foreign Powers; but he came around in due time. Yuan Shih-kai's position was particulary difficult. That he was more or less on the fence at the beginning of the troubles is not to be wondered at, but his attitude, though seemingly contradictory in some respects, was clear enough to the observant foreigner. His province of Shantung had cradled the Boxer movement, and was situated next door to Chihli province. Moreover, the Governor, like Li Hung-chang, was on good terms with the Empress Dowager and even with the reactionary Court officials. And Yuan was too shrewd a statesman and too clever a politician openly to alienate the sympathy or support of either party, or, above all, to become *persona non grata* to the rulers of his country. However, Yuan Shih-kai's course, as has been intimated, was correctly read by the diplomats and consuls; in fact, he rendered invaluable aid. As the confidant of the Court, he was the only one in touch with the situation in Peking, but just how he got his news no one seemed to know. He faithfully transmitted his scraps of information to the foreigners in central and south China and to the Admirals at Taku, and through his agency the world knew that the tragedy in the capital was being strung out instead of ended at a single blow, as most had feared.

No less remarkable in preventing the spread of the anti-foreign movement was Liu Kun-yi, the Viceroy of Nanking, at this time 77 years of age, having for 35 years served in this high official rank. He was regarded as the leader of the Hunanese, the most warlike Chinese in the central provinces. Having been summoned to Peking for an Imperial audience, he had the rare courage to tell the Empress Dowager in outspoken terms that her policy would be the ruin of the country. He succeeded in incurring the enmity of Prince Tuan, Kang Yi and all the reactionaries. These tried their best to prevent his reappointment in the south, but Liu Kun-yi was too firmly established in the friendship of Tzu Hsi, and so was permitted to resume his duties. He was instrumental in arranging the league of the Viceroys in south and central China, which was now responding so favorably to the views of the foreign Ministers and Consuls. More than that, he associated himself at the capital with the liberals, in opposition to the reactionaries. That the unfortunate Rebellion did not spread throughout the Empire was due to these half-dozen Viceroys and Governors, who saw beyond the events of the moment and were not blinded by hate or prejudice in their views as to what was best for China and the Chinese.

It was not to be expected that all of the provinces affected would unite against the Boxers. Honan and Shansi joined the anti-foreign movement, which was natural, considering their proximity to Chihli province and the influence of the reactionary party upon their leaders.

The Chinese Minister at London had despatched a *memorandum* to the Downing Street Office which read in part:

The Viceroy (of Huquang) tenders his grateful acknowledgments to Lord Salisbury for his friendly offer (of sending ships and also giving asylum for the Viceroys on board British vessels in case of personal danger), and will gladly avail himself of it in case of need. He, however, is persuaded that he and his colleague, the Viceroy of Nanking, with whom he has been in communication on the subject, will be more than able to cope with the " Boxers " or any other elements of disorder who, contrary to his expectations, may attempt to disturb the peace and tranquility of the Yangtse provinces.

To the British offer of troops to assist in quelling any outbreaks, the answer was:

The Viceroys have at their disposal very sufficient, well-equipped and well-disciplined forces, on which they can implicitly depend, and these they will so dispose and employ as to give the fullest measure of protection to all residing within their respective jurisdictions, whether native or foreigners, and of whatever religion.

The Viceroys well knew that any display of force on the part of the Powers in central and south China would immediately inflame the passions of the people. Therefore, they " would deprecate any obtrusive demonstration of British naval force on the Yang-tse as being calculated rather to make difficulties for the Chinese authorities than to aid them in maintaining tranquility and good order in the riverine provinces ".[1] Lord Salisbury credited these Chinese officials with understanding the peculiarities of the situation, and so refrained from any demonstration or show of force for the purpose of intimidation.[2] But to make doubly sure, the *Hermione* was ordered to Nanking " to communicate with the Viceroy, assuring him of the support of her Majesty's Government in preserving order and protecting British interests ".[3] For the same purpose, the *Linnet* was ordered to Hankow and the *Undaunted* to Woosung.

By July 3rd, the Viceroys Liu Kun-yi and Chang Chihtung made the following definite pledge:

[1] *China No. 3 (1900)*, no. 153.

[2] When the revolt began, the natural inference had been at first that the best way to prevent its spread would be by an " adequate force " to prevent " possible disturbances." This force would undoubtedly have been much larger than the few ships sent had not the Viceroys effectively discouraged such action and, by proving it to be highly injurious, prevented undue augmentation.

[3] *China No. 3 (1900)*, Inc. in no. 140.

We, the Viceroys of the Liang Kiang and Liang Hu provinces, undertake to hold ourselves responsible for the security of foreign life and property within our respective jurisdictions, as well as in the province of Chekiang, so long as the Treaty Powers do not land troops in either the Yang-tse Valley or the province of Chekiang.[1]

The American Department of State observed with pleasure the trend of events in central and south China, and Secretary Hay informed the Chinese Minister at Washington, Wu Ting-fang, that the President was " much gratified at the assurances contained in these telegrams (as the one above)".[2]   Hay further informed Wu that the United States had " no intention of sending any military or naval forces into regions where their presence is not needed ". In addition, the position of the United States in this matter was communicated to the American Ambassadors at London, Paris, Berlin and St. Petersburg and to the American Minister at Tokyo.

The Consular Body at Shanghai was able to inform the *Taotai,* Yu Lien-yuen, that the Admirals at Taku were ex-

---

[1] *China No. 3* (*1900*), no. 244.

[2] A further cable was sent, June 25, in part as follows:

"As no war decree has been received by any of the Viceroys or Governors (thus ignoring Prince Tuan's *Edict* of June 20, already referred to), it is evident that the Imperial Government has no intention of breaking off friendly relations. . . . The Viceroys and Governors of the provinces bordering on the Yang-tse and the coast have assumed full responsibility and are doing all in their power to afford protection (to life and property). Foreigners of all nationalities need fear no solicitude. If there should be further conflict of arms in or about Tientsin it would necessarily follow that southern China would also be involved. . . . The above has the concurrence of all the Viceroys and Governors, and a like message has been communicated, by cable, to the Ministers of Foreign Affairs of the different countries."

Cable from Chang Chih-tung to Minister Wu Ting-fang at Washington. U. S. *For. Rel.,* 1900, pp. 274, 275.

erting themselves likewise to restrict the field of operations, that " they only fight against the Boxers and those who strive to prevent the rescue of the foreigners in danger at Peking and other places ".[1] The Consuls were able to re-assure the Viceroys with the further comforting statement:

Our Governments have had no intention, and now have no intention, either individually or collectively, to take any hostile action or land any hostile force in the Yangtse Valley so long as their Excellencies are able to, and do, maintain the rights of the foreigners in their provinces as provided for in the treaties with the Government of China.[2]

The prompt action of the Viceroys and Governors and the fair spirit in which Europe and America met their advances and adhered to their wishes received its reward. Barring a few outlying skirmishes and riots, the Boxer Rebellion was thus confined to the siege of the Legations, to the capture of Taku and Tientsin, to the two relief expeditions, and to various punitive expeditions in the neighborhood of the above places. Though consequently limited to a comparatively small area and to relatively few objectives, this was a large enough task, as the Allies soon found out, and a great deal more than they had anticipated. Of course, had all the Eighteen Provinces joined in the anti-foreign movement, the result in the end would have been exactly the same, with a still greater humiliation for

[1] TAKU, JUNE 20, 1900.
The Admirals and senior officers of the Allied Powers in China desire to let it be known to all Viceroys and authorities on coast, river provinces, and cities in China, that they intend use of their arms only against the Boxers and those people who oppose them in their march to Peking for the rescue of their fellow countrymen.
Published by request of the Senior Admiral at Taku.
U. S. *For. Rel.*, 1900, pp. 251, 252; *China No. 3 (1900)*, Inc. in no. 164.
[2] U. S. *For. Rel.*, 1900, no. 267, p. 249.

China and an indemnity not only greater but possibly including territory. But in that case, with a united revolt from one end of the vast Empire to the other, such as very nearly took place, its subjugation would have been infinitely more arduous and the loss of life and destruction of property immeasurably greater. The attitude of China's great Viceroys simplified the situation. Had they joined the Boxers. it is safe to say that with their support the Court, the Yamen and the reactionaries would have thrown off all restraint, and every member of the Legations would have shared the fate of Baron von Ketteler and the Japanese Chancellor.[1]

The policy of the United States throughout this period did not deviate a hair's breadth from the one consistently followed ever since it was enunciated in Webster's instructions to Cushing. In fact, the Far Eastern program of the Department of State may be favorably compared in definiteness and singleness of purpose to the attitude of Great Britain in always opposing the strongest power on the mainland of Europe. Both these policies seem to have become permanent fixtures in international politics and diplomacy. The American Minister at Peking, while given authority to coöperate with the Diplomatic Body in the demand for an Imperial audience and in other matters, was nevertheless told to " act independently in protection of American interests when practicable, and concurrently with representatives of other Powers if necessity arise ". Later followed the most definite of instructions:

We have no policy in China except to protect with energy

---

[1] U. S. *For. Rel.*, 1900, pp. 248-252, 265, 273, 274, 276, 277; *China No. 3*, (*1900*), nos. 128, 130, 135, 137, 140, 161, 162, 165, 166, 168, 172, 177, 179, 194-196, 198, 199, 204, 205, 222, 226, 240, 244, 249, 251, 261, 262, 270, 271.

American interests, and especially American citizens and the
Legation. There must be nothing done which would commit
us to future action inconsistent with your (Conger's) standing instructions. *There must be no alliances.*[1]

Thus the national dictum of the United States, first enunciated by Washington and thoroughly established in American diplomacy by the Genêt experience and the mistakes of
the treaty of 1776 with France,[2] has been followed with
scarcely a deviation ever since. This policy is, in effect, to
avoid all entangling alliances and to keep American foreign
affairs distinct and separate from the interests of Europe.
The *Circular* of July 3rd, sent by Secretary Hay to the
American representatives at London, Paris, Berlin, Vienna,
Rome, St. Petersburg and Tokyo for presentation to the
respective Foreign Offices epitomized the course the United
States would pursue at present and upon the restoration of
order:

DEPARTMENT OF STATE,
WASHINGTON, JULY 3, 1900.

In this critical posture of affairs in China it is deemed appropriate to define the attitude of the United States as far as
present circumstances permit this to be done. We adhere to
the policy initiated by us in 1857 (the Reed treaty), of peace
with the Chinese nation, of furtherance of lawful commerce,
and of protection of lives and property of our citizens by all
means guaranteed under extraterritorial treaty rights and by
the law of nations. If wrong be done to our citizens we propose to hold the responsible authors to the uttermost accountability. We regard the condition at Peking as one of virtual

[1] U. S. *For. Rel.*, 1900, p. 143.

[2] Another exception to the general American policy was Article
XXXV of the treaty with New Granada (Colombia) in 1846.

anarchy, whereby power and responsibility are practically de-
volved upon the local provincial authorities. So long as they
are not in overt collusion with rebellion and use their power
to protect foreign life and property we regard them as representing the Chinese people, with whom we seek to remain in
peace and friendship. The purpose of the President is, as it
has been heretofore, to act concurrently with the other Powers,
first, in opening up communication with Peking and rescuing
the American officials, missionaries, and other Americans who
are in danger; secondly, in affording all possible protection
everywhere to American life and property; thirdly, in guarding and protecting all legitimate American interests; and
fourthly, in aiding to prevent a spread of the disorders to the
other provinces of the Empire and a recurrence of such disasters. It is, of course, too early to forecast the means of
attaining this last result; but the policy of the Government of
the United States is to seek a solution which may bring about
permanent safety and peace to China, preserve Chinese territorial and administrative entity, protect all rights guaranteed
to friendly Powers by treaty and international law, and safe-
guard for the world the principle of equal and impartial trade
with all parts of the Chinese Empire.

You will communicate the purport of this instruction to the
Minister for Foreign Affairs.

HAY.[1]

[1] It is necessary to remark that the general principles outlined in
Hay's *Circular* of July 3, were on that same day and again on July 8
enunciated by Delcassé in the French Chamber, and that for the preceding month Delcassé had made this position of France clear to the
diplomatic world. The American Ambassador at Paris, Mr. Horace
Porter, in sending to Hay the statements of the French Minister,
remarked that " his (Delcassé's) definition of the policy of France
in China substantially agrees with us."

Said Delcassé on July 3 to the Chamber of Deputies: " I have
in my previous declarations, particularly last month, clearly explained
the tendencies of our policy in China. The Chamber will remember
that during the past two years I have repeatedly stated that France,
as mistress of Indo-China, has no interest in provoking or desiring
the break-up of China, which is, perhaps without sufficient reflection,

This statement of the various purposes of the American diplomatic policy, being in the main already well-known, met with no opposition in Europe.[1]   The only difficulty seems to have been experienced with the Allied Admirals at Taku, when it was decided in conference to attack and

spoken of. What I can affirm is that France has no wish for war with China, but she cannot evade the duty of protecting her citizens and of obtaining for her merchants the guaranties obtained by others. It is for this and this alone that the Government has taken the measures necessitating these credits. France is certainly anxious for the maintenance of the equilibrium in the Far East. She will see that it is not broken to her detriment, but she cherishes no secret designs. I know not, moreover, who could have particular objects. What I see is that a common peril demands a common aim, and this is comprehended by all the Powers. This is the reassuring feature of the situation, the difficulties of which it would be as childish to deny as it would be to be disturbed by them. I descend the Tribune after repeating the assurance that France, whose efforts are already employed in facilitating the *rapprochement* of the Powers, will continue to neglect nothing for maintaining and strengthening those sentiments of internal and humane solidarity which would prevent them, if necessary, from thinking of what might divide them."

See U. S. *For. Rel.*, 1900, pp. 312, 313.

As far as Germany's plans in China were concerned, these had been sufficiently expressed by Count von Bülow in the Reichstag as far back as April 27, 1898. Said the Count: "Mention has been made of the partition of China. Such a partition will not be brought about by us, at any rate. All we have done is to provide that, come what may, we shall not go empty-handed"; then adding, with the characteristic German fondness for proverbs: "The traveller cannot decide when the train is to start, but he can make sure not to miss it when it does start. The devil takes the hindmost." By this the Count intimated that the Powers could take the initiative in the partition of China, and what they would do, that likewise would be the course pursued by Germany, who was prepared for any event. See *China No. 1 (1899)*, p. 67.

Naturally it was to the interest of Japan to have a free and united China as neighbor, with the hope of future domination, if not politically at least commercially. Russia on her part was slowly advancing at this time by exceedingly shrewd and brilliant moves in the diplomatic conquest of Manchuria.

[1] *Ibid.*, p. 299.

capture the Forts. To this action the American commander, Admiral Kempff, was opposed, on the ground that there had been no declaration of war against China, and that the attack would be tantamount to such declaration. In the bombardment which followed, June 16th, he had the courage to stand aside and take no part in the action or in the capture which followed. He reasoned correctly. The immediate effect of the injudicious conduct of the Allied Admirals was to place the Seymour relief expedition, then about half-way to Peking, in an exceedingly perilous position from which it emerged with difficulty. The attack on Taku further gave the Chinese troops the necessary excuse for joining the Boxers; in fact, it united the Government at Peking, the Imperial army, and the Boxer sympathizers against the Powers, with the convenient argument that Europe had started the war. It is significant to note that immediately after the Chinese Court received news of the bombardment and loss of the Forts, an edict [1] was pub-

---

[1] From the *Edict* of June 29:

" To our surprise on the 20th of the fifth moon (June 16) foreign (naval?) officers at Taku called upon Lo Jung-kwang, the General commanding, and demanded his surrender of the Forts, notifying him that failing to receive compliance they would, at 2 o'clock the next day, take steps to seize the Forts by force. Lo Jung-kwang being bound by the duties of his office to hold the Forts, how could he yield to the demand? On the day named they actually first fired upon the Forts (this was not true; the Forts fired first), which responded and kept up a fighting all day and then surrendered. Thus the conflict of forces began, but certainly the initiative did not come from our side. Even supposing that China were not conscious of her true condition, how could she take such a step as to engage in war with all the Powers simultaneously, and how could she, relying upon the support of an anarchistic populace, go into war with the Powers? Our position in this matter ought to be clearly understood by all the Powers. The above is a statement of the wrongs we have suffered, and how China was driven to the unfortunate position from which she could not escape."

U. S. *For. Rel.*, 1900, pp. 277, 278.

lished which meant practical affiliation with the Boxers,[1] while coincidently all members of the Legations were summarily ordered to leave Peking; and a few days afterwards occurred the distressing murder of the German Minister.[2] Admiral Kempff had defended his position on the ground that neither his Government nor that of any other Power was at war with China; that China could not be considered otherwise than at peace with the world, in spite of internal disorders over which the Chinese Government presumably had no control. In this he was supported by the Administration at Washington.

The refusal of the American Admiral to join the Allied fleet in the bombardment of Taku raises the very interesting question whether war existed between China and the Powers. It seems that the solution of the argument must be left with the individual reader. We have seen that the United States was reluctant to make such interpretation of the difficulties,[3] and that China herself did not regard the disturbances as approaching the dignity and magnitude of an armed conflict until forced to do so by the warships of

[1] This soon developed into a certainty. A *decree* issued June 25 announced that "a sum of 100,000 taels is granted in reward to each of the following army corps: Sheng Tzu Ying, Fu Shang Ying, *and the corps of the Boxers, etc.*"

In addition, four *edicts* on June 27 each promised pecuniary rewards to the Boxers, "as a stimulus to exertion."

See *ibid.*, pp. 169, 170.

[2] Von Ketteler entered upon his last visit to the Yamen against the advice of the entire Diplomatic Corps. For a graphic account of the murder, see *China No. 4* (*1900*), no. 2, pp. 22, 23. As MacDonald observed, the event strengthened the position of "a powerful party determined on war at all hazards," since now there was no escape from it.

[3] Secretary Hay told Lord Pauncefote that the United States "did not think that a state of war necessarily exists." *China No. 3* (*1900*), no. 178.

Europe. Lord Salisbury was of the opinion, June 22d, that, " if the Forts at Taku fired without orders from the Government at Peking, and the attacks on the international troops (Seymour's expedition) are without authority, there is no reason that it should be considered that a state of war exists ".[1] Count Lamsdorff of the Russian Foreign Office was then of the same opinion. Later, however, the relief measures changed to a distinct state of hostilities, call it a punitive expedition or international police or what not. This was inevitable when it gradually leaked out that the Legations were surrounded by *Imperial troops*; that the Court had sided with the Boxers; that the authorities had ordered the Ministers from Peking; had endeavored to entice them into the open by false promises; had tried to ambush them; and had subjected them from June 21st to July 27th to a continued storm of shot, shell and firecrackers. From then on the attacks became more intermittent. Possibly the Court realized the futility of trying to exterminate the diplomats; at any rate, on July 21st the hungry defenders received " three bags of flour, a few watermelons, cucumbers, eggplants, and squashes ", but nothing more, " no arms or any other defence ".[2] The situation was doubly curious because of the half-hearted policy of the Chinese Government, alternately striving to feed and to destroy the Legations, thus trying, so it appeared, to be both at war and at peace with the world. No doubt what held the Court back from decisive action were the momentary spasms of fear at the terrible price which eventually would have to be paid. Especially hesitating and spasmodic grew the attacks when it was realized that China could not possibly be victorious. What all this really amounted to

[1] *China No. 3 (1900)*, no. 176. See also nos. 173-175.
[2] U. S. *For. Rel.*, 1900, p. 199.

was well expressed by Count Lamsdorff in conversation with the British Ambassador at St. Petersburg. Said the Count:

We were at present dealing with a country which was in a complete state of anarchy, and which had no Government or constituted authority which it could be useful to menace, or even address, but we were in a state of war with anarchists, and not with China.[1]

By these " anarchists " Count Lamsdorff was referring to Prince Tuan and the reactionaries; yet these, it must in all candidness be admitted, were for the time being in complete possession of the Chinese Government.

The first expedition of the Allies from Tientsin to the relief of the Legations was prompted to hasty action by a telegram, June 10th, from MacDonald, which dissipated any favorable illusions the Admirals may have entertained concerning the state of affairs. " Situation extremely grave ", wrote the British Minister, " unless arrangements are made for immediate advance to Peking it will be too late ".[2]   That was sufficient warning, and all discussions were dropped in the hurry of the moment. This initial relief column, with Admiral Seymour as Commander and the Russian Colonel as Chief-of-Staff, consisted of 900 British, 500 French, 200 Germans, 200 Russians, 120 Americans,[3] 100 Italians, 25 Austrians, and 200 Japanese. Later, a party of 65 Frenchmen overtook them by rail.[4]

[1] Count Lamsdorff to Sir C. Scott, *China No. 3* (*1900*), no. 246.

[2] *China No. 3* (*1900*), Inc. in no. 103.

[3] Under command of Captain McCalla of the *Newark*.

[4] Cordier, *op. cit.*, vol. iii, pp. 508, 509: " Le 11 juin, le commandant de Marolles, du *d'Entrecasteaux*, avec 50 hommes et un cannon, remonte à Tien-tsin, trouve l'admiral Seymour parti, et le rattrappe avec 65 hommes par chemin de fer."

With little difficulty they penetrated inland to the half-way points, Langfang, Lofa Station and Anting, and there they were decisively checked. It was impossible to advance further, with every village full of Boxers, with Imperial troops barring the way, with the railway line from there on utterly destroyed, with scarcity of food and drink and the knowledge that it was courting annihilation to persist because of the unexpected and overwhelming forces opposing them. In fact, though they marched 30 miles the first day, on the second they covered only three, while it took almost every available man to care for the sick and wounded. There was no alternative but to retreat, greatly to the disappointment of the officers and men, who feared that the return to the coast would seal the doom of the Legations.[1] Indeed, the outlook for the besieged Ministers and their families was gloomy enough, when, assembled at the railway station to welcome the expected Allies, they met instead the taunts and jeers of the Boxer crowd and their sympathizers. The abortive expedition, hard pressed on the way back, was forced to deflect its course so as to capture the Imperial Hsiku Arsenal, a few miles from their objective, where they found a goodly supply of arms, ammunition and provisions.[2] Here they were augmented by

---

[1] Minister Conger: " It is now eight days since the relief party under Admiral Seymour and Captain McCalla left Tientsin. We know they have been within thirty miles of Peking, and we can not understand why, if they find it impossible to readily repair the railway, they do not, with the larger part of their command, march directly here." U. S. *For. Rel.*, 1900, p. 151. Conger was of course unaware of the opposition offered Seymour, both Boxer and Imperial troops, in addition to an already inadequate commissary.

[2] " The capture of this Arsenal virtually saved the force from almost certain annihilation (there were only a few rounds of ammunition left per man), for in it they found abundance of three things of which they were most in need—ammunition, food, and medical stores." H. C. Thomson, *China and the Powers*, p. 15. See also *China No. 3* (*1900*), nos. 206, 227.

a mixed force of 1,800 men commanded by the Russian Lieutenant-Colonel Shirinsky, who had hastened to reinforce their weakened ranks, and together they retreated safely to Tientsin, reaching that city on the 26th of June. Admiral Seymour's column had been in the field for 16 days, some of which had been spent in hard fighting and in imminent peril, and returned with the respectable casualty list of 62 killed and 228 wounded.[1] It was a noble effort but failed because Chinese resistance, which no one had thought at all likely or possible in such degree, was underestimated.

It was fortunate for the small number of Allies then at Tientsin that the 1,800 Russian troops on their way from Port Arthur did not arrive in time to join Seymour's column, as had been intended. Their coming too late was a stroke of fortune, for on June 17th, at three o'clock in the afternoon, the Chinese attacked in force the foreign concessions in the city and reduced them to a state of siege. The day before, at one in the morning, the great Roman Catholic Cathedral had been burned and scores of native Christians butchered. This siege of the concessions in Tientsin was glorious enough in itself, a companion act to the drama which was being so curiously strung out in Peking.

[1] The killed and wounded of the Seymour expedition:

	Killed	Wounded
British	27	97
American	4	25
French	1	10
German	12	62
Italian	5	3
Japanese	2	3
Austrian	1	1
Russian	10	27
Total	62	228

Report of Seymour to Admiralty, *China No. 3* (*1900*), no. 219.

Only 2,500 soldiers and marines were on hand to maintain a position some ten miles in length, with all communication with the fleet cut off for a considerable time. But the troops of the Powers were being rushed to the scene with the utmost dispatch possible. Not, however, until July 14th [1] had enough reinforcements arrived from the coast to relieve after severe fighting the beleaguered force and to capture the entire city, which was indispensable as a base of operations against Peking.[2]

Then came another distressing wait before the advance on the capital could begin. This was largely on account of the changed opinions regarding Chinese valor and the effectiveness of their resistance to the Seymour expedition. As it was, the Allies would have tarried at Tientsin for additional reinforcements some weeks longer had not the British and American commanders threatened to proceed alone with their contingents and risk the consequences. Although it was felt, so had the estimation of Chinese prowess been increased, that at least 50,000 troops were necessary, some thought 70,000, successfully to invade the interior, the second relief expedition to Peking finally got under way, August 4th, with an impressive total of 18,800 men. This number included 8,000 Japanese, 3,000 British, 4,500 Russians, 2,500 Americans, and 800 French. The Germans were unrepresented, as it was judged best to reserve some strength for Kiaochau and the coast, in case of

[1] About 200 Americans and 300 Russians on June 22 made a desperate attempt to enter Tientsin by following the railway. When within two miles they were ambushed and forced to retire, the Americans losing 3 killed and 13 wounded. But upon receiving reinforcements they returned on the 24th and forced their way in, causing the Chinese to withdraw from their position on the east, which enabled the besieged again to have communication with Taku.

[2] See the interesting *Report* by U. S. Consul Ragsdale on the " Siege of Tientsin " in U. S. *For. Rel.*, 1900, pp. 268-273.

the failure to relieve Peking and the need of further hostilities. For the same reasons the British concentrated half their number at Hong Kong and elsewhere. To Germany, however, fell the honor of commanding the Allied forces in China,[1] and the choice of Field-Marshal Count von Waldersee as Generalissimo, to please the Kaiser, gave entire satisfaction.

The start was made at last, and once having been put in motion, the Allied army progressed rapidly enough, in spite of the determined opposition of the Boxers and Imperial troops *en route,* especially at Pehtang and Yangtsung. With the object of the expedition constantly in mind, the Allies kept up a persistent advance, undiscouraged by hunger, thirst, heat, and the discomforts of a trying climate. In two days, by August 13th, Peking was reached, stormed at different points and entered, and the Legations relieved, or rather what was left of them.[2] The following day the work of conquest was completed; the entire city, Tatar and Chinese, was occupied by the invaders, and the war of China with the world was over.

[1] Cordier, *op. cit.*, vol. iii, pp. 536, 537: "Au commencement d'août, l'Empereur d'Allemagne presentait les gouvernements au sujet de la nomination du feld-maréchal comte Waldersee comme commandant en chef des troupes internationales en Chine. L'Empereur Nicolas répondit qu'étant données la si grave offense faite à l'Allemagne par l'assassinat de son ministre en Chine et la haute situation militaire du comte d'Waldersee, li ne voyait pas, en ce qui le concernait, d'inconvénient à cette désignation. L'Italie le 9 et l'Angleterre le 10 août acceptèrent la création d'un généralissime et le choix proposé du maréchal de Waldersee.

[2] The Belgian, Austrian, Italian, Dutch, and most of the French Legations had been burned; also the Post Office, three foreign banks, the houses and offices of all the customs officials, and all the missionary compounds except the Peitang (Catholic Cathedral). The Legation forces had lost 65 killed, 135 wounded, and 7 deaths by disease.

See *Report* of Minister Conger to Secretary Hay, U. S. *For. Rel.*, 1900, pp. 161-167.

PART III

THE RESTORATION OF ORDER AND THE
PEACE PROTOCOL OF SEPTEMBER, 1901

PART III

The Restoration of Order and the Peace Protocol of September, 1901

Letter of Emperor of China to President McKinley—Reply of the President — Letters to Europe and Replies — Li Hung-chang appointed Commissioner—His Proposed Armistice—Prince Ching Co-Plenipotentiary—Their Credentials—Renewal of Punitive Expeditions—Paotingfu—Chuchow—Situation at Shanghai—Proposed Resumption of Hostilities—Foreign Extensions at Tientsin—Attitude of the United States—Occupation of Imperial Palace at Peking—Beginning of Negotiations—The German Proposal for Punishment—Replies of the Powers—Edict of September 25 Inadequate—The French Proposals—Acceptance by the Powers—Bases of Negotiations—The Joint Note—Elaboration by Diplomatic Body at Peking—Further Imperial Decrees—Final Protocol of September 7, 1901.

ON July 19, 1900, with the Boxer complications at their height and the conviction already rooted in the mind of the Chinese Court that a heavy reckoning with the Powers would assuredly come in the near future, there was addressed to President McKinley, in the name of the Emperor, a letter which again illustrated that trusting faith in American friendship and fairness which China had expressed since her international relations began:

China has long maintained friendly relations with the United States, and is deeply conscious that the object of the United States is international commerce. Neither country entertains the least suspicion or distrust toward the other. Recent outbreaks of mutual antipathy between the people and Christian missions caused the foreign Powers to view with unwarranted suspicion the position of the Imperial Government as favorable to the people and prejudicial to the missions, with the result that the Taku Forts were attacked and captured. Consequently, there has been clashing of forces, with calamitous consequences. The situation has become more and more serious and critical. We have just received a telegraphic memorial from our envoy, Wu Ting-fang, and it is highly gratifying to us to learn that the United States Government, having in view the friendly relations between the two countries, has taken a deep interest in the situation. Now China, driven by the irresistible course of events, has unfortunately incurred well-nigh universal indignation. For settling the present difficulty China places special reliance in the United States. We address this message to your Excellency in all sincerity and candidness, with the hope that your Excellency will devise measures and take the initiative in bringing about a concert of the Powers for the restoration of order and peace. The favor of a kind reply is earnestly requested and awaited with the greatest anxiety.[1]

July 23rd, President McKinley, through Secretary Hay, answered this appeal for help by a skillfully constructed letter which intimated plainly enough that it was within China's power to remedy her situation, and that this, once done, would lead to immediate and universal peace:

I have received Your Majesty's message of the 19th of July, and am glad to know that Your Majesty recognizes the fact that the Government and people of the United States desire of China nothing but what is just and equitable. The purpose for which we landed troops in China was the rescue of our Legations from serious danger and the protection of the lives and property of Americans who were sojourning in China in the enjoyment of rights guaranteed them by treaty and by international law. The same purposes are publicly declared by all the Powers which have landed military forces in Your Majesty's Empire.

I am to infer from Your Majesty's letter that the male-

[1] U. S. *For. Rel.*, 1900, p. 294.

factors who have disturbed the peace of China, who have murdered the Minister of Germany and a member of the Japanese Legation, and who now hold besieged in Peking those foreign diplomatists who still survive, have not only not received any favor or encouragement from Your Majesty, but are actually in rebellion against the Imperial authority. If this be the case, I most solemnly urge upon Your Majesty's Government to give public assurance whether the foreign Ministers are alive, and if so, in what condition.

2. To put the diplomatic representatives of the Powers in immediate and free communication with their respective Governments and to remove all danger to their lives and liberty.

3. To place the Imperial authorities of China in communication with the relief expedition so that coöperation may be secured between them for the liberation of the Legations, the protection of foreigners, and the restoration of order.

If these objects are accomplished it is the belief of this Government that no obstacles will be found to exist on the part of the Powers to an amicable settlement of all the questions arising out of the recent troubles, and the friendly good offices of this Government will, with the assent of the other Powers, be cheerfully placed at Your Majesty's disposition for that purpose.[1]

To this guarded response there was no immediate reply, and there the matter rested. China was of course unable to conform to the President's stipulations, as by July 19th the policy pursued against the Boxers, at first one of indirection and inactivity, then indifference, and finally open encouragement to the rebels, had resulted in the movement reaching the proportions of a whirlwind which not even a united Imperial Court could have quelled. It was necessary for the revolt to burn itself out and then trust to the magnanimity of the Powers when the time for settlement came.

[1] U. S. *For. Rel.*, 1900, pp. 294, 295. See also *China No. 1* (*1901*), no. 74.

The principal Powers received communications similar to the letter to America. The President of France took advantage of the occasion to outline terms such as the French later insisted upon as bases of negotiations.[1]   The responses of France and the United States were made quickly, and answers from the other Powers came in due time.   Lord Salisbury informed the Chinese Minister in the course of a conversation:

Whenever the European Ministers should return to us unhurt, we should be very glad to discuss, and to discuss in the most favorable manner, any appeal which the Imperial Government of China might have to make to Her Majesty's Government, but as long as there remained this terrible doubt as to the fate which they might have incurred at the hands of the Chinese soldiery or the Boxers, it was impossible for Her Majesty's Government to enter into further negotiations with that of the Empire.[2]

Count von Bülow, in his *note verbale* to the Chinese Legation at Berlin, was not able to

find himself in a position to submit this telegram (the Emperor's letter) to His Majesty the Emperor and King so long

[1] " 1° Qu'une protection efficace et l'entière liberté de leurs communications avec leurs Gouvernements sont assurées au représentant de la République et à ses collègues du corps diplomatique:

" 2° Que le prince Touan et les hauts fonctionnaires responsables des événements actuels ont été éloignés du Gouvernement, en attendant le châtiment inévitable:

" 3° Que les autorités et les corps de troupes, dans toute l'étendue de l'Empire, ont reçu l'ordre de cesser les hostilités contre les étrangers."

" 4° Que des mesures ont été prises pour la répression rigoureuse du mouvement insurrectionnel des Boxeurs:

Cordier, *op. cit.*, vol. iii, pp. 522, 523. See also *China No. 1 (1901)*, Inc. in no. 79 and Trans., *Letter* to the President of France, reprinted from *"Agence Havas"* of July 25, 1900.

[2] *China No. 1 (1901)*, no. 69.

as the fate of the foreign Missions shut up in Peking and of the other foreigners there has not been cleared up, and so long as the Imperial Chinese Government have not made atonement for the outrageous murder of the Imperial Minister, and given adequate guarantees that their conduct in the future will be in accordance with the law of nations and with civilization.[1]

Russia, reluctant to let the splendid chance for diplomacy slip by, returned an answer which was at once a declination and a veiled acceptance. The *Official Gazette* of August 2nd published the reply of the Russian Government to Kuang Hsu's letter begging the Czar to take the initiative in securing a cessation of hostilities (as the Chinese Court similarly begged the other Powers). The Russian statement was to the effect that the Government, while " deploring the serious events now happening in China ", found that " the absence of news respecting the fate of the Russian and foreign representatives " rendered " all idea of mediation in favor of China very difficult at the present time ". However, in spite of all this:

The efforts of Russia have but one object in view, namely, to assist in the re-establishment of order and tranquility in the Chinese Empire, and, inspired by their traditional friendship for China, the Imperial Government have decided to render to the Chinese Government every assistance with a view to repressing the present troubles.[2]

Japan returned a curt refusal, Viscount Aoki replying through the Chinese Minister at Tokyo that " the gravest breach of international law which any country could commit was an attack on diplomatic representatives ", and that, " until the suppression of the insurrection there could be no question of amicable negotiations ".[3] Thus there was

---

[1] *China No. 1 (1901)*, no. 79 and Inc.

[2] *Ibid.*, no. 105.   [3] *Ibid.*, no. 51.

small consolation in these responses to the letters and telegrams which Governor Yuan Shih-kai had sent over the
world at the bidding of the Peking Court.   A crumb of
comfort might have been found in the Russian answer
were it not for the fact that China was already becoming
wary of Russia's constant "traditional friendship" with
"but one object in view", especially when applied to a case
such as the present, where China had been so grievously at
fault.[1]

[1] Later, October 14, 1900, the Emperor, or rather the Chinese Court,
sent another letter to McKinley:

"We are extremely grateful to your Excellency for taking the
initiative in the withdrawal of troops (from Peking) and for consenting, in the interest of friendly relations, to use your kindly offices
between China and the friendly Powers who have been offended on
account of the recent unexpected uprising in China.

"We therefore especially delegate our Envoy Extraordinary and
Minister Plenipotentiary, Wu Ting-fang, to personally deliver this
telegraphic letter to your Excellency conveying our sincere expressions of thanks.

"We beg that your Excellency, in the interest of peace and international good relations, will exert your friendly influence with the
other Powers toward the complete effacement of all ill feeling and the
speedy determination on their part to negotiate for a peaceful settlement. For this we shall feel unbounded gratitude toward your Excellency, whose good offices we are now earnestly beseeching."

To which the President replied:

"I cordially share Your Majesty's wish that there may be a peaceful
settlement of all questions between China and the Powers whose interests and nationals have so grievously suffered wrong in Your Majesty's
dominions, and that the outcome may be the complete effacement of
ill feeling between them. The desire of this Government that such a
settlement may be brought about speedily has been made known to all
the Powers, and I trust that negotiations may begin so soon as we and
the other offended Governments shall be effectively satisfied of Your
Majesty's ability and power to treat with just sternness the principal
offenders, who are doubly culpable, not alone toward the foreigners, but
toward Your Majesty, under whose rule the purpose of China to dwell
in concord with the world has hitherto found expression in the welcome
and protection assured to strangers."

See U. S. For. Rel., 1900, pp. 295, 296.

Obviously, the first prerequisite of universal peace would be the appointment on the part of China of plenipotentiaries to treat with the Powers, and for this delicate and extremely difficult task Li Hung-chang, the grand old man of Chinese diplomacy, was again called upon to aid his country in its extremity. As early as August 8th, roughly speaking a week before the Legations were relieved, an Imperial edict announced:

We hereby appoint Li Hung-chang as our Envoy Plenipotentiary, with instructions to propose at once by telegraph to the Governments of the several Powers concerned for the immediate cessation of hostile demonstrations pending negotiations which he is hereby authorized to conduct for our part for the settlement of whatever questions may have to be dealt with. The questions are to be severally considered in a satisfactory manner and the result of the negotiations reported to us for our sanction.[1]

The Government of the United States was particularly well pleased with the appointment of Li, partly because of the fact that, aside from Prince Ching and probably Yuan Shih-kai, the hero of Shimonoseki was one of the few statesmen in the Empire, if not the only one, who possessed the requisite ability, training and characteristics to press

[1] Imperial *Edict* forwarded by the Privy Council at Peking, Aug. 8, to Governor Yuan Shih-kai at Tsinan, Shantung, and transmitted by him, Aug. 11, to the Taotai at Shanghai, by whom it was re-transmitted to Minister Wu at Washington, who received it on the night of the same day (Aug. 11). See U. S. *For. Rel.*, 1900, pp. 285, 286.
The same edict is given with different wording in *China No. 1 (1901)*, no. 167. As to the need for negotiations, says the decree: "The present hostilities between certain Chinese subjects and foreign nations are caused partly by the misunderstandings of the foreign Powers and partly by the mismanagement of the Chinese local authorities. It would be a misfortune to the whole world, and contrary to the wishes of China, should such a complication be allowed to evolve out of itself." Therefore the appointment of Li.

such negotiations on China's part as much as possible to a successful conclusion. The Department of State, it was declared, " learned with satisfaction of the appointment of Earl Li Hung-chang as Envoy Plenipotentiary to conduct negotiations with the Powers, and will, on its part, enter upon such negotiations with a desire to continue the friendly relations so long existing between the two countries ".[1] Other Powers also seemed satisfied, and offered no objection if, as M. Delcassé expressed it, Li " really can furnish *bona fide* credentials ". That was an important point, considering the state of governmental affairs in China, and later will be touched upon again.

Sir Claude MacDonald, on being sounded by Downing Street as to Li's appointment, replied that Li seemed to have " full powers to arrange all matters with the Foreign Officers of the Powers ". MacDonald must have realized the possible trend of the preliminary negotiations in his warning that the " march of troops on Peking should not be delayed by any negotiations whatever ". This message, dated from Peking August 10th, goes on to say: " We are still being fired at daily, and our supplies are and have been entirely cut off, so that we must surrender unless we are shortly relieved ".[2] Things turned out as the British Minister feared, for as early as July 30th (unknown of course to MacDonald because of the siege) Li had made a " suggestion to the United States " that " the Ministers might be sent under safe escort to Tientsin, provided the Powers would engage not to march on Peking ". The Secretary of State gave a skillful answer to this proposition, and also to the proposal of Li that the march on Peking should be halted during the negotiations. He said:

[1] U. S. *For. Rel.*, 1900, p. 286; *China No. 1* (*1901*), no. 328.

[2] Peking, August 10, *via* Shanghai August 14; received telegraphic at London, August 14. *China No. 1* (*1901*), no. 192.

I do not think it expedient to submit the proposition of Earl Li to the other Powers (at this time the United States was the only one approached) ; free communication with our representatives in Peking is demanded as a matter of absolute right, and not as a favor.   Since the Chinese Government admits that it possesses the power to give communication, it puts itself in an unfriendly attitude by denying it.   No negotiations seem advisable until the Chinese Government shall have put the diplomatic representatives of the Powers in full and free communication with their respective Governments, and removed all danger to life and liberty.   We would urge Earl Li earnestly to advise the Imperial authorities of China to place themselves in friendly communication and coöperation with the relief expedition; they are assuming heavy responsibility in acting otherwise.[1]

That ended the matter for the time being, as Lord Salisbury, on being approached by Ambassador Choate, found that he " entirely concurs in the terms of the reply of the Secretary of State ".[2]

At this early stage of affairs, it must be remembered that Li was at Canton and had received at that place the notification of his designation as peace commissioner.   Communication with the north was uncertain and news of the progress of the Allies very meagre; and for some time Li remained unaware of the capture of Peking by the Allied forces on August 14th.   From Canton, Li went to Shanghai and there, August 15th, sent a message to Sir Chihchen Lofenglu, Chinese Minister at London, in which he stated that by this time it must be certain " the treaty Powers fully appreciate the difficult position in which both the Emperor and Empress Dowager are now situated ".   He was under the impression that so far the Allies had only reached

---

[1] *China, No. 1 (1901)*, no. 99.
[2] *Ibid.*, no. 108.

the village of Tungchow, on the road to Peking. Therefore he asked the British Government "most respectfully"
not to proceed further, assuring Salisbury that to persist
would " shed the blood of innocents " and " cause irre-
parable damage to the present dynasty ", and in addition
would " hurt the feelings of 400,000,000 of the Chinese
population ".[1]   The same request was telegraphed to Russia, France, Germany, the United States and Japan.

The proposed armistice met with no favor.   To Li's
suggestion that the Legations be sent to Tientsin (a
suggestion later elaborated by Russia), Great Britain
replied that, " until the British Legation has been allowed to return to Tientsin under the escort of an adequate European force, Her Majesty's Government can
enter into no such negotiations ".[2]   The actual removal of
the Legation from Peking, Downing Street seems never to
have considered seriously, and Minister MacDonald distinctly discouraged the idea.   Delcassé, in his answer to Li,
said that, " the only means of proving the good faith shown
by the Chinese Government in their arrangements with regard to the foreign Ministers was to command the soldiers
to give in to the international troops ".[3]   Russia would act
only as the other Powers acted.[4]   The United States never
considered the idea of removing the Legation.[5]

Later, the idea of leaving Peking and thus sparing as
much as possible the feelings of China met with much favor
with the Russian Foreign Office and was adopted as one of
the cardinal points of the Russian program.   With this
end in view the Russian Legation was for a time actually

[1] *China No. 1* (*1901*), no. 202.

[2] *Ibid.*, no. 209.

[3] *Ibid.*, no. 213.

[4] *Ibid.*, no. 245.

[5] U. S. *For. Rel.*, 1900, p. 204.

removed to Tientsin.[1]   But Russia's method of thus ingra-
tiating herself with China was frowned upon by the other
Powers.   They considered it a serious diplomatic mistake
to leave Peking, as it certainly was.   Said Lord Salisbury,
in commenting on the Russian proposal for this purpose:
" The present moment (September 29th) did not seem to
me opportune for the withdrawal to Tientsin of Her Majesty's Minister ".[2]   Italy likewise did " not favor the proposal ", but was willing to join the Powers in united action;
while the United States had no " present intention " to ac-
commodate the Russian Government in this regard.   All
the foreign Ministers at Peking, except the Russian representative, agreed with Sir Claude MacDonald in his opinion
that, " the departure of the Legations now would be most
inexpedient, and I think that their withdrawal from the
capital would hinder future negotiations ".[3]   But Russia
had a purpose, and in spite of these adverse replies proceeded with her plan.   By October 19th, having produced
the desired effect upon Chinese sympathies, the Russian
Minister, M. de Giers, received instructions to return, bag
and baggage, to Peking.[4]

Li Hung-chang, meanwhile, was at Shanghai on his journey to the north, which seemed to be much delayed.   Differences soon arose because of the divergent views held by

[1] *Journal de Saint-Pétersbourg*, Sep. 12 (25) : " Several members of
the Russian Legation and the first divisions of the expeditionary detachments have already started for Tientsin; the departure of the rest
of the troops is being gradually carried out, and will be completed as
soon as the local conditions permit."
Reprinted in *China No. 1 (1901)*, no. 397 and Inc.

[2] *Ibid.*, no. 401.

[3] *Ibid.*, no. 327.

[4] On the removal of the Russian Legation to Tientsin, see *China No. 1*
(*1901*), nos. 140, 172, 281, 287, 318, 327, 356, 383, 397, 403; *China No. 5*
(*1901*), nos. 64, 77; U. S. *For. Rel.*, 1900, pp. 205, 214, 375-377.

Li and the foreign Ministers.   Naturally, it was Li's ambition to begin the peace proposals at once, the sooner the better, but to this plan the British Minister was strongly opposed.   At this date, August 24th, the situation in Peking was described by MacDonald as " very complicated ", while " rumors of intended attacks are prevalent".   He continued : " It is useless to attempt serious negotiations with the Chinese Government until the Chinese military power is disheartened and completely crushed, and communications with Tientsin are made thoroughly secure ".[1]

Then it developed that Li's powers to negotiate were incomplete, and "we (the Ministers) must ask him to produce fresh powers ", or at least have his credentials re-affirmed. Japan was unwilling to recognize Li's powers on the ground that there was no responsible and " no representative Government in Peking ".   These difficulties were removed by two decrees, one of which, August 24th, said : " Li Hung-chang must act at Plenipotentiary, and make the best terms he can as quickly as possible.   Being at this distance (Sianfu) we (the Court) will not interfere ".[2]   Three days later another edict announced : " We hereby summon the Grand Secretary, Li Hung-chang, who has been furnished with full powers to negotiate with the Plenipotentiaries of the Allied Powers, to come, without delay, to Peking, in order to coöperate with Prince Ching in the transaction of important State affairs ".[3]

Li had announced that he would leave Shanghai for Tientsin after the Chinese festival of September 8th.   Why the Grand Secretary delayed his arrival at Peking in this fashion it is somewhat hard to understand, all the more

[1] *China No. 1 (1901)*, no. 240.

[2] *Ibid.*, no. 313.

[3] *Ibid.*, no. 319.

since everyone in the capital was on edge to receive him. However, the two decrees just mentioned, ordering him to proceed " without delay ", settled the matter, as a command from the Court was not to be disobeyed. In explanation of Li's dilatory tactics, it must be remembered that at this time he was a very old man who had sacrificed his health and strength in the service of his country.[1] Considering the unsettled conditions, with all sorts of rumors flying around in south China of the terrible events in the north, it was but natural that, at his advanced age, Li should have had serious misgivings in undertaking the journey. As a precaution he applied to both the British and American Governments for protection in case his person was not respected, and both Powers gave him their generous support. Finally, September 14th, under a safe-conduct furnished by Sir Robert Hart, Li at last set sail in a British vessel for Tientsin, the " steamer flying a flag denoting that he is a Plenipotentiary ". He arrived without mishap in Peking, where Prince Ching, escorted by " Bengal and Japanese cavalry ", had already preceded him.

One side was by this time about as impatient as the other to begin negotiations. Already a whole month had passed since Peking had been relieved and as yet nothing had been done. One Power seemed to be waiting for another to act decisively. The news that Prince Ching had also been appointed peace commissioner[2] gave universal satisfaction, for the Prince was highly esteemed by Europe as a diplomat and broad-minded Chinese statesman.

But the question of credentials was not yet settled. It seemed that Japan was the most dubious of all over the ade-

---

[1] Li Hung-chang's death occurred on Nov. 7, 1901.

[2] Li had memorialized the Throne for co-Plenipotentiaries. **See** *China No. 1 (1901)*, nos. 282, 285.

quacy of Li's and Ching's " full powers ". The British
representative at Tokyo wrote Lord Salisbury of the following conversation with Viscount Aoki:

Viscount Aoki went on to say that the only credentials which
could be considered satisfactory would be a document signed
by the Emperor of China himself.   The Chinese Imperial edicts
were usually issued in the name of the Emperor by some of the
Ministers or by some Board, but his Excellency thought that
in this case the Emperor's autograph signature should be insisted on.   At the same time, unless some Government had
been formed and had gained power in China, from which the
violently anti-foreign elements, such as Prince Tuan, Kang-yi,
and General Tung had been eliminated, and unless Li Hung-
chang could show that he represented such a Government,
negotiations with him would be quite useless.   The above-
named men, who were to blame for the recent disturbances,
would keep their hold upon the persons of the Emperor and
the Empress Dowager as long as they possibly could, and no
other authoritative Government could be formed so long as
they succeeded in doing so.[1]

Li had applied first to Japan for a warship to carry him
north, but Viscount Aoki had answered that " he would do
better to apply to Her Majesty's Government for such escort ".   At the same time Aoki " once more warned him
against proceeding to the north without fresh credentials,
as he might thereby lay himself open to humiliating re-
buffs ".[2] But now it appeared that Japan would be satisfied provided Li's credentials were satisfactory to Great
Britain.   MacDonald intimated to Lord Salisbury: " We
had better, I should say, accept both above-mentioned (Li
and Ching), with an understanding that these are purely
preliminary negotiations, and reference will be made to the

[1] *China No. 5 (1901)*, no. 31.   [2] *Ibid.*, no. 126.

Governments of the Powers ".[1] To which Downing Street replied, September 27th: " If the powers of Prince Ching and Li Hung-chang are deemed sufficient and on clear understanding that negotiations are purely preliminaries for reference to Governments, you are authorized, in conjunction with your colleagues, to commence negotiations with them ".[2]

The final outcome of this tiresome but highly important discussion was that the sufficiency of the powers of the Chinese Plenipotentiaries [3] should be determined by the Diplomatic Corps of the Powers at Peking. This was really not done until late in December, when the demands of the Powers were first handed to Prince Ching and Li Hung-chang. The Grand Secretary unfortunately was prevented by illness from attending the meeting mentioned, so Prince Ching exchanged all formalities. Upon being requested to produce his credentials, Prince Ching submitted eleven documents, one of which was given to each of the Minis-

---

[1] *China No. 1 (1901)*, no. 372.   [2] *Ibid.*, no. 396.

[3] By an *Edict* of August 31, the Viceroys of Nanking and Wuchang were ordered to coöperate with Prince Ching and Earl Li. The *Decree* of September 9 further appointed Jung Lu, Yuan Shih-kai's blood brother, as Minister Plenipotentiary to assist Li, Ching, and the Yangtse Viceroys.

Jung Lu was reluctant to serve but obeyed the summons. The British Minister did not relish his appointment, " several of whose troops were killed by us on the barricades opposed to us during the siege." Furthermore, " one of Ching's standards was also captured by us," yet to Prince Ching there seemed to be no objection on the part of the British Minister. Li came to the rescue with the suggestion that Jung Lu " confess his complicity " in the Legation attacks and then see whether the Powers would have him.

By the *Edict* of September 12, Prince Ching was made Plenipotentiary with full powers, the same as with Li, while the Yangtse Viceroys were made Ministers Plenipotentiary, the same as Jung Lu. These were all admonished to " loyally coöperate one with the other, and to have no differences."

See *China No. 1 (1901)*, nos. 323, 331; *China No. 5 (1901)*, no. 112.

ters, and then he asked " that they might be examined and returned to him ". After that was done, Prince Ching naturally demanded their powers in return and a curious situation developed, a situation almost laughable when we consider the ado the Powers had made over the credentials of the Chinese commissioners. All of the foreign representatives, with the sole exception of the German Minister, were " equally unprepared ", in other words, had neglected to bring their papers with them. The following interesting predicament was brought to light:

The French and Russian Ministers have received telegraphic full powers, and documentary full powers are on their way to the Italian Minister; the others seem disposed to rely on the fact that they have formerly presented letters of credence in the usual manner.[1]

However, as this was but a preliminary meeting, with no treaty to sign, the conclusion was reached that the matter did " not seem to press for a solution ", although there is no denying the fact that the Diplomatic Body was at fault for the very thing for which they had been holding China " to a strict accountability ". And so ended, at the last moment to the advantage of the Chinese Plenipotentiaries, the long and wearisome dispute over credentials, in which it seemed throughout that the Powers were as much sparring for time in formulating their demands as they were concerned over the authority of Prince Ching and Li Hung-chang to negotiate with them.[2]

[1] *China No. 6 (1901)*, no. 91.

[2] On the question of the Chinese Plenipotentiaries, see *China No. 1 (1901)*, nos. 31, 35, 45, 46, 99, 108, 132, 166, 167, 173, 176, 190, 192, 202, 209, 213, 225, 230, 238-240, 245, 254, 268, 276, 292, 302, 313, 314, 318-320, 323, 326, 328, 331, 333, 341, 356, 357, 371, 372, 374, 382, 385, 396; *China No. 5 (1901)*, nos. 31, 68, 111, 112, 125, 126, 200, 207, 209, 216, 226, 252; *China No. 6 (1901)*, no. 91; U. S. *For. Rel.*, 1900, pp. 161, 200, 202, 259, 285, 286, 291-293.

With the two leading Chinese Plenipotentiaries now at Peking ready for business, it was felt that at last the negotiations for settlement could begin in earnest. But such was not to be the case. North China was yet far from pacified, and proposals for peace were temporarily sidetracked by the renewal of punitive expeditions in the neighborhood of the capital. Most prominent of these was the military excursion of the Allied troops to Paotingfu and Chengtingfu,[1] October 12, 1900. Some 4,000 soldiers participated, under the command of von Waldersee, the German Commander-in-chief of the international forces in China. At first Li Hung-chang could not do otherwise than order the Imperial troops " not to oppose the advance on any account ".[2] Later, November 5th, he changed his attitude and complained of the "conduct of the international troops", alleging that the " villages had been attacked by Chinese Christians " and that these primarily were to blame for the initial disturbances. This note of remonstrance was returned by the German, British and Italian Ministers with the answer that they " were unable to accept it ".[3] The French Minister followed with similar action.[4] The other representatives contented themselves with stating that they would " merely refrain from acknowledging its receipt ".[5] The expedition itself was of course a huge success. The

[1] In Chihli province, southwest of Peking.

[2] *China No. 5 (1901)*, no. 80.

[3] Minister Conger, though acting in unison with the other diplomats, feared that "negotiations will be delayed" by the expedition. U. S. *For. Rel.*, 1900, p. 213.

[4] The news that the French Minister agreed in being "unable to accept" the note was sent by Lord Salisbury in a *Circular* to the British Ambassadors at Paris, Berlin, Vienna, Rome, St. Petersburg and Washington.

[5] The Russian Minister seems at first to have objected to the expedition.

imperiled Christians were relieved; a fine of 100,000 taels was levied on Paotingfu with a month to pay it in; and it was decided to execute three officials of high rank and to quarter German and French troops upon the town for the duration of the winter.[1]

This expedition and others either following or contemplated were not regarded with any excess of favor by the Powers. It was well known that the United States was disinclined towards further punitive measures; and as regarded Great Britain, the Marquis of Lansdowne, who had succeeded Lord Salisbury as head of the Foreign Office, judged it highly desirable that " pending negotiations, no further expeditions should take place unless the conduct of the Chinese should render them necessary ".[2] Count Lamsdorff deprecated the advance into Chihli, as it offered the " danger of utterly destroying the independence and traditional prestige of the only central authority which the Chinese recognized, and of putting in its place a titular puppet Government acting under foreign dictation and compulsion, and imposed by foreign bayonets ",[3] which was a strikingly apt observation. Great Britain agreed with Lamsdorff in " deprecating the renewal of military activity in Pechihli, unless there be urgent reasons ". The British Foreign Office also called attention to the fact that since October no British troops had taken part in any punitive expeditions.[4]

Still more serious than in the north was the situation at Chuchow, south of Shanghai in Chekiang province. In a

[1] See *China No. 5* (*1901*), nos. 29, 54, 80, 118, 119, 123, 210, 257; *China No. 6* (*1901*), no. 40.

[2] *Ibid.,* no. 1.

[3] *China No. 6* (*1901*), nos. 60, 61.

[4] Which was slightly incorrect. A small military surveying party had been sent by Gen. Gaselee with the Paotingfu expedition.

Boxer outbreak which occurred as far back as July 28, 1900, nine British subjects had been killed,[1] in addition to the magistrate of Hsinan, who met his death in attempting to pacify the mob. The British Foreign Office immediately demanded redress of Li Hung-chang, while Sir Ernest Satow informed the Chinese Plenipotentiary that " such misdeeds should be wiped out by a fitting expiation ". The Yamen acted quickly enough in dismissing the Governor from office, removing him on November 30th, and thus getting rid of the " prime cause of the massacres ". China did not seem inclined to do more, however, and the result was that the " gentry and other ill-disposed people " in the province, so Acting Consul-General Warren informed the Home Office, " are being encouraged to further acts of violence by the delay which has taken place in punishing the officials and others who are responsible for the murders ". It was made clear to the Chinese authorities that drastic action was necessary. Final British demands took the form of the " banishment and degradation of the ex-Governor (Liu Shu-tang) and the ex-Provincial Judge; their property to be confiscated "; and in addition the confinement of the Brigadier, " who is out of his mind ", the execution of the Taotai and of the Commandant of the Volunteers, the degradation and imprisonment of the Prefect, and finally the degradation and banishment of three gentry concerned and the confiscation of their property. Though the outbreak was deplorable enough, possibly Great Britain was demanding too much at this stage of affairs. The Chinese peace commissioners were exerting their utmost to readjust the entire situation, and in consequence were overwhelmed with the demands, notes, and opinions of the foreign repre-

---

[1] Total victims were eleven in number; two men, six women and three children. Nine of these were British and two American.

sentatives. In this mass of correspondence the items for punishment were considerable, and these further formed the prelude for extension of these same negotiations. Also, each new or recent disturbance added a fresh quota of victims to the long list of Chinese already indicted, which list, steadily growing, all the more delayed the final settlement. At any rate, the " fitting expiation " which China paid for the Chuchow grievances was a long time in coming, and this through no fault of Prince Ching and Li Hung-chang, laboring as they did under great disadvantages.[1]

Shanghai at this time similarly exhibited a lack of tranquility. The alarm had been general throughout the revolt because of ominous reports that Boxer influence was spreading southward, and during the reconstruction these fears remained manifest. It was felt in middle 1900 that troops would have to be sent by the Powers to keep the Yangtse region in order. Fortunately, Viceroy Chang Chih-tung saw no reason for a large force but agreed to a moderate one from Great Britain, say about 3,000. At the same time, as has previously been noted, the Yangtse Viceroys vigorously opposed the idea of sending troops inland, or stationing warships on the Yangtse or at the riverine ports. In this contention they received the support of Admiral Seymour of the China Station. As regarded Shanghai, the British were in favor of garrisoning that city, as such a concentration of military power would be far better " than keeping a force at a distant spot such as Weihaiwei", which was in reality entirely outside British influence and had been leased only as a check on Russia at Port Arthur, directly opposite. The Powers finally arrived at a sort of international agreement in sending troops and warships to

---

[1] On the Chuchow massacre and negotiations, see *China No. 1 (1901)*, nos. 82, 119, 127, 329, 393; *China No. 5 (1901)*, nos. 12, 20, 132, 145, 190, 218, 219, 221; *China No. 6 (1901)*, nos. 36, 38, 86, 146, 147, 223, 229.

Shanghai, though none to the riverine ports,[1] and these, the majority of which were British ships and a regiment of native Indian soldiers, produced that wholesome effect needed to prevent entire Chekiang, in spite of the Chuchow massacre, from following the example of the northern provinces.[2]

The Rebellion, it will be remembered, had early been kept under control in Shantung, which province, under the discipline of the energetic Yuan Shih-kai, was kept in a fair state of order during the remaining period of the disturbances. However, the Powers for the sake of security decided to hold Tientsin and seven districts to the south, all bordering on Shantung. This led to the belief that Shantung itself was again to be invaded and occupied by Allied troops. The Consular Body at Shanghai was quick in its disapproval. So also the Yangtse Viceroys, who said:

Yuan Shih-kai frequently memorialized the Throne to suppress the rebels and rescue the Ministers, and joined with themselves (the Viceroys of Nanking and Wuchang) in refusing to be a party to the Rebellion, so that they are unable to sit by and see his dominions endangered without speaking on his behalf.[3]

[1] Vice-Admiral Seymour intimated to the Foreign Office that if ships and troops were sent through the Yangtse region, the Chinese population "might think foreigners had come to seize their country," and if such fears were once aroused, "the Chinese would fight to prevent their country being taken away from them." This was also the view of Viceroy Chang Chih-tung.
See *China No. 1 (1901)*, no. 110.

[2] *Ibid.*, nos. 50, 68, 72, 89, 94, 104, 106, 109, 110, 117, 125, 137, 145, 162, 177, 178, 198, 201, 205, 208, 214, 273, 283, 286, 295, 366; *China No. 5 (1901)*, nos. 30, 148.

[3] Acting Consul-General Warren to Marquis of Salisbury, October 10, 1900, *China No. 5 (1901)*, no. 37.

Fortunately, no such move was made, or even contemplated by the Allies, as it was clearly recognized that Yuan Shihkai had accomplished all that was possible at the time.[1]

The province of Shansi likewise was in doubt, due particularly to the brutality and unconcealed hostility of the Governor, the infamous Yu Hsien, toward the missionaries and foreigners. In Shansi alone, up to October 2, 1900, the foreign death list had reached 140, mainly British. As the disturbances seemed to continue, an expedition to Shansi was contemplated late in the year. To this the Viceroys of Nanking and Hankow strongly objected, and wrote, November 28th, to Sir Chihchen Lofenglu, the Chinese Minister at London, deprecating the intention of the Allies, as they " feared that new difficulties might crop up at any time ". At this opportune moment they further advised the British Foreign Office to " stick to the peace agreement of the southern and eastern provinces ", and better yet, " to hasten the opening and conclusion of peace negotiations ". They explained that the new Governor (Yu Hsien had been removed, soon to be decapitated) was doing all he could and already had " executed more than eighty of the Boxer insurrectionists ". Lord Lansdowne was able to assure the Viceroys that he was " not aware of any proposal for an expedition to Shansi ", and in case one was contemplated, he would use British influence to the contrary.[2]

Thus it can be seen that affairs in China were far from tranquil for a long time after the Legations had been relieved and China apparently had been crushed. Because of these punitive expeditions and their inevitable conse-

[1] *China No. 5 (1901)*, nos. 37, 52, 53, 95, 159, 217.

[2] *China No. 1 (1901)*, nos. 220, 344; *China No. 5 (1901)*, nos. 4, 15, 28, 62, 179, 183, 184. See also *ibid.*, Inc. 2 and Subinc. 1-5 in no. 62.

quences, namely, prolonging the period of uncertainty and
unrest and delaying the peace negotiations, China remained
in an unsatisfactory state even after the year 1901 was
well advanced.   So serious was the outlook that it was
deemed possible by some to alleviate the situation only by a
renewal of hostilities.   This impression was intensified as
the months flew past with little or nothing accomplished.
The most critical period was apparently the middle of February, 1901.   At that time it became known that Field-
Marshal von Waldersee, " in view of the dilatory and obstructive tactics of the Chinese ", considered that " renewal
of operations on a large scale may become necessary ", and
General Sir A. Gaselee telegraphed to Downing Street for
instructions.[1]

Minister Conger did not take kindly to the proposed renewal of punitive expeditions, and came out with the following declaration:

A report is current that the possibility of an early active

[1] See *despatch* of Lieut.-Gen. Sir A. Gaselee to Lord Hamilton of the
India Office, Feb. 18, 1901, *China No. 6 (1901)*, no. 100.

Following is the *Army Order* of Feb. 15, issued by Field Marshal
von Waldersee:

"Although the peace negotiations still continue to be carried on, their
course, up to the present, induces me to point out that a resumption
of larger operations may shortly become necessary.   I request, therefore, that, as the favorable season is approaching, such prompt measures
be taken as to insure the mobilization of all the troops by the end of the
month.   It will be necessary in the first place to take care that the
troops possess sufficient means of transport to carry with them about
eight days' military stores and provisions on difficult mountain roads.

"Although the greater portion of the Commissariat can be supplied
from the field of operations, the circumstances are not sufficiently
known to allow of this being counted on with certainty.   Transport
columns for sending on the necessary additional supplies should therefore be formed and fitted out, such as will be capable of surmounting
considerable difficulties of ground."

Ibid., no. 105.

resumption of operations by the military on a large scale, on account of the course taken by the peace negotiations, is being discussed by some of the military commanders, and that preparations are being made.   Criticism of the military authorities is far from my intention, but it is hardly competent that any of the Powers should, seeing that negotiations for a peaceful settlement have been jointly commenced by all the Governments, take such action as to endanger the concert, disturb the harmony, or place the result of the peace negotiations in jeopardy—*i. e.*, by the resumption of military operations without the consent of all parties.

At the time of the signature of the joint note formulating our demands, I made, in signing it, an express stipulation that my Government should thereby in no way be committed to undertake further military operations.   When our British colleague's addition to the last clause was adopted on the declared understanding that it limited the military operations to the occupation of Peking and this province (Chihli), the note was finally agreed to.

I would propose, supposing that the report I have heard proves true with regard to the proposed military operations, and if my colleagues agree with me, that we should recommend either to our Governments or to our respective military commanders to wait till the peace negotiations have arrived at such a stage as to warrant, in the united opinion of the Governments, the resumption of military operations as now contemplated.[1]

Sir Ernest Satow informed Minister Conger that " no official information " of this extreme step had reached him. However, he found it necessary first, as Conger had intimated, to consult the Foreign Office at home.   M. Pichon, the French Minister, seemed decidedly in favor of an avowed resumption of military operations, and thought that

[1] *China No. 6 (1901)*, no. 105.

" such a warning might be of assistance to the negotiations ". Furthermore, he discovered that some 35,000
Chinese " were threatening the French troops in the south
of the province ", and that their advance (from Shansi
presumably, for in that neighboring province von Waldersee seemed disposed to renew hostilities) has to be kept
in check ". The idea of a punitive expedition appealed to
him, and he did not think that " we ought to make any en-
gagements not to take military movements, and thus tie our
hands ". The Russian Minister agreed that the situation
was " a grave one ", yet was of the opinion that " the Governments ought to arrive at an understanding with regard
to the question now raised ", thus placing himself in favor
of the fundamental idea underlying Minister Conger's declaration.[1]

This serious difficulty seems to have arisen mainly from
the exasperation of the military at the way in which negotiations were being dragged out, although this cannot be
considered a sufficient provocation. The final stand of
Downing Street was in opposition, although it was intimated that " we were sincerely anxious to give Count Waldersee all the support in our power ", and for this reason
the Foreign Office would " regret very much to spoil the
effect of any demonstration which he might deem necessary by an appearance of disapproval ". But Lord Lansdowne made it clear that Great Britain was " not prepared
to sanction employment of force under your (Gaselee's)
command on expeditions to places remote from the capital ".[2] It soon developed that Count von Waldersee " acted
without special instructions from the German Government".
But Count Hatzfeldt informed Lord Lansdowne that the
object of the Commander-in-Chief " was to induce the

[1] *China No. 6 (1901)*, no. 105.   [2] *Ibid.*, nos. 110, 118.

Chinese Government to comply with the demands of the Powers ", and he " earnestly trusted " that the British Foreign Office would not refuse support if such action became necessary.   Lord Lansdowne replied that " His Majesty's Government was most anxious to avoid any appearance of reluctance to support Count Waldersee ", yet was disinclined to join and did not desire to join unless no other course were possible.[1]

No doubt the German Commander-in-Chief intended his order as nothing more than a threat to China, to make it clear to the Chinese Plenipotentiaries that the patience of the Powers, both diplomatic and military, was well-nigh exhausted.   If such were the case, a " good effect " was immediately produced by the proposal, " to which publicity was given, and by the movement of troops, for a telegram urging prompt acceptance of our demands with regard to punishment (of officials and Boxers) has been sent by the Chinese Plenipotentiaries to Hsi-an " (Sianfu),[2] the city in Shensi where the Imperial Court was sojourning during the occupation of Peking.

Before reviewing the final peace negotiations, it is advisable to consider the situation at Tientsin and its outcome.   With the capture of that city, the Allied army remained in possession, and after the fall of Peking still remained.   Ulterior motives of the European Governments developed about the middle of November, 1900.   The following month, Minister Conger " confirmed " his previous telegrams that the Powers were seeking permanent extensions to the concessions which they already occupied. Conger rightly regarded this action as a " dangerous precedent ", and added his opinion that " all extensions of for-

[1] *China No. 6 (1901)*, no. 120.

[2] *Ibid.*, no. 105.

eign settlements should be international ".[1]	As Russia
had started the fracas, Conger directed the United States
consul at Tientsin, Mr. Ragsdale, to " enter a protest ",
while he himself prepared to remonstrate with the Russian
Minister at Peking.[2]	These proposed extensions of the
Russians and Belgians, and those later demanded by the
Germans, French, Austrians, and Japanese, were denounced
by the American representative as a " grab game " which
was " neither fair nor consistent ".	It may be remarked
in passing that throughout his tenure of office, in this most
difficult period of modern Chinese history, Minister Conger
was an able exponent of the American policy, as followed
from the beginning and elaborated by Secretary Hay, of
friendship for and justice to China, and of unselfish protection of American and Chinese interests, especially at this
time when China was practically friendless and knew not
what to do or where to turn.	Of course, in this Tientsin
affair, Conger admitted that, "since there are so many regu-
larly established concessions at Tientsin an international
one is hardly to be expected ", but he contended that " all
action in relation to securing new or extending old concessions should be deferred until order is restored, the Chinese
Government re-established, and the rights and interests of
all can be considered ".

As regarded the policy of the United States in this matter, Conger remarked:

It would be advantageous to us in many ways to have an
American concession at Tientsin, but we have learned by ex-
perience that it takes both money and citizens to own and oper-
ate a concession.	We have not enough there of either.	The
Department (of State) is familiar with our former efforts to

[1] Like the one at Shanghai.
[2] U. S. *For. Rel.*, 1901, p. 39.

sustain the desirable concession which had to be abandoned in
1896. If, however, the United States Government can in any
way take upon itself part of the burden, as the other Governments do, it may be advisable for us to demand consideration
of our rights to a concession while the others are taking and
dividing up all available territory.[1]

It was plainly Conger's intention to play safe until the
matter had been definitely determined.

The Russian *Circular* announcing the occupation of the
left bank of the Peiho river, opposite the foreign concessions already established, was the first to appear, early in
November. Said this typically Russian document:

Since the 17th of June last the Imperial Chinese troops have
joined the rioters (Boxers) who attacked the foreign concessions and the railway station occupied by the Russian troops,
and that on the 23d of June the Russian reinforcements, who
came to raise the blockade, swept the left bank of the Peiho
. . . and have established themselves there *by right of conquest* [2] in having taken possession by force of arms and at the
price of Russian blood spilled, in order to prevent the Chinese
from returning to resume the firing. His Excellency (Lieu-
tenant-General Linevitch) considers all this tract of land . . .
as having become the property of the Russian troops on the
23d of June by *act of war.*
The Russian flags have been planted, and notice posted upon
boards in many places within the territory, which has been
occupied and protected by the Russian military authorities.
Therefore his Excellency *can not and will not* recognize, except by his special authorization, any cession whatever of this
territory of which he has taken *entire and complete possession.*[3]

On November 20th, the French Consul-General, G. du

[1] U. S. *For. Rel.*, 1901, p. 40.
[2] The *italics* are the author's.
[3] U. S. *For. Rel.*, 1901, p. 41.

Chaylard, who also was the president of the municipal council of Tientsin, undertook " to warn foreign residents
against the consequences they would expose themselves to
by buying ground in the quarter *presently* annexed to the
French concession ", and declared that he would not "recognize as valid any contract subsequent to June 17th, the
date on which hostilities began ". However, " all land
holders, bearers of *regular* titles issued *before* the 17th of
June ", were " requested to exhibit them at the French Consulate, where they shall be duly verified and registered ".[1]
Then followed a designation of the area of the proposed
extension.

Belgium likewise grabbed all in sight that was possible
for so small a kingdom, and " appropriated to its sole use
and benefit " a large tract east of the Peiho river. Then
followed the other Powers, each in every instance with its
additions carefully defined and all others solemnly warned
not to interfere with its squatter rights.[2] Here again we
find that Russia was the prime mover and set the example
for the rest, and that then as now, when there is any territorial complication in the Far East as well as in certain other parts of the world, it is advisable first to examine the Russian attitude. Generally, it will be the key
to the whole situation.

The United States, in its not altogether enviable position
as guardian of Chinese territorial integrity, soon had its
hands full and, rather to its regret, was forced to take a
seemingly inconsistent stand which needs careful explanation to be seen in the right light. On February 26, 1901,
Minister Conger reported to the Department of State that,

[1] U. S. *For. Rel.*, 1901, p. 42.

[2] For the Belgian *circular* see *ibid.*, p. 42; Austrian, p. 46; Italian,
p. 47; Japanese, p. 47; German, p. 52.

notwithstanding his protests, all available territory except
the small tract which in 1896 had formed the American
concession, had been seized by the land-hungry Powers.
With an eye to the future, Conger found it necessary to in-
struct Consul Ragsdale to serve notice on the other Consuls
that " that tract must be left for part of an international
settlement or a United States concession, which will be determined when order is restored ". He emulated the European notes in finalty of argument by adding, as they had
done in every instance, " that the United States will not
recognize seizure or adverse occupation ".[1] This was the
wisest course, considering the circumstances, and was fully
approved by Secretary Hay.

Minister Conger strengthened his position by submitting
to the Department of State a communication solicited from
Major-General Chaffee, commanding the American troops
in China. The General was of the following opinion:

Owing to recent events in this section of China and with a
view to the future expansion of trade by the United States
at Tientsin and adjacent country, I think it not improbable
our Government would be willing to recover, if it can be done
without friction, its old concession at Tientsin. Further, it
might wish or consent to do so for a few years at least, as a
military necessity, in order to afford undisputed footing for
its troops and stores in case of renewal of disturbance pending
a few years of trial of the Chinese Government to restore and
maintain public order.

*   *   *   *   *   *   *   *   *

It is my opinion that our Government should recover this
concession if it can do so at once and without serious difficulty. I leave the subject with you (Conger), however, to
represent to Washington. As the matter is now in such condition that delay might bring about the threatened absorption

[1] U. S. *For. Rel.*, 1901, p. 58.

before report could be made and received by mail, the disposition of the Government might be obtained by using the cable.[1]

Minister Conger was careful to inform Consul Ragsdale in regard to this delicate matter:[2]

[1] U. S. *For. Rel.*, 1901, p. 49. Major Foote of the American force at Tientsin gives further information, *ibid.*, pp. 49, 50. Reply of Minister Conger to General Chaffee, *ibid.*, pp. 51, 52.

[2] The history of the American "concession" is an interesting one. According to Consul Ragsdale (to Major Foote) it is as follows:

"Sir: With reference to the old American concession at Tientsin, and in compliance with your request, I have the honor to submit that in the year 1869 there was laid out at Tientsin three tracts of land for English, French, and American residents, and that for some years our Government exercised in a way jurisdiction over the same.

"On October 12, 1880, the concession was relegated to its former status (meaning back to China) "with the understanding that if at some future time it shall become desirable to establish suitable municipal regulations therein it shall be competent for the consular authorities to do so."

"Under date of October 14, 1880, the Taotai Cheng acknowledged receipt of the dispatch sent to him by the Consul two days before, and it stated that if any American consul in future should "desire to have the settlement revert to the present system of administration he must first arrange with the customs taotai as to the mode of administration, and if there be nothing objectionable in same there should be nothing to prevent the settlement from reverting to the original Government."

"Sometime in the year 1896 a movement was on foot to cede this territory to the Germans, against which action a protest was filed and correspondence in relation thereto with the State Department followed, and finally on April 2, 1896, the Minister (Denby) advised that all jurisdiction over the property be abandoned, and on June 25 instructed the United States Consul at Tientsin to advise the taotai to that effect."

Then Consul Ragsdale gives an opinion of his own. "It has never been the policy of our Government to acquire territory abroad, and that policy may be a wise one in most instances, but at Tientsin I think it would be wise for our Government to have some place over which they could exercise some control. The trouble in north China is not over (this was Feb. 15, 1901), and final settlement day is a long ways off, etc."

It is against the declared policy of our Government in any way to make the military movement in China a pretext for seizing or obtaining territory; and it is for this reason that I have instructed you to make the protests which you have made against the seizures by other Powers.

Then came the first definite announcement of the American policy:

But in order that we may prevent every possible place being occupied by others, so that if the Government desires to apply for a concession after order is restored, we may be able to reoccupy at least the small tract that was formerly the United States concession, or, preferably, have it included in an international settlement, and still be consistent with the position we have already taken (meaning the protests to the other Powers), you may send the enclosed, in the form of a note from yourself, to each of your colleagues.[1]

The " inclosed " was a brief communication stating that the United States had *revived its right* to its former concession, to be used either as such or as part of an international one.[2]

(*Continued from previous page.*)   See U. S. *For. Rel.*, 1901, p. 50.
Minister Denby, October 15, 1896, made a pertinent observation: "As there is no record showing that any concession was ever actually made to the United States, and in view of the further fact that we, many years ago, relinquished whatever control we may have been allowed to exercise over the land, it would seem that we are not in a position to maintain that we are entitled to resume jurisdiction over the tract, even if it is considered desirable to do so." *Ibid.*, p. 50.

[1] U. S. *For. Rel.*, 1901, p. 51.

[2] Copy of Notice to be Served on Foreign Consuls by United States Consul at Tientsin Relative to Preservation of the Tract of Land Known as the United States Concession in Tientsin.
For the purpose of preserving the tract of land known as the United States concession in Tientsin, to be with other tracts organized into an international settlement if possible, but, if not, then at the proper time whenever it may legally be done, to be reoccupied as a United States

However, the United States seemed disinclined to appropriate this ground, although it was occupied temporarily in the hope that it could be converted into an international settlement. As the other Powers did not care for such an arrangement, it was next proposed to come to terms with Great Britain. Immediate action was imperative, as this " no man's land " was " rapidly filling up with bad characters, making some control absolutely necessary ".[1] Sir Ernest Satow offered to arrange the matter on these conditions to be observed:

1. The United States Government to reserve the right to exercise exclusive military control over the concession in case of necessity.

2. The United States Government to reserve the right to moor a gunboat or gunboats at the bund of the United States concession in case of necessity.

3. At least one American citizen to be on the extra concession council. In the event of there being no American citizen on the extra concession council in the ordinary way, the United States Consul should have the right to nominate one by virtue of this arrangement.

4. All transfers of land in the United States concession to be registered at the United States Consulate.

5. No special regulations which apply to the United States concession and not to other parts of the British extra concession to be made without the approval of the United States Consul.

concession, the undersigned, by direction of the United States Legation at Peking, hereby serves this formal notice of such intention on the part of his Government, and requests that it be in every way respected. No adverse seizure or occupancy of any part of this tract can be recognized or allowed.

JAMES W. RAGSDALE,
United States Consul.

[1] U. S. *For. Rel.*, 1901, p. 53.

6. The United States Government to reserve the right to terminate the arrangement with the British extra concession on giving one year's notice and assuming any financial liabilities which may have been incurred for the development of the concession with the consent of the United States Consul.[1]

The next step was the formal application of Minister Conger for a retrocession of this land to the United States. Quite unexpectedly, difficulties arose. Foreign interests, Li Hung-chang explained, were in possession; at any rate, it seemed certain that some foreign concerns were decidedly adverse to having the United States resume its former title. Li Hung-chang offered to compromise the matter by urging Conger to " accept a much larger and unoccupied tract a long way down the river ", but this, the American Minister insisted, " would not satisfy us ", since the other tract, even with its present occupants, " exactly suited our purpose and was the only tract we desired ". The " present occupants", according to Li, were " some of the foremost and wealthiest Chinese in the Empire ". However, it seems certain that some foreign investment companies were causing the real difficulty. Minister Conger wore himself out over the matter, and finally Secretary Hay likewise became disgusted, as the land after all was of little value. Therefore, November 27th, he notified Conger that " it seems undesirable to press the matter further at present ", in view of the difficult situation which had arisen since the United States had relinquished possession.[2] It was indeed curious that when the United States, through force of circumstances, endeavored to deviate just a hair's-breath from its traditional policy, this was found to be impossible. Fate

---

[1] U. S. *For. Rel.*, 1901, pp. 53, 54.

[2] See especially *ibid.*, Inc. no. 769, pp. 54-56, also the correspondence with the Chinese officials, pp. 56-58, and Secretary Hay's reply of November 27, 1901, pp. 58, 59.

seemed to have decreed that the American Power, to its everlasting credit, should be utterly landless in China.

We can now turn to Peking and follow the many and complicated issues confronting China and the Powers to their conclusion in the Peace Protocol of September 7, 1901. China was now completely cowed into submission, the final touch having been given by the occupation of the Imperial City where the court palaces and grounds were situated, and into which heretofore no ordinary mortal had entered. At first the Allies were a bit dubious about attacking this hallowed quarter, and deemed such action beyond their military instructions. So the Generals left the matter with the Diplomatic Body for settlement, and the latter were " of unanimous conviction that failure to crush the resistance of the Chinese troops, holding the Forbidden City, would have disastrous consequences in prolonging a state of anarchy, and diminishing the chances for peace ". Therefore it was decided to take the Imperial Palace, but before the attempt could be made the Chinese troops evacuated it. Nevertheless, the Generals decided to march the Allied army through it, " lest the Chinese, with their infinite capacity for misrepresentation, should infer that some supernatural power had intervened, so that the Allied forces had been affected by fear of the consequences of invading the sacred precincts ". The final decision was to go through the Imperial Palace in complete military array, then close the gates and keep them closed until the Court, which had gone " westward on a tour ", in other words fled the city, should come back. On August 28th, the impressive ceremony was gone through, to the infinite humiliation of the Chinese populace, which had never heard of nor witnessed such an act of sacrilege. That the harsh conduct of the Allies was, however, both necessary and desirable is beyond dispute. The British Minister wisely refrained from giving a graphic description of the event, as he would " not attempt to compete with the numerous newspaper corres- pondents who took part in the ceremony ".[1]

The Summer Palace of the Emperor, a short distance from the capital, likewise came in for its share of attention. A report had reached the Russian military authorities that the Boxer bands in the neighborhood were using the Pal- ace as a sort of target, firing volleys into it every night. The Russians, by the way, had occupied the Palace imme- diately after the capture of Peking, but in their policy of making friends with China they left no stones unturned, particularly in actions such as these, to bring about desired results.   Therefore, on their own initiative and without consulting the Allies, they had marched out and handed over both the Summer and the Winter Palaces to the Chi- nese.   Field-Marshal von Waldersee though this the best plan, but the British Minister emphatically objected to it as " most undesirable " at this juncture of affairs.   The upshot of the matter was that the British decided to move into the Summer Palace themselves and hold it until order was restored.   Probably in order to have some company they extended an invitation to the Italian contingent to join them, and these welcomed the opportunity to take part. That some minor Chinese officials were already in posses- sion might have seemed rather embarrassing at first glance, but it further developed that the native custodians " were only too glad to hand the Palace over ", as they were " un- armed, and had also nothing to eat ".   Minister MacDon- ald considered it his duty to take over the Palace upon evacuation by the Russians " in order to maintain the con- sistent attitude which the combination of western Powers had assumed ", which attitude, so it appeared, would not

[1] See *China No. 5 (1901)*, no. 209. See also U. S. *For. Rel.*, 1900, p. 198.

allow of the abandonment of any action or precedent after it had once been established.[1]

By the acceptance of the credentials of Prince Ching and Li Hung-chang the situation had at last reached the point where definite negotiations could begin.   Naturally, the punishment of the guilty was the question uppermost in the earliest stage of settlement.   In regard to this, the first attempt at solution, the German Government had the honor of making the first move.   Count von Bülow was of the conviction that, " before entering into negotiations for peace, public opinion in Germany would require that the Government should obtain some satisfaction for the outrages committed in China ".[2]   For argument von Bülow harked back to the times of 1860 and said that if the leaders responsible for the outrages of that period had been " adequately punished ", the present lamentable state of affairs would never have occurred.

Accordingly, September 18, 1900, the German *Chargé* at Washington presented a *Circular* to the Department of State as follows:

The Government of His Majesty the Emperor considers as a preliminary condition for entering into diplomatic negotiations with the Chinese Government a surrender of such persons as are determined upon as being the first and real perpetrators of the crimes committed in Peking against international law.   The number of perpetrators who served as tools is too great; a wholesale execution would be adverse to the civilized conscience.   Furthermore, circumstances would not allow that even the group of leaders could be completely ascertained. But the few among them whose guilt is notorious should be surrendered or punished.   The representatives of the Powers

[1] See *China No. 5* (*1901*), nos. 75, 208, 211 and Inc. 1 and 2 in no. 211.

[2] *China No. 1* (*1901*), no. 365.

in Peking will be in a position to make or adduce in this investigation fully valid testimony. The number of those punished is of less importance than their character as principal instigators and leaders. The Government of His Majesty the Emperor believes that it can depend in this matter upon the concurrence of all the Cabinets; for indifference toward the idea of a just expiation would be equivalent to indifference toward a repetition of the crime.

Germany further proposed that the Diplomatic Body at Peking should " designate the principal Chinese personages whose guilt in the instigation or execution of the crimes is beyond a doubt ".[1]

To which Acting Secretary David J. Hill replied:

The Government of the United States has from the outset proclaimed its purpose to hold to the uttermost accountability the responsible authors of any wrongs done in China to citizens of the United States and their interests, as was stated in the Government's *circular* communication to the Powers of July 3 last. These wrongs have been committed not only in Peking, but in many parts of the Empire, and their punishment is believed to be an essential element of any effective settlement which shall prevent a recurrence of such outrages and bring about permanent safety and peace in China. It is thought, however, that no punitive measures can be effective by way of reparation for wrongs suffered and as deterrent examples for the future as the degradation and punishment of the responsible authors by the supreme Imperial authority itself; and it seems only just to China that she should be afforded in the first instance an opportunity to do this, and thus rehabilitate herself before the world. Believing thus, and without abating in any wise its deliberate purpose to exact the fullest accountability from the responsible authors of the wrongs we have suffered in China, the Government of the United States is not

[1] U. S. *For. Re'.*, 1900, p. 341. See also p. 306.

disposed, as a preliminary condition to entering into diplomatic negotiations with the Chinese Government, to join in a demand that said Government surrender to the Powers such persons as, according to the determination of the Powers themselves, may be held to be the first and real perpetrators of those wrongs. On the other hand, this Government is disposed to hold that the punishment of the high responsible authors of these wrongs, not only in Peking, but throughout China, is essentially a condition to be embraced and provided for in the negotiations for a final settlement. It is the purpose of this Government at the earliest practicable moment to name its plenipotentiaries for negotiating a settlement with China, and in the meantime to authorize its Minister in Peking to enter forthwith into conference with the duly authorized representatives of the Chinese Government with a view to bringing about a preliminary agreement whereby the full exercise of the Imperial power for the preservation of order and the protection of foreign life and property throughout China pending final negotiations with the Powers shall be assured.[1]

The American reply was the most unfavorable and about the only one out and out opposed to the proposal of the German Government. This was because the Department of State frankly doubted the advisability, or even the success, of this preliminary diplomatic procedure.

Replies from the other Powers were more reassuring to the German Government. Austria, as of course everyone expected, accepted the German proposition "without reserve".[2] Japan also believed that punishment should first take place and so was ready to coöperate in the spirit suggested by Germany, although the Tokyo Government anticipated "grave difficulties" in this undertaking.[3] Count

[1] U. S. *For. Rel.*, 1900, pp. 341, 342. See also *China No. 1 (1901)*, no. 385.

[2] U. S. *For. Rel.*, 1900, p. 394.   [3] *China No. 1 (1901)*, no. 370.

Lamsdorff answered unofficially for the Russian Government at one of his famous weekly receptions in St. Petersburg. The Count intimated that the German proposals were " somewhat vague " as to whether the prescribed persons were to be punished by the Powers or by China. As far as he was concerned, he " would prefer that the rôle of executioner, if necessary, should be undertaken by the Chinese Government, who appeared to have a special aptitude for such a task ". But no more than Russia, it may be remarked, in the light of the massacre of Blagovestchensk in July, 1900, when the progress of the Amur was choked by the corpses of 5,000 unoffending civilian Chinese, driven into the river at the point of the bayonet. Count Lamsdorff was of opinion that exile would be sufficient punishment for those Boxer leaders and sympathizers of high rank who might be declared guilty. Later, September 26th, the Russian Government agreed " in principle " to the German proposal, which the United States practically had not done. But Russia asked for more particulars on the subject of surrender of the guilty, whether these were to be handed over to the Diplomatic Body or were to be punished by China.[1] Italy " accepted the German note in principle and replied to that effect ".[2] Naturally, the entire Triple Alliance would adhere to the policy suggested by its leader.

Lord Salisbury wanted time " for a few day's reflection ". He admitted that the proposal awakened "profound sympathy" as to contents, and that the retribution suggested was " not only richly deserved, but that an element of security for the future will be lost if that punishment cannot be inflicted ". Although France had given an affir-

[1] *China No. 1 (1901)*, nos. 376, 388, 395.

[2] *Ibid.*, no. 398.

mative reply,[1] Lord Salisbury decided that, while ordinarily he would have given " an unreserved assent ", yet the nature of the proposal was of such consequence that first he wished to communicate with the British Minister at Peking on the following points:

1. Whether he (Minister MacDonald) and the other foreign representatives could with any certainty and on clear evidence designate those who were really responsible for the recent outrages.
2. Whether, in the event of the Chinese Government refusing to surrender or to punish these persons, or returning evasive answers, it would be practicable to seize them.[2]

To which MacDonald replied, September 29th:

1. It is quite possible to designate the guilty with certainty, and is likely that the list of each of my colleagues would be identical with the others.
2. Prince Tuan, being one of the chief offenders, and seeming to be *de facto* the Chinese Government at the present time, it will be most difficult to seize the guilty.[3]

On the same day that the British Foreign Office received these answers from Peking, the second of which must be regarded as rather unfavorable to the German proposal, the news also came of a Chinese edict, promulgated September 25th, in which punishment was defined and prescribed for a number of the most guilty. Evidently, China was doing the best under the circumstances to anticipate the German action and to propitiate the Powers. The edict read:

[1] Delcassé approved " with much satisfaction of the German *Circular* " as it practically coincided with his own views as he had expressed them to the Chinese Government in July last. *China No. 1 (1901)*, no. 394.
[2] *Ibid.*, nos. 386, 387.
[3] *Ibid.*, no. 399.

The present troubles have been occasioned against the will of the Throne. The Boxer brigands have been incited by Princes and Ministers, and war with friendly natives (nations?) has been the result. The Court has had to flee (to Sianfu), and although the Throne is itself to blame, the Princes and Ministers are largely culpable in various degrees. Accordingly, four Imperial Princes are deprived of office and rank. Prince Tuan is degraded from office, but given the privilege of trial by the Clansmen's Court. Kang Yi and Chao Shu-chiao are handed over to the Censorate for punishment.[1]

[1] *China No. 1* (*1901*), no. 400. See also *China No. 5* (*1901*), no. 9.

Regarding the *Edict* of September 25, Lord Salisbury expressed to the Chinese Minister at London his " satisfaction with the results that had so far been attained by the issue of the Edict of the Emperor of China in regard to the most guilty of the Chinese statesmen." But Lord Salisbury admitted that the edict's " real value would ultimately be decided by the practical effect which the Chinese Government should give to its provisions." *China No. 5* (*1901*), no. 6.

Sir Claude MacDonald was not so sure. " The various Boards (of the Yamen) are left to decide the penalties to be inflicted." He noticed too that, although punishment of Prince Tuan was included, " Yu Hsien, Governor of Shansi, Tung Fu-hsiang and others are omitted." In criticism of the *Edict* he said: "Although this decree does not in itself prove that the Throne has either the will or the power to inflict adequate punishment, it may be accepted as a step in the right direction." *China No. 5* (*1901*), no. 16.

Said Acting Consul-General Warren at Shanghai: " This (referring to the Edict of September 25), in the opinion of the Wuchang Viceroy, is the first step in the real policy of the Court." Unfortunately, " the general impression among Chinese here is that these edicts, professing to punish the reactionaries, are really intended only to mislead the foreign Powers as to the sincerity of the Court's regret, and there is evidence to support this idea." Also, " the fact that Yu Hsien should be awarded no punishment, and that Prince Tuan should be replaced by an official equally as bad as, if not worse than, himself, seems to show that the Court has not the power to punish those who deserve punishment most. The immunity from censure enjoyed by Jung Lu and Tung Fu-hsiang, both of whom are supported by large forces of troops, is also an argument in favor of this conclusion." *Ibid.*, no. 18.

The appearance of the above decree altered the situation to an appreciable extent and forced Germany to add to her note the following questions, asking the Powers for a consideration and opinion of them:

1. Whether the list of persons to be punished, as contained in the Chinese edict (the above decree of September 25) is sufficient and correct.

2. Whether the proposed punishments are suitable.

3. In what manner the Powers will be able to control the execution of these punishments.[1]

As regarded these questions, Italy decided " to accept ", but would " reserve the right of instructing their representative in Peking to come to an agreement with his colleagues as to the manner of ascertaining these three points".[2] France notified her *Chargé* at Berlin "to inform the German Government that the Government of the Republic accept the proposals made by them in connection with China ".[3] The British Ambassador at Berlin, Sir F. Lascelles, was able to inform von Bülow on October 4th, " on the arrival of the Queen's messenger ", that Lord Salisbury substantially agreed with the German views.[4] Japan also expressed approval, in fact was very friendly about it, assuring von Bülow that he had " the cordial support and approval of the Imperial Japanese Government ", which would be " pleased " to have him " accept that assurance as

[1] *China No. 5 (1901)*, Inc. in no. 5, giving French version and trans. For the same in German and trans., see no. 10, Inc.

[2] Further: " The Italian Government do not desire to put themselves in a prominent position in China in view of their slight interests there, but to maintain the concert by giving such replies to proposals of the other Powers (France and Russia up to this date) as help in this direction." *Ibid.*, no. 14.

[3] *Ibid.*, no. 19.

[4] *Ibid.*, no. 25.

a full and satisfactory response to the proposal ". However, Japan suggested " that the sphere of usefulness of the foreign representatives in Peking would be greatly enlarged if all the questions which are to serve as the basis of negotiations with China were to be presented to them for collective examination ". In this, it may be remarked, Japan anticipated a later development in the negotiations. But as regarded Germany's efforts, Japan was convinced they were " a step in the right direction ",[1] which was comforting to von Bülow, as the United States in particular did not regard them as such.

Meanwhile, the Diplomatic Body at Peking held a meeting to consider the three German questions, and the following answers were unanimously [2] adopted :

1. As far as it goes the list is a correct one, though the names of Tung Fu-hsiang and Yu Hsien should be inserted.

2. The penalties imposed are not sufficiently severe.

3. It is advisable that the punishments be carried out in Peking in the presence of the military or civil foreign representatives.[3]

September 27th, Count Lamsdorff gave the definite reply of Russia to the German note. As regards the first two points, these Russia "accepted in principle", but the *"modus procedendi,* as traced in the German *Circular,* presented, however, certain difficulties ". Lamsdorff did not believe that China would hand over the principal offenders to the Powers for punishment, " since the guilty persons would probably be found to be in the entourage of the Emperor

[1] *China No. 5 (1901)*, no. 60 and Inc. 1 in no. 60.

[2] The Russian Minister was not present, as at this time the Russian Legation staff was sojourning at Tientsin. Germany and Austria were represented by their *Chargé d'Affaires.*

[3] *Ibid.,* no. 35.

and Dowager Empress ". And so, " as their surrender
would almost certainly be refused, the negotiations would
be indefinitely postponed ". As the best way out of the
difficulty, in the opinion of Count Lamsdorff:

The punishment of the leaders of the movement should, during
the course of the negotiations, be demanded from the Chinese
Plenipotentiaries as one of the guarantees to be exacted from
the Emperor of China as security against any further repetition
of the attacks on the representatives of foreign Powers, and
upon the lives and property of foreigners in China.

Lamsdorff further remarked:

Apart from the anomaly of asking China to hand over its subjects to the foreign Powers for punishment . . . their punishment by the central Imperial authority would have a far greater
effect throughout the whole of the Chinese Empire than the
infliction by the Allied Powers of just retribution upon the
guilty—a task which, to the Russian Government at least,
would be extremely distasteful.

The British Ambassador, Mr. C. Hardinge, then ventured
to suggest to Lamsdorff that, " for all practical purposes,
the views of the Russian Government coincided with those
of the United States ". This drew from the Count the reply that, " the Russian Government had by no means rejected the German proposal, nor had replied to it in such
categorical terms as those in which the American reply had
been couched ".[1]

Germany, however, had at least succeeded in starting the
negotiations, which was accomplishing not a little; but
now the German note was overshadowed in importance by
the French proposals. These were more inclusive and to
the point than the single proposition advanced by Germany.

[1] *China No. 5 (1901)*, no. 22.

The suggestions of France as a basis for negotiations read as follows:

1. Punishment of the principal culprits, to be designated by the representatives of the Powers at Peking.

2. Maintenance of the prohibition of import of arms.

3. Equitable indemnities for States, Societies, and individuals.

4. Establishment of a permanent Legation guard at Peking.

5. Dismantlement of the Forts at Taku.

6. Military occupation of two or three points on the road from Tientsin to Taku, which would thus be always open in the event of the Legations wishing to reach the sea, or for forces coming from the sea with the object of proceeding to the capital.[1]

The simplest way of discussing these French proposals would be to run them through to their acceptance by the Powers [2] and China, and then to take them up in detail,

---

[1] *China No. 5 (1901)*, no. 11 and Trans.; U. S. *For. Rel.*, 1900, p. 322.

[2] Notice the following version of the French *note* as desired by the Russian Government, given by the Russian Embassy at Washington, September 21 (October 4) to Secretary Hay:

" In the opinion of the Imperial Government, as well as of the Government of the French Republic, the programme upon which the several Cabinets may succeed in reaching an accord should comprise:

" First. The punishment of the principal authors or instigators of the outrages committed in China, and notably of Prince Tuan, the dignitaries Tung Fu-hsiang, Kang Yi, Li Ping-heng, and the Governor of Shansi, Yu Hsien.

" Second. The continued interdiction of the importation of arms into China.

" Third. The granting to the Governments, corporations, and private individuals of all indemnities, the adjustment of which, in the event of protracted divergence, might be confided to the International Peace Bureau at The Hague.

" Fourth. Guarantees for the future, as to which it would be permissible to consult the diplomatic representatives of the Powers in China. My French colleague has doubtless specified in the note he has addressed to you what these guarantees might be."

M. de Wollant to Secretary Hay, U. S. *For. Rel.*, 1900, pp. 381, 382.

along with the suggestions and propositions from other nations.

Said the United States, October 10th:

The President is glad to perceive in the bases of negotiations put forward in the memorandum of October 4 the spirit that has animated the declaration heretofore made by all the Powers interested, and would be pleased to see the negotiations begun immediately upon the usual verification of credentials.

Regarding clause 1, comment was made: " The Chinese Government has already indicated its intention to punish a number of those responsible for the recent disorders.[1] The representatives of the Powers at Peking may suggest additions to that list when negotiations are entered upon ". As regards clause 2: " It is not understood (by the Department of State) that this interdiction (against the importation of arms) is to be permanent, and the duration of it and the details of its regulation seem a proper subject of discussion by the negotiators ". As regards clause 3:

This (equitable indemnity) is an object desired by all the Powers. The Russian Government has suggested that in case of protracted divergence of views, the matter might be commended to the consideration of the International Court of Arbitration of the Hague. The President thinks this suggestion worthy the attention of the Powers.

As regards clause 4 (Legation guards) : " The Government of the United States is unable to make a permanent engagement of this nature without the authorization of the legislative branch,[2] but in the present emergency we have stationed in Peking an adequate Legation guard ". As regards

[1] Referring here to the Imperial *Edict* of September 25.

[2] This would be an act of a military nature requiring the consent of Congress.

clause 5 (dismantling the Taku Forts) : " The President reserves the expression of his opinion as to this measure, pending the receipt of further information in regard to the situation in China ".[1] As regards clause 6 (on military occupation of points between Tientsin and Peking) : The same observation here as in clause 4, *i. e.*, the President "is unable to commit the United States to a permanent participation in such occupation ",[2] although it was thought desirable that " the Powers shall obtain from the Chinese Government the assurance of their right to guard their Legations in Peking and to have the means of unrestricted access to them whenever required ".

It must be kept in mind that all of the above was only a detailed criticism of the French note and not a condemnation. In fact, Secretary Hay expressed the hope that " the Government of France and the other Powers will see in the reserves we have made here no obstacle to the initiation of negotiations on the lines suggested ".[3] A week later the French Government announced at Washington that it " highly appreciated " the attitude of the Department of State, and Secretary Hay replied that he was " gratified to learn that all the interested Powers have adhered to the essential principle of the French note of October 4th ". He trusted that the reservations made by the United States and other nations would " prove no embarrassment to the progress of the negotiations, in the course of which they

[1] The answer of the Department of State to this clause remained unfavorable during the entire negotiations. This was because the Powers later stood for the destruction of the Taku Forts, while the United States only desired their dismantlement. In art. viii of the Final Protocol it was agreed that these famous forts were to be razed.

[2] Again the desire of the United States, as with Minister Reed in 1858 and Admiral Kempff at Taku, to avoid all entanglements or temporary alliances of a military nature with Europe.

[3] U. S. *For. Rel.*, 1900, pp. 322, 323; *China No. 5 (1901)*, Inc. in no. 100.

can be frankly discussed with a view to a common agreement ".[1] These various reservations had, of course, nothing to do with the acceptance by all concerned of the French note as the basis of negotiations. However, M. Delcassé did not count upon unqualified adherence by the Powers. The most he hoped for was their assent in general.[2] Delcassé's sole purpose was to embody the " collective ideas of the Powers in a compendious form ". In doing so, he had " no wish to push his country into the foremost place ",[3] nor had he " any unavowed objects to serve ". But he " dreaded the mischief that might be caused by allowing events to drag on ", and therefore he was of the opinion that " expedition should be used in defining the objects and methods upon which the Powers interested might agree ".[4] Delcassé's efforts deserved and received the hearty commendation and support of Europe and America.

Great Britain agreed likewise, excepting the last point. Lord Salisbury was of the opinion, regarding the road from Peking to Taku being held by an international force, that it was " safer and more effective that each Power that wished should hold a fort of its own, which should be within reach of the sea so far as practicable ".[5] The Russian views

---

[1] U. S. *For. Rel.*, 1900, pp. 323, 324.

[2] Sir E. Monson to Lord Salisbury, Paris, Oct. 10, *China No. 5 (1901)*, no. 36.

[3] Neither had Germany for that matter, although Germany's grievances were aggravated out of all proportion to the others by the murder of Minister von Ketteler. American and British policies were also unselfish, but with Russia there is more doubt, as Russia almost always had either ulterior motives in view or an eye to future developments favorable to the Russian Government. It must be remembered that at this period the Government at St. Petersburg was assiduously cultivating the friendship of China in order to cloak Russian territorial ambitions.

[4] *China No. 5 (1901)*, no. 42.

[5] *Ibid.*, no. 43.

were identical with the British, also as regarded the single British objection. Furthermore, Russia " had always considered that each Power should have its own guard for its Legation ".[1] Italy accepted, " subject to such modifications as may be rendered necessary by the unforeseen in the development of negotiations with China ".[2] Japan expressed " general agreement, observing, however, that in a permanent prohibition of arms (clause 2) China might find a difficulty as regards the fulfilment of her treaty obligations to protect foreigners and maintain order,[3] or at least an excuse for her failure to do so ". Further, Japan considered " impracticable the organization of an international guard", but would agree to separate guards ".[4]

[1] *China No. 1 (1901)*, no. 90.   [2] *Ibid.*, no. 55.

[3] A very good point. It must be remembered that, because of the Boxer movement, not a single Power believed in China's immediate regeneration, although this actually happened. Therefore the possibility of the Chinese military patterning entirely after Yuan Shih-kai's foreign-drilled and equipped troops was incomprehensible to Europe at this time. Also, Japan's idea for only a temporary prohibition of arms was not an altruistic one regarding China but merely to afford greater security to foreigners.

[4] *China No. 5 (1901)*, no. 60.

Mr. Whitehead reported to Lord Salisbury from Tokyo, October 5, that, in an interview with Viscount Aoki, the Japanese statesman informed him: " Japan would demur to the second point in the French proposals, viz., the maintenance of the prohibition to import arms and ammunition, because such prohibition, if effective, would deprive the Chinese authorities of the means of maintaining order.

Mr. Whitehead continued: " His Excellency added, however, that he did not think the prohibition was likely to be effective, because it would be impossible to prevent the Chinese Government from engaging foreign instructors and manufacturing what they required in the interior of the country. Viscount Aoki stated further that he agreed to the proposal to destroy the Forts at Taku. As regards the organization of a guard for the Legations at Peking, he thought that if this meant a body of troops recruited from different nationalities, the idea was impracticable, but that there would be no objection if it meant that each Legation was to have its own guard." *China No. 5 (1901)*, no. 196.

The Powers having agreed to accept the French proposals [1] as bases for negotiations, they were next taken up
by the Diplomatic Body at Peking, by whom they were
finally to be presented to the Chinese Plenipotentiaries. A
meeting of the foreign representatives was called, October
10th, by Sir Claude MacDonald, at which the Russian Minister was absent, still at Tientsin, while the Austrian and
Netherlands Legations were unrepresented.

The French proposals were threshed out in a very satisfactory manner. Regarding punishments of the " principle offenders designated by the representatives of the
Powers ", it was suggested that the condemnations "should
include all officials who took an active part, in country districts, and in abetting massacres; the foreign representatives to ascertain their names subsequently ". Still more
important was the proposal that " there should be no official examinations held during five years in districts and
towns where foreigners had suffered maltreatment ". This
in itself was felt to afford an effective check on the disaf-
fected localities against further outbreaks, as it would strike
at the root of the entire Chinese system and public life.

At the meeting of October 16th, after some discussion,
the diplomats reached the following unanimous agreement:

The penalty to be demanded in the case of the persons guilty
of directing the attacks on the Legations and the massacre of
foreigners [2] in the interior ought to be *capital punishment*,[3] and

---

[1] On the introduction and acceptance of the French proposals, see
China No. 5 (1901), nos. 11, 17, 36, 42-45, 55, 60, 66, 67, 70, 71, 73, 81,
83, 84, 86, 90, 94, 99, 100, 104, 109, 117, 154-156, 196.

[2] At the meeting on October 31 it was decided to add to the above
the words " or have suffered cruel treatment " after the phrase " massacre of foreigners."

[3] The *italics* are the author's. This question of capital punishment
later caused a prolonged correspondence among the Powers.

that the list should include, besides the Princes and officials mentioned in the Imperial edict,[1] the names of Tung Fu-hsiang and Yu Hsien [2] . . . To these we considered it would be necessary to add the names of the officials responsible for the murder and cruel treatment of foreigners at Paotingfu, in this province (Chihli), and Chuchow, in the province of Chekiang, which are gradually being ascertained, as well as others equally guilty that may be authentically reported to us.

At the meeting of October 31st, Minister Conger of the United States pointed out to the Diplomatic Body:

Although protection was promised by the treaties to foreigners residing in China, innumerable cases had occurred in recent years of attacks against their lives and property, for which no adequate reparation had been obtained. When the dismissal of officials, who, by connivance or apathy, had favored such attacks, had been obtained, they had usually been transferred elsewhere, and even promoted.

Therefore Conger proposed as addition to base no. 1 the following clause:

As a further guarantee against future trouble, an Imperial edict shall be issued and published everywhere in the Empire, mak-

[1] *Edict* of September 25.

[2] Sir Claude MacDonald: "The former of these is the General responsible for the continuance of the bombardment of the Legations at the same time that assurances were being communicated to your Lordship (Salisbury), and to the Governments of the other Powers, that the Chinese Government continued to protect the foreign Ministers. The latter is the notorious Governor of Shansi, who is reported to have boasted to the Chinese Government that he had caused fifty-one foreigners to be killed in his Yamen at Tai Yuan-fu." Resentment against Yu Hsien was particularly bitter because of the public beheading of many of his victims in this instance cited by MacDonald.

Sir E. Satow had succeeded MacDonald at the time this dispatch was forwarded (November 8), but he reported it, as he said, almost literally in words of the former Minister.

ing all Viceroys, provincial and local officials responsible for
order in their respective jurisdictions, and, whenever anti-
foreign disturbances or any infractions of treaty occur therein,
they, the said officials, shall be immediately removed, and forever prohibited from holding any office or honor.

This clause was accepted by the Diplomatic Body.[1]

Regarding base no. 2: It has already been mentioned
that the foreign representatives had decided it to be " very
necessary to prohibit the importation of arms ". In addition it was unanimously agreed to refer to their respective
governments " to determine subsequently the duration of
the prohibition, as we (the Ministers) conceived that it is
intended to prevent the importation of ammunition and any
substances exclusively intended for use in its manufacture".

Regarding base no. 3: The conclusion reached was that
the Powers " should come to a preliminary agreement as to
the extent of indemnities ", which should include compensation to friendly and Christian Chinese " who have lost by
their connection with foreigners ".[2] As to the manner of
payment and the necessary guarantees, it was suggested that
" an institution might be created in the nature of a *Caisse
de la Dette* ", although this need not include all revenues.

The idea of the indemnity claims " to be investigated by
a commission composed of Consuls of each nation concerned " did not appeal to Minister MacDonald, who suggested instead that the claims " should be entrusted to a
commission of persons not resident in China to be sent out

---

[1] Later amended by inserting "which are not forthwith suppressed
and the guilty persons punished " after " occur therein."

[2] " It seemed obviously right to demand compensation in the case of
Chinese writers and servants in the employ of the Legations, foreign
residents of Peking, or it may be elsewhere, who have suffered, as also
for those refugees whose labor on the defences of the Legation so
greatly contributed to rendering resistance effectual against the attacks
of the besiegers."

from neutral countries, such as Switzerland, Denmark, and Sweden ". Such a commission would, of course, work far better. The British Minister evidently was ot the opinion that the various Consuls would be too biased in their individual governmental perspectives. It was then mentioned by Conger that the United States had received a proposal from Russia to send these claims to the Hague Tribunal, and this was received with favor.

Regarding base no. 4, for permanent Legation guards: It was suggested that " a defensible Legation quarter would be a useful addition ". The formula finally adopted by unanimous vote was the " right of each Power to maintain for its Legation a permanent guard, and of putting the Legation in a defensible position, while the right of residence therein would not be accorded to Chinese ". It will be noticed that the Diplomatic Body placed itself on record in favor of separate Legation guards.

As regards base no. 5 : Several of the diplomats were of the opinion that the expression " Taku Forts " should as well include others, as from Taku to Tientsin, and from Tientsin to Peitang (halfway to Peking). This would make secure the entire route of communication from the coast to the capital. The formula was accordingly amended to include the whole distance.

In regard to keeping the route from Taku to Peking open, *etc.*: the Diplomatic Body observed :

Taku is inaccessible from the sea during at least the three months of December, January and February, and that the only practicable landing-places at that season are Chinwangtao and Shanhaikwan. Also that as the distance from Peking to Taku is 107 miles, and of Shanhaikwan 153 miles more, fortified posts in the vicinity of these two places would not help us much.

Therefore the British Minister offered this opinion, given to him " by a high military authority " :

The establishment of a garrison at Tientsin and the occupation of some principal railway station from Peking to Shanhaikwan for some months to come would probably meet the case. . . . In order, therefore, to have these points entirely free to be determined hereafter by the Governments, the following alteration was suggested: The Powers may arrange between themselves for the military occupation of certain points for the maintenance of communication between the capital and the sea.

This suggestion of Sir E. Satow [1] met with unanimous approval.

So much for the criticism, extension and final adoption of the French proposals by the foreign representatives at Peking. It developed, however, that the Diplomatic Body had certain ideas distinctly its own, as follows:

Base no. 7: It should be agreed by the Chinese Government to post for two years in every district an Imperial Edict, prohibiting, under pain of death, any membership of " Boxer " Societies, and stating what punishments had been inflicted, including the suspension of examinations suggested above.

Base no. 8: A Minister for Foreign Affairs should be appointed, and the Tsung-li Yamen abolished.

Base no. 9: Relations with the Court on a sensible basis should be established.

The seventh proposal was agreed to without a dissenting voice. Sir E. Satow reported that, at the meeting of October 31st, some of the diplomats were under the impression that a proclamation of religious liberty had been incorporated, but Satow, in looking through MacDonald's notes, happily found no such suggestion. Therefore the religious

---

[1] Sir E. Satow succeeded Sir C. MacDonald, October 25, as British Minister, and himself directed the British policy on Oct. 26, 28, 31, Nov. 5, while MacDonald was present Oct. 10 and 17.

idea was not adopted, as the diplomats wisely resolved to steer clear of the missionary question and its many unnecessary complications.

The eighth and ninth proposals, originally offered by M. Salvago Raggi, the Italian Minister, were " generally accepted in principle ". There was some doubt, however, as to whether these two provisions should be inserted " in the note which we are to present in the name of our Governments ". Austria-Hungary, Great Britain, Germany, Italy and the United States voted for the inclusion, while France, Japan and Russia voted contra. Belgium and Spain did not vote, preferring to recommend their Governments to adopt the view which would ultimately be taken by the majority of the Powers.

At the meeting of November 5th, A. von Mumm, the German Minister, came forward with the following additional article:

The dispatch of a special mission to Berlin, headed by an Imperial Prince, in order to express the regret of His Majesty the Emperor of China and of the Chinese Government with respect to the murder of Baron von Ketteler.

On the spot where the murder was committed the erection of a monument to the memory of the deceased Minister, appropriate to his rank, and bearing an inscription in Latin, German and Chinese expressing the regret of the Emperor of China for the murder committed.

There was no discussion over the German addition and it was accepted unanimously.

However, this proposed monument to von Ketteler led the Japanese Minister to make a similar addition to commemorate the Japanese Chancellor, Mr. Sugiyama, who also lost his life during the siege. It was agreed that the Diplomatic Body would support his request in similar fashion.

Next, Sir E. Satow was of the opinion that an article should be inserted " which would entitle the Powers to obtian a satisfactory revision of the existing treaties of commerce and navigation, and a settlement of various pending questions of importance to commercial interests ".[1] The Russian Minister was of the belief that commercial questions did not enter into these negotiations. Satow replied that the Rebellion had resulted in " the destruction of the foreign settlements at Tientsin and to the complete severance of all foreign commercial relations with every part of the country ". On putting the article to vote, the Ministers of Austria-Hungary, Belgium, Germany, Italy, Japan, United States and Great Britain were in favor of it. The Russian Minister maintained his objection, and was supported by the French Secretary of Legation, acting in the absence of the French Minister.

On October 10th, the Italian Minister, recurring to base no. 3, gave it as his opinion that, as China's " existing Customs revenue is almost entirely absorbed by the service of existing foreign loans ", therefore, " in order to provide for the indemnities which China will be called upon to Governments and subjects ", it would be necessary that " other sources of income will have to be appropriated ". To meet this difficulty he proposed :

China will take financial measures on the lines which will be indicated by the Plenipotentiaries in order to guarantee the payment of the indemnities and the service of the loan.

The Russian Minister thought that this clause was unnecessary, " considering that the Plenipotentiaries would concert among themselves the means of insuring the pay-

[1] This clause explains why so many commercial treaties were entered into by China and other countries in the years immediately following the adoption of the Boxer Peace Protocol.

ment of the indemnities when fixed ". The Japanese Government " reserved " by its Minister's action " the expression of an opinion on this point ". All the rest recommended M. Raggi's proposal to their respective Foreign Offices as desirable of adoption.[1]

This ended the discussions of and additions to the French proposals by the Diplomatic Body.[2] Lastly, a committee was appointed, consisting of the Ministers of Austria-Hungary and Italy and the Secretary of the French Legation, to draft a preamble to this Joint Note which should recount China's violations of international law and their results.[3]

However, it soon developed that there was great difference of opinion among the Powers as to several provisions of this Joint Note to the Chinese Government. It must be remembered that as yet China had not been consulted in the matter. All discussions had been among the various foreign governments and among their representatives at Peking. It had been felt in the beginning by the Diplomatic Body that this Joint Note should be a sort of " ultimatum " with " irrevocable conditions ", which China should be forced to accept unconditionally and without reserve. With such object in view, it was fortunately seen in time that some of the provisions were entirely too severe, in particular as regarded the " irrevocable " nature of the Note and the punishment of the Boxer leaders. The punishment

[1] Later, the proposal of the Italian Minister was amended, and "financial measures acceptable to the Powers" was substituted for "on the lines which the Powers will indicate."

This made a unanimous agreement among the Ministers as to the entire proposals and additions. See *China No. 5 (1901)*, no. 173. See also no. 117.

[2] The meeting of the Diplomatic Body for the above discussions and proceedings relative to the French bases for negotiations are reported in *ibid.*, nos. 107 and 255.

[3] For the text of the *Joint Note* see Appendix I, reprinted from *China No. 5 (1901)*, no. 188.

clause especially was overdrawn, the diplomats in their zeal having condemned princes of the blood to death for complicity in the Rebellion when calm reflection should have convinced them that China never would have agreed to so drastic a retribution for members of the royal family. In general the tone of the Joint Note was too harsh, and after the various provisions had circulated among the Powers for a few months, this was clearly seen to be the case. Modifications urgently needed were fortunately agreed upon, helped and encouraged, of course, by hints from and discussions with the Chinese Plenipotentiaries.

Germany was strongly opposed to referring any of the questions involved to the Hague Tribunal for settlement. The United States objected to " irrevocable " conditions and instructed Minister Conger to that effect. The two great Yangtse Viceroys, of Nanking and Hankow, firm friends of the Powers during the darkest days of the Rebellion, pointed out that the death sentence for members of the Imperial family should be commuted to perpetual banishment, which was punishment enough. Commissioners Li Hung-chang and Prince Ching were not at all disposed to agree to articles no. 6 and 11 of the Joint Note relating to indemnities and the amendment of the existing commercial treaties. Because of their objection to these two clauses the United States proposed to refer the articles to a conference at Washington. This idea found no favor with Germany, who preferred, instead, a commission of financial and commercial experts to meet at Peking. Japan agreed with Germany on this point, and because of this opposition the United States withdrew its proposal.[1] Austria was

---

[1] Marquis of Lansdowne to Sir E. Satow (*Circular*), Jan. 11, 1901: " I am informed by the United States' Ambassador that the President withdraws his proposal for a conference to deal with points 6 and 11 of the peace conditions, owing to the decided opposition of the German and Japanese Governments." *China No. 6 (1901*, no. 27). For the Japanese objections, see *ibid.*, no. 28.

loath to see the death penalty of all the Boxer leaders dispensed with, while Russia was of the opinion that, in reference to this, the proposed phrase *la peine de plus sévère* might be construed to mean death after all, a construction the connections of which it is a little difficult to see. Germany, of course, because of the murder of von Ketteler, wanted the existing phrase *la peine de mort* to stand without change. France, like the United States, " never liked " the word " irrevocable ", while Great Britain desired it. It was finally agreed that the word " irrevocable " as to the contents of the Joint Note should be withdrawn, only to be replaced afterwards, while the phrase *la peine de mort* should be changed to *la peine de plus sévère*.

On December 19, 1900, the Joint Note was signed by all the foreign Ministers at Peking, with the exception of Mr. Conger, who misread the instructions from Washington regarding " irrevocable ", but who signed later.

So much for the Joint Note,[1] as far as its composition was concerned. Several of its provisions were carried through readily enough with the Chinese Plenipotentiaries, but with others there was much difficulty, as was to be expected. From the first, the Powers were united on presenting the Note jointly, and solemnly warned the Chinese commissioners against concluding any separate agreements.[2] The understanding as to the prohibition of import of arms gave trouble until it was decided that the clause should be only temporay in nature. To have made it permanent

[1] On the Joint Note, see *China No. 5 (1901)*, nos. 69, 88, 137, 153, 177, 188, 192-194, 198, 199, 201-206, 220, 224, 225, 227-229, 231-234, 236-244, 258, 261, 265, 266; *China No. 6 (1901)*, nos. 2, 4, 7, 8, 10, 12, 18-28, 32, 33, 37, 39, 47, 49, 51, 54, 56, 63, 70-73, 82, 90, 91, 96, 98, 117, 143, 145, 178, 180, 185, 201, 234; *China No. 1 (1902)*, nos. 41, 114, 172; U. S. *For. Rel.*, 1900, pp. 235, 237, 238, 240-243, 246, 248.

[2] On the warnings to China against concluding separate agreements, see *China No. 6 (1901)*, nos. 79, 80, 101, 106, 153, 164, 197, 202, 213.

would have been nonsensical, an utter impossibility in the nature of things.[1]

The demands for punishment and the indemnity question caused the greatest difficulties. It will be remembered that the decree of September 25th, visiting punishment upon several of the Boxer leaders, was regarded by the Powers as inadequate and incomplete. Therefore a new edict appeared on November 13th, which was more stringent in tone than the preceding. According to its commands, Prince Tuan and Prince Chuan were to be deprived of their offices and rank and immured for life at Moukden. Prince Yi and Secondary Prince Tsai Yin were likewise to suffer life imprisonment. Secondary Prince Tsai Lien was to be deprived of his hereditary rank and confined to his house. Duke Tsai Lan was to be degraded one step in rank and was to lose all his emoluments. Kang Yi was dead, therefore penalty was waived in his case. Ying Nien was to be degraded, likewise Chao Shu-chiao, who was to lose his nominal rank but was to remain in office. Yu Hsien was to be banished to the most remote frontier and put to work on the most distant military post road. The punishment of Tung Fu-hsiang, " on account of his being in command of Imperial troops ", was to be reserved for future consideration.[2]

But this new decree gave little satisfaction to Europe,

[1] It had early been recognized that it would have been undesirable to have allowed an unrestricted importation of arms into China for some period after the Boxer troubles. Of course the Powers realized that they could not prevent China from manufacturing arms and ammunition, but all outside supplies were to be cut off until the entire Empire again was in a state of peaceful intercourse with the world.

See *China No. 1 (1901)*, nos. 97, 115, 116, 129, 142, 186, 206, 345; *China No. 5 (1901)*, nos. 73, 151; *China No. 6 (1901)*, no. 131; *China No. 1 (1902)*, nos. 12, 145, 159, 210, 220.

[2] *China No. 5 (1901)*, nos. 140, 142.

and the Diplomatic Body pronounced it " inadequate and absurd ". Particularly was criticism directed against the alleged mild sentences of Prince Tuan, the arch-conspirator, and the infamous Yu Hsien, Governor of Shansi, whose acts during the Rebellion had been peculiarly atrocious. An ultimatum was contemplated by the representatives at Peking, by which they would refuse to consider further negotiations until the death sentence had been pronounced against all the Boxer leaders, including Yu Hsien and Tung Fu-hsiang. Japan was strongly opposed to this ultimatum idea, and doubted whether China would sanction such wholesale penalties. Further, if China were to refuse, the Powers by virtue of the ultimatum would be placed in an embarrassing position. Less eager than Japan for these extreme punishments was the United States, in fact, had declared so throughout the negotiations. Russia was also opposed, to extreme punishment and to the ultimatum, "for how was such a demand to be enforced? ". The Triple Alliance Ministers were in favor of punishment as outlined, although willing to compromise. The situation was somewhat relieved when it was reported that Yu Hsien had committed suicide by " swallowing gold ".[1] But concerning the guilty Princes, Li Hung-chang made it clear that the Empress Dowager would never consent to their death because of their rank, much less those who were in command of the Imperial troops. Li was frank in admitting that personally he had suffered risk by denouncing them to the Throne at the behest of the Diplomatic Body.

The final agreement was a compromise, as follows:[2]

Imperial Edicts of the 13th and 21st of February, 1901

[1] The report of the death of Yu Hsien was untrue; he was finally executed February 22, 1901.

[2] Article II of the Protocol of September 7, 1901.

(Annexes nos. 4, 5 and 6 to the Peace Protocol), inflicted the following punishments on the principal authors of the outrages and crimes committed against the foreign Governments and their nationals:

Tsai-I Prince Tuan and Tsai Lan Duke Fu-kuo were sentenced to be brought before the autumnal court of assize for execution, and it was agreed that if the Emperor saw fit to grant them their lives, they should be exiled to Turkestan and there imprisoned for life, without the possibility of commutation of these punishments.[1]

Tsai Hsun Prince Chuang, Ying Nien, President of the Court of Censors, and Chao Shu-chiao, President of the Board of Punishments, were condemned to commit suicide.

Yu Hsien, Governor of Shansi, Chi Hsiu, President of the Board of Rites, and Hsu Cheng-yu, formerly Senior Vice-President of the Board of Punishments, were condemned to death.

Posthumous degradation was inflicted on Kang Yi, Assistant Grand Secretary, President of the Board of Works, Hsu Tung, Grand Secretary, and Li Ping-heng, formerly Governor-General of Szechwan.

An Imperial Edict of February 13th, 1901 (Annex no. 7), rehabilitated the memories of Hsu Yung-yi, President of the Board of War, Li Shan, President of the Board of Works, Hsu Ching-cheng, Senior President of the Board of Works, Lien Yuan, Vice-Chancellor of the Grand Council, and Yuan Chang, Vice-President of the Court of Sacrifices, who had been put to death for having protested against the outrageous breaches of international law of last year.

Prince Chang committed suicide the 21st of February, 1901, Ying Nien and Chao Shu-chiao the 24th, Yu Hsien was executed the 22nd, Chi Hsiu and Hsu Cheng-yu on the 26th. Tung Fu-hsiang, General in Kansu, has been deprived of his

[1] Prince Tuan went no farther than Manchuria for exile, and was heard of there in 1908. Tung Fu-hsiang's sentence was made banishment (to Turkestan, presumably), but he came back to Kansu province in 1906, and lived there in harmless old age.

office by Imperial Edict on the 13th of February, 1901, pending the determination of the final punishment to be inflicted on him.

Imperial Edicts dated the 20th of April and 19th of August, 1901, have inflicted various punishments on the provincial officials convicted of the crimes and outrages of last summer.[1]

Now as to the indemnity which China was to pay for her brief excursion into lawlessness. The Powers early decided that this was to be paid in a lump sum, which the various Governments would later divide among themselves. The United States, from information gathered at Washington, was of the opinion that China could not possibly pay more than around $150,000,000, and Special Commissioner Rockhill[2] was instructed to demand $25,000,000 as the share of the American Government.[3] Instead of this severe enough indemnity, the total for all the Powers leaped to 450,000,000 Haikwan taels, or $333,900,000.[4] This in-

[1] On the question of punishments, see *China No. 5* (*1901*), nos. 6, 9, 16, 18, 63, 96, 98, 102, 105, 106, 121, 122, 140-142, 144, 150, 151, 157, 158, 163-167, 172, 180-182, 186, 187, 207, 220, 236, 248, 251; *China No. 6* (*1901*), nos. 16, 42, 48, 49, 52, 55, 57, 63, 64, 67, 69, 77, 78, 83, 103, 104, 108, 114, 119, 121-123, 126, 127, 135, 232-234; *China No. 1* (*1902*), no. 21, 39, 40, 42, 88, 112, 146, 186, 243, 245, 246, 256, 257, 259; U. S. *For. Rel.*, 1900, pp. 210, 211, 213, 214, 220, 221, 223, 224, 226-229, 232, 297, 298.

[2] Commissioner Rockhill's *Report* is contained in U. S. *For. Rel.*, 1901, Appendix I.

[3] The United States remitted about $10,000,000 of its share of the Boxer indemnity, and China as a mark of gratitude agreed to use the funds in sending Chinese students to this country every year for education. See U. S. 60th Cong., 1st Sess., *Hse. Rept.*, no. 1107; U. S. 60th Cong., 2d Sess., *Hse. Doc.*, no. 1275.

[4] Gardner L. Harding, in his "The Peril of China," *Century*, July, 1915, estimates that the Boxer indemnity "will have swelled to something between $650,000,000 and $700,000,000 by the time the usurious methods of juggling its deferred interest by annual payments stretching to 1939 are fully worked out." P. 459.

cluded everything due to the foreign Governments, to companies, societies, private individuals, missionaries and native Chinese. The interest to be paid was fixed at 4 per cent per annum, capital and interest to be paid by China in thirty-nine years, with amortization beginning January 1, 1902, and ending in the year 1940. The amortizations were to be paid annually, the first payment to be made on January 1, 1903.[1] The revenues set aside as security for China's bond were the following:

1. The balance of the revenues of the Imperial Maritime Customs, after the payment of the interest and amortization of preceding loans secured on these revenues, plus the proceeds of the raising of five per cent effective of the present tariff, on maritime imports, including articles until now on the free list but exempting foreign rice, cereals, flour, gold and silver bullion and coin.

2. The revenues of the native customs, administered in the open ports by the Imperial Maritime Customs.

3. The total revenue of the salt gabelle, exclusive of the fraction previously set aside for other foreign loans.

With punishment and indemnity out of the way the greatest difficulties were removed. All the other provisions of the bases for negotiations, built up by the Diplomatic Body from the French proposals, were agreed to in their entirety. In addition to the mission to Germany to apologize for the murder of the German Minister, Baron von Ketteler, a like mission of regret was despatched to Japan to offer reparation for the death of Mr. Sugiyama, the Japanese Chancellor of Legation at Peking. It was also arranged that the Forts of Taku were to be razed. On this point the United States had objected, having stood merely for

[1] On amortization, see *China No. 1 (1902)*, nos. 107, 124, 175, 176, 180, 183-185, 187, 189, 199.

dismantlement, but without success. Lastly, the famous
Tsung-li Yamen, a sort of foreign council established
through the pressure of the Powers in 1860, was transformed into a Ministry for Foreign Affairs called the Waiwupu (now the Waichiaopu), which has at last become a
most important division of the Chinese Government. Attached to the final Protocol were nineteen annexes, fully
explaining the preceding articles and also containing the
various decrees on punishment, *etc.*, referred to in the main
body of the document.

In consideration of the above, the Powers agreed that,
with the exception of the new Legation guards provided
for in article VIII of the Protocol, the international troops
would evacuate Peking on September 17, 1901, and also
from the other points which they were holding, with the exception of those mentioned in article IX, where they were
to maintain open communication between the capital and
the sea until order was completely restored.

The Boxer Rebellion was the last protest of China
against the inevitable, and, in the completeness of its failure, was the final lesson necessary in that series of international events ever since 1840 to teach China that, however excellent her civilization may be in some respects, it
was inadequate when judged by the spirit and achievements
of the XXth century. Through the agency of unparalleled
national disasters, it was finally brought home to the intelligent classes and in a lesser degree to the entire people that,
successfully to withstand European aggression, it was necessary to have recourse to Europe's ways, to adopt in the
new scheme of things whatever heretofore had been lacking, whether for good or for evil. The awakening did not
come all at once. For the ensuing two or three years China
remained crushed by the succession of humiliations heaped
upon her since 1895. It even fell to other nations, notably

Japan, to save China from Russian ambitions, the result of which was the Russo-Japanese war, fought equally in Chinese interests, on Chinese territory, and with the violation of Chinese integrity and neutrality. This momentous conflict, in which an Oriental race triumphed over one of the greatest of European Powers, besides changing the course of history in the Far East, left an indelible impression upon the Chinese national consciousness, and from then on the awakening of China began in a truly nationalized form. Once fairly started, the advance was rapid enough, too rapid in some respects to suit the convenience of Europe. What part the modern China will play in the international economics, politics and diplomacy of the future it would be presumptuous to predict. China is not yet ready for such a rôle, nor will be ready for many years to come. But the possibilities of China are almost limitless, considering the wealth and resources of the country and the national characteristics of the Chinese themselves. However, the future historian, in examining and estimating the causes and events which gave rise to this new Far Eastern power, will look back to the period from 1895 to 1902 and the subsequent years to trace those ideals, ambitions and sacrifices which took the world by surprise in the revolution of 1911, a revolution which resulted in the establishment of the present Republic, and which, most significant fact of all, was pressed by Chinese arms alone to a successful conclusion.

APPENDIX I

The Joint Note [1]

During the months of May, June, July, and August of the present year, serious disturbances broke out in the northern provinces of China, and crimes unprecedented in human history, crimes against the law of nations, against the laws of humanity and civilization, were committed under peculiarly odious circumstances. The principal of these crimes were the following:

1. On the 20th of June, His Excellency Baron von Ketteler, German Minister, proceeding to the Tsung-li Yamen, was murdered while in the exercise of his official duties by soldiers of the regular army acting under orders of their chiefs.

2. The same day the foreign Legations were attacked and besieged. These attacks continued without intermission until the 14th of August, on which date the arrival of foreign troops put an end to them. These attacks were made by regular troops who joined the Boxers and who obeyed orders of the Court, emanating from the Imperial Palace. At the same time the Chinese Government officially declared by its representatives abroad that it guaranteed the security of the Legations.

3. The 11th of June, Mr. Sugiyama, Chancellor of the Legation of Japan, in the discharge of an official mission, was killed by regulars at the gates of the city. At Peking and in several provinces foreigners were murdered, tortured, or attacked by Boxers and regular troops, and only owed their safety to their determined resistance. Their establishments were pillaged and destroyed.

---

[1] Version in English agreed upon by the British and American Ministers. See U. S. *For. Rel.*, 1900, p. 244; Moore's *Digest*, vol. v. pp. 514-516; *China No. 5 (1901)*, no. 188; Rockhill, *op. cit.*, pp. 63-65.

4. Foreign cemeteries, at Peking especially, were desecrated, the graves opened, the remains scattered abroad.

These events led the foreign Powers to send their troops to China in order to protect the lives of their representatives and their nationals, and to restore order. During their march to Peking the Allied forces met with the resistance of the Chinese armies, and had to overcome it by force. China having recognized her responsibility, expressed her regrets, and manifested the desire to see an end put to the situation created by the disturbances referred to, the Powers have decided to accede to her request on the irrevocable conditions enumerated below, which they deem indispensible to expiate the crimes committed and to prevent their recurrence:

I. (A) Dispatch to Berlin of an extraordinary mission. headed by an Imperial Prince, to express the regrets of His Majesty the Emperor of China and of the Chinese Government, for the murder of his Excellency the late Baron von Ketteler, German Minister.

(B) Erection on the place where the murder was committed of a commemorative monument suitable to the rank of the deceased, bearing an inscription in the Latin, German, and Chinese languages, expressing the regrets of the Emperor of China for the murder.

II. (A) The severest punishment in proportion to their crimes for the persons designated in the Imperial Decree of September 25, 1900, and for those whom the representatives of the Powers shall subsequently designate.

(B) Suspension of all official examinations for five years in all the towns where foreigners have been massacred or have been subjected to cruel treatment.

III. Honorable reparation shall be made by the Chinese Government to the Japanese Government for the murder of Mr. Sugiyama, Chancellor of the Japanese Legation.

IV. An expiatory monument shall be erected by the Imperial Chinese Government in each of the foreign or international cemeteries which have been desecrated, and in which the graves have been destroyed.

V. Maintenance, under conditions to be settled between the Powers, of the prohibition of the importation of arms, as well as if material used exclusively for the manufacture of arms and ammunition.

VI. Equitable indemnities for governments, societies, companies, and private individuals, as well as for Chinese who have suffered during the late events in person or in property in consequence of their being in the service of foreigners. China shall adopt financial measures acceptable to the Powers for the purpose of guaranteeing the payment of said indemnities and the interest and amortization of the loans.

VII. Right for each Power to maintain a permanent guard for its Legation and to have the Legation quarter in a defensible condition. Chinese shall not have the right to reside in this quarter.

VIII. The Taku and other forts which might impede free communication between Peking and the sea shall be razed.

IX. Right of military occupation of certain points, to be determined by an understanding between the Powers, for keeping open communication between the capital and the sea.

X. (A) The Chinese Government shall cause to be published during two years in all subprefectures an Imperial decree embodying—

Perpetual prohibition, under pain of death, or membership in any anti-foreign society.

Enumeration of the punishments which shall have been inflicted on the guilty, together with the suspension of all official examinations in the towns where foreigners have been murdered or have been subjected to cruel treatment.

(B) An Imperial decree shall be issued and published everywhere in the Empire, declaring that all governors-general, governors, and provincial or local officials shall be responsible for order in their respective jurisdictions, and that whenever fresh anti-foreign disturbances or any other treaty infractions occur, which are not forthwith suppressed and the guilty persons punished, they, the said officials, shall be immediately removed and forever prohibited from holding any office or honors.

XI. The Chinese Government shall undertake to reform the Office of Foreign Affairs, and to modify the Court ceremonial relative to the reception of foreign representatives in the manner which the Powers shall indicate.

Until the Chinese Government have complied with the above to the satisfaction of the Powers the undersigned can hold out no expectation that the occupation of Peking and the province of Chihli by the general forces can be brought to a conclusion.

PEKING, *December 22, 1900.*

For Germany:	A. MUMM.
For Austria-Hungary:	M. CZIKANN.
For Belgium:	JOOSTENS.
For Spain:	B. F. DE COLOGAN.
For United States of America:	E. H. CONGER.
For France:	S. PICHON.
For Great Britain:	ERNEST SATOW.
For Italy:	SALVAGO RAGGI.
For Japan:	T. NISSI.
For Netherlands:	F. M. KNOBEL.
For Russia:	MICHEL DE GIERS.

APPENDIX II

[Translation]

Under date of December 24, 1900, the Plenipotentiaries of
Germany, Austria-Hungary, Belgium, Spain, the United States,
France, Great Britain, Italy, Japan, the Netherlands, and
Russia, have sent Us the following Note:

(The Joint Note is here quoted textually and in its entirety):

We hastened to transmit the full text of this note to His
Majesty the Emperor who, having taken cognizance of it, rendered the following decree:

" We have taken cognizance of the whole of the telegram of
Yi Kuang (Prince Ching) and Li Hung-chang. It behooves
Us to accept, in their entirety, the twelve articles which they
have submitted to Us."

Consequently, we, Ching, Prince of the first rank, Plenipo-
tentiary, President of the Council of Foreign Affairs, and Li,
Earl of the first rank, Su-yi, Plenipotentiary, Tutor to the
Heir Apparent, Grand Secretary of the Wen-hua Tien Throne
Hall, Minister of Commerce, Superintendent of trade for the
northern ports, Governor-General of Chihli,

Declare that we accept in their entirety the twelve articles
which we have been requested to insure the transmission of
to His Majesty the Emperor.

In witness of which we have signed the present protocol

[1] Rockhill, *op. cit.*, p. 66.

and we transmit to the foreign Plenipotentiaries a copy of the Edict of His Majesty the Emperor, bearing the Imperial Seal.

It is understood that in case of disagreement, the French text shall be authoritative.

PEKING, *16 January, 1901.*

(Signed)   YI KUANG

(Prince Ching).

[L. S.]   LI.

APPENDIX III

Peace Protocol of September 7, 1901 [1]

The Plenipotentiaries of Germany, His Excellency M. A. Mumm von Schwarzenstein; of Austria-Hungary, His Excellency M. M. Czikann von Wahlborn; of Belgium, His Excellency M. Joostens; of Spain, M. B. J. de Cologan; of the United States, His Excellency M. W. W. Rockhill; of France, His Excellency M. Paul Beau; of Great Britain, His Excellency Sir Ernest Satow; of Italy, Marquis Salvago Raggi; of Japan, His Excellency M. Jutaro Komura; of the Netherlands, His Excellency M. F. M. Knobel; of Russia, His Excellency M. M. de Giers; and of China, His Highness Yi-Kuang Prince Ching of the first rank, President of the Ministry of Foreign Affairs, and His Excellency Li Hung-chang, Earl of Su-i of the first rank, Tutor of the Heir Apparent, Grand Secretary of the Wen-hua Throne Hall, Minister of Commerce, Superintendent of the northern trade, Governor-General of Chihli, have met for the purpose of declaring that China has complied to the satisfaction of the Powers with the conditions laid down in the note of the 22d of December, 1900 (the Joint Note), and which were accepted in their entirety by His Majesty the Emperor of China in a decree dated the 27th of December. (Annex No. 1).

[1] U. S. *For. Rel.*, 1901, Appendix I, pp. 306-312 for official French version and pp. 312-339 for English with the 19 Annexes; Chinese Maritime Customs, III, no. 30, *op. cit.*, vol. i, pp. 1-49 for French and Chinese texts; Cordier, *Histoire des Rélations, etc.*, vol. iii, pp. 537-545 for official French copy; Moore's *Digest*, vol. v, pp. 517-524; Rockhill, *op. cit.*, pp. 66-96 for text and Annexes; U. S. *Consular Reports*, vol. lxviii (Washington, 1902), pp. 19-26.

ARTICLE I^a

By an Imperial Edict of the 9th of June last (Annex no. 2), Tsai Feng, Prince Chun, was appointed Ambassador of His Majesty the Emperor of China, and directed in that capacity to convey to His Majesty the German Emperor the expression of the regrets of His Majesty the Emperor of China and of the Chinese Government for the assassination of his Excellency the late Baron von Ketteler, German Minister.

Prince Chun left Peking the 12th of July last to carry out the orders which had been given him.

ARTICLE I^b

The Chinese Government has stated that it will erect on the spot of the assassination of his Excellency the late Baron von Ketteler a commemorative monument, worthy of the rank of the deceased, and bearing an inscription in the Latin, German, and Chinese languages, which shall express the regrets of His Majesty the Emperor of China for the murder committed.

Their Excellencies the Chinese Plenipotentiaries have informed his Excellency the German Plenipotentiary, in a letter dated the 22nd of July last (Annex No. 3) that an arch of the whole width of the street would be erected on the said spot, and that work on it was begun the 25th of July last.

ARTICLE II^a

Imperial Edicts of the 13th and 21st of February, 1901 (Annexes nos. 4, 5, and 6), inflicted the following punishments on the principal authors of the outrages and crimes committed against the foreign Governments and their nationals:

Tsai-I Prince Tuan and Tsai Lan Duke Fu-kuo were sentenced to be brought before the autumnal court of assize for execution, and it was agreed that if the Emperor saw fit to grant them their lives, they should be exiled to Turkestan and there imprisoned for life, without the possibility of commutation of these punishments.

Tsai Hsun Prince Chuang, Ying Nien, President of the

Court of Censors, and Chao Shu-chiao, President of the Board of Punishments, were condemned to commit suicide.

Yu Hsien, Governor of Shansi, Chi Hsiu, President of the Board of Rites, and Hsu Cheng-yu, formerly senior Vice-President of the Board of Punishments, were condemned to death.

Posthumous degradation was inflicted on Kang Yi, Assistant Grand Secretary, President of the Board of Works, Hsu Tung, Grand Secretary, and Li Ping-heng, formerly Governor-General of Szechwan.

An Imperial Edict of February 13th, 1901 (Annex no. 7), rehabilitated the memories of Hsu Yung-yi, President of the Board of War, Li Shan, President of the Board of Works, Hsu Ching-cheng, senior Vice-President of the Board of Works, Lien Yuan, Vice-Chancellor of the Grand Council, and Yuan Chang, Vice-President of the Court of Sacrifices, who had been put to death for having protested against the outrageous breaches of international law of last year.

Prince Chuang committed suicide the 21st of February, 1901, Ying Nien and Chao Shu-chiao the 24th, Yu Hsien was executed the 22nd, Chi Hsiu and Hsu Cheng-yu on the 26th. Tung Fu-hsiang, General in Kansu, has been deprived of his office by Imperial Edict of the 13th of February, 1901, pending the determination of the final punishment to be inflicted on him.

Imperial Edicts dated the 29th of April and 19th of August, 1901, have inflicted various punishments on the provincial officials convicted of the crimes and outrages of last summer.

ARTICLE II[b]

An Imperial Edict promulgated the 19th of August, 1901 (Annex no. 8), ordered the suspension of official examinations for five years in all cities where foreigners were massacred or submitted to cruel treatment.

ARTICLE III

So as to make honorable reparation for the assassination of

Mr. Sugiyama, Chancellor of the Japanese Legation, His Majesty the Emperor of China by an Imperial Edict of the 18th of June, 1901 (Annex no. 9), appointed Na Tung, Vice-President of the Board of Revenue, to be his Envoy Extraordinary, and specially directed him to convey to His Majesty the Emperor of Japan the expression of the regrets of His Majesty the Emperor of China and of his Government at the assassination of the late Mr. Sugiyama.

ARTICLE IV

The Chinese Government has agreed to erect an expiatory monument in each of the foreign or international cemeteries which were desecrated and in which the tombs were destroyed.

It has been agreed with the representatives of the Powers that the Legations interested shall settle the details for the erection of these monuments, China bearing all the expenses thereof, estimated at ten thousand taels for the cemeteries at Peking and within its neighborhood, and at five thousand taels for the cemeteries in the provinces. The amounts have been paid and the list of these cemeteries is enclosed herewith. (Annex no. 10.)

ARTICLE V

China has agreed to prohibit the importation into its territory of arms and ammunition, as well as of materials exclusively used for the manufacture of arms and ammunition.

An Imperial Edict has been issued on the 25th of August, 1901 (Annex no. 11), forbidding said importation for a term of two years. New Edicts may be issued subsequently extending this by other successive terms of two years in case of necessity recognized by the Powers.

ARTICLE VI

By an Imperial Edict dated the 29th of May, 1901 (Annex no. 12), His Majesty the Emperor of China agreed to pay the Powers an indemnity of four hundred and fifty millions of Haikwan Taels. This sum represents the total amount of the indemnities for States, companies or societies, private individuals, and Chinese referred to in Article VI of the note of December 22nd, 1900.

(a) These four hundred and fifty millions constitute a gold debt calculated at the rate of the Haikwan tael to the gold currency of each country, as indicated below:

Haikwan tael = marks 3.055
            = Austro-Hungary crown 3.595
            = gold dollar 0.742
            = francs 3.750
            = pound sterling .... 3s. 0d.
            = yen 1.407
            = Netherlands florin 1.796
            = gold rouble (17.424 dolias fine)... 1.412

This sum in gold shall bear interest in 4 per cent per annum, and the capital shall be reimbursed by China in thirty-nine years in the manner indicated in the annexed plan of amortization. (Annex no. 13.)

Capital and interest shall be payable in gold at the rates of exchange corresponding to the dates at which the different payments fall due.

The amortization shall commence the 1st of January, 1902, and shall finish at the end of the year 1940. The amortizations are payable annually, the first payment being fixed on the 1st of January, 1903.

Interest shall run from the 1st of July, 1901, but the Chinese Government shall have the right to pay off within a term of three years, beginning January, 1902, the arrears of the first six months, ending the 31st of December, 1901, on condition, however, that it pays compound interest at the rate of four per cent per annum on the sums the payment of which shall have thus been deferred. Interest shall be payable semi-annually, the first payment being fixed on the 1st of July, 1902.

(b) The service of the debt shall take place in Shanghai, in the following manner:

Each Power shall be represented by a delegate on a commission of bankers authorized to receive the amount of interest and amortization which shall be paid to it by the Chinese authorities designated for that purpose, to divide it among the interested parties, and to give a receipt for the same.

(c) The Chinese Government shall deliver to the Doyen of the Diplomatic Corps at Peking a bond for the lump sum, which shall subsequently be converted into fractional bonds bearing the signatures of the delegates of the Chinese Government designated for that purpose. This operation and all those relating to issuing of the bonds shall be performed by the above-mentioned commission, in accordance with the instructions which the Powers shall send their delegates.

(d) The proceeds of the revenues assigned to the payment of the bonds shall be paid monthly to the commission.

(e) The revenues assigned as security for the bonds are the following:

1. The balance of the revenues of the Imperial Maritime Customs after payment of the interest and amortization of preceding loans secured on these revenues, plus the proceeds of the raising to five per cent effective of the present tariff on maritime imports, including articles until now on the free list, but exempting foreign rice, cereals, and flour, gold and silver bullion and coin.

2. The revenues of the native customs, administered in the open ports by the Imperial Maritime Customs.

3. The total revenues of the salt gabelle, exclusive of the fraction previously set aside for other foreign loans.

The raising of the present tariff on imports to five per cent effective is agreed to on the conditions mentioned below.

It shall be put in force two months after the signing of the present protocol, and no exceptions shall be made except for merchandise shipped not more than ten days after the said signing.

1. All duties levied on imports " ad valorem " shall be converted as far as possible and as soon as may be into specific duties. This conversion shall be made in the following manner: The average value of merchandise at the time of their landing during the three years 1897, 1898, and 1899, that is to

say, the market price less the amount of import duties and incidental expenses, shall be taken as the basis for the valuation of merchandise.   Pending the result of the work of conversion, duties shall be levied " ad valorem."

2. The beds of the rivers Peiho and Whangpu shall be improved with the financial participation of China.

ARTICLE VII

The Chinese Government has agreed that the quarter occupied by the Legations shall be considered as one specially reserved for their use and placed under their exclusive control, in which Chinese shall not have the right to reside and which may be made defensible.

The limits of this quarter have been fixed as follows on the annexed plan (Annex no. 14) :

On the west, the line 1, 2, 3, 4, 5.

On the north, the line 5, 6, 7, 8, 9, 10.

On the east, Ketteler street (10, 11, 12).

Drawn along the exterior base of the Tatar wall and following the line of the bastions, on the south the line 12.1.

In the protocol annexed to the letter of the 16th of January, 1901, China recognized the right of each Power to maintain a permanent guard in the said quarter for the defence of its Legation.

ARTICLE VIII

The Chinese Government has consented to raze the forts of Taku and those which might impede free communication between Peking and the sea; steps have been taken for carrying this out.

ARTICLE IX

The Chinese Government has conceded the right of the Powers in the protocol annexed to the letter of the 16th of January, 1901, to occupy certain points, to be determined by an agreement between them, for the maintenance of open communication between the capital and the sea.   The points occupied by the Powers are :

Huangtsun, Langfang, Yangtsun, Tientsin, Chunliangcheng, Tangku, Lutai, Tangshan, Lanchou, Changli, Chinwangtao, Shanhaikwan.

ARTICLE X

The Chinese Government has agreed to post and to have published during two years in all district cities the following Imperial Edicts:

(a) Edict of the 1st of February (Annex no. 15), prohibiting forever, under pain of death, membership in any anti-foreign society.

(b) Edicts of the 13th and 21st February, 29 April, and 19th August, enumerating the punishments inflicted on the guilty.

(c) Edict of the 19th August, 1901, prohibiting examinations in all cities where foreigners were massacred or subjected to cruel treatment.

(d) Edict of the 1st of February, 1901 (Annex no. 16), declaring all governors-general, governors, and provincial or local officials responsible for order in their respective districts, and that in case of new anti-foreign troubles or other infractions of the treaties which shall not be immediately repressed and the authors of which shall not have been punished, these officials shall be immediately dismissed, without possibility of being given new functions or new honors.

ARTICLE XI

The Chinese Government has agreed to negotiate the amendments deemed necessary by the foreign Governments to the treaties of commerce and navigation and the other subjects concerning commercial relations, with the object of facilitating them.

At present, and as a result of the stipulation contained in Article VI, concerning the indemnity, the Chinese Government agrees to assist in the improvement of the courses of the rivers Peiho and Whangpu, as stated below.

(a) The works for the improvement of the navigability of the Peiho, begun in 1898 with the coöperation of the Chinese

Government, have been resumed under the direction of an international commission. As soon as the administration of Tientsin shall have been handed back to the Chinese Government, it will be in a position to be represented on this commission, and will pay each year a sum of sixty thousand Haikwan taels for maintaining the works.

(b) A conservancy board, charged with the management and control of the works for straightening the Whangpu and the improvement of the course of that river, is hereby created. This board shall consist of members representing the interests of the Chinese Government and those of foreigners in the shipping trade of Shanghai. The expenses incurred for the works and the general management of the undertaking are estimated at the annual sum of four hundred and sixty thousand Haikwan taels for the first twenty years. This sum shall be supplied in equal portions by the Chinese Government and the foreign interests concerned. Detailed stipulations concerning the composition, duties, and revenues of the conservancy boards are embodied in Annex no. 17.

ARTICLE XII

An Imperial Edict of the 24th of July, 1901 (Annex no. 18), reformed the Office of Foreign Affairs (Tsung-li Yamen), on the lines indicated by the Powers, that is to say, transformed it into a Ministry of Foreign Affairs (Waiwupu, and now called the Waichiaopu), which takes precedence over the six other Ministries of State. The same Edict appointed the principal members of this Ministry.

An agreement has also been reached concerning the modification of Court ceremonial as regards the reception of foreign representatives, and has been the subject of several notes from the Chinese Plenipotentiaries, the substance of which is embodied in a memorandum herewith annexed (Annex no. 19).

Finally, it is expressly understood that as regards the declarations specified above and the annexed documents originating with the foreign Plenipotentiaries, the French text only is authoritative.

The Chinese Government having thus complied to the satisfaction of the Powers with the conditions laid down in the above-mentioned note on December 22nd, 1900 (the Joint Note), the Powers have agreed to accede to the wish of China to terminate the situation created by the disorders of the summer of 1900. In consequence thereof the foreign Plenipotentiaries are authorized to declare in the names of their Governments that, with the exception of the Legation guards mentioned in Article VII, the international troops will completely evacuate the city of Peking on the 17th of September, 1901, and with the exception of the localities mentioned in Article IX, will withdraw from the province of Chihli on the 22d of September.

The present final Protocol has been drawn up in twelve identical copies and signed by all the Plenipotentiaries of the conteacting countries. One copy shall be given to each of the foreign Plenipotentiaries, and one copy shall be given to the Chinese Plenipotentiaries.

Peking, 7th September 1901.

BIBLIOGRAPHY

CHINA. Maritime Customs, III—Misc. Ser., no. 30. *Treaties, Conventions, etc., between China and Foreign States.* 2 vols., Shanghai, 1905.

FRANCE. Affaires Etrangerès, Ministère des
—— *Documents Diplomatiques, Chine, 1894-1901.* Paris, 1898-1901.
—— *Documents Diplomatiques, Chine, 1898-1899.* Paris, 1900.
—— *Documents Diplomatiques, Chine, 1899-1900.* Paris, 1900.
—— *Documents Diplomatiques, Chine, Juin-Octobre, 1901.* Paris, 1901.

GREAT BRITAIN. Parliamentary Papers, " Blue Books."
—— *China No. 1 (1898): Correspondence respecting the Affairs of China.*
—— *China No. 2 (1898): Notes exchanged with the Chinese Government respecting the Non-Alienation of the Yang-tsze Region.*
—— *China No. 3 (1898): Despatch from Her Majesty's Minister at Peking forwarding a Report by the Acting British Consul at Ssumao on the Trade of Yunnan.*
—— *China No. 1 (1899): Correspondence respecting the Affairs of China.*
—— *China No. 2 (1899): Correspondence between Her Majesty's Government and the Russian Government with Regard to their Respective Railway Interests in China.*
—— *China No. 1 (1900): Further Correspondence respecting the Affairs of China.* In continuation of " China No. 1 and 2 (1899)."
—— *China No. 2 (1900): Correspondence with the United States' Government respecting Foreign Trade in China.*
—— *China No. 3 (1900): Correspondence respecting the Insurrectionary Movement in China.*
—— *China No. 4 (1900): Reports from Her Majesty's Minister in China respecting Events at Peking.*
—— *China No. 5 (1900): Correspondence respecting the Anglo-German Agreement of October 16, 1900, relating to China.*
—— *China No. 1 (1901): Correspondence respecting the Disturbances in China.* In continuation of " China No. 3 (1900)."
—— *China No. 2 (1901): Despatch from His Majesty's Ambassador at St. Petersburgh respecting the Russo-Chinese Agreement as to Manchuria.*
—— *China No. 3 (1901): Further Correspondence respecting Events at Peking.* In continuation of " China No. 4 (1900)."

—— *China No. 4 (1901): Plans referred to in China No. 3 (1901). Further Correspondence respecting Events at Peking.*

—— *China No. 5 (1901): Further Correspondence respecting the Disturbances in China.* In continuation of " China No. 1(1901)."

—— *China No. 6 (1901): Further Correspondence respecting the Disturbances in China.* In continuation of " China No. 5 (1901)."

—— *China No. 7 (1901): Correspondence respecting the Imperial Railway of North China.*

—— *China No. 1 (1902): Correspondence respecting the Affairs of China.* In continuation of " China No. 6 (1901)."

UNITED STATES. Department of State.

—— *Consular Reports,* vols. from year *1895* to *1902.*

—— *Foreign Relations,* vols. from year *1895* to *1902.*

UNITED STATES. War Department.

—— U. S. Adjutant-General's Office. Military Information Division. *Notes on China, August, 1900.* Publ. XXX, War dept. doc. no. 124.

Hertslet, Sir Edward (Editor)
Treaties, etc., between Great Britain and China; and between China and Foreign Powers; and Orders in Council, Rules, Regulations, Acts of Parliament, Decrees, etc., affecting British Interests in China. In Force on the 1st of January, 1908. 3d ed., 2 vol., London, 1908.

Mayers, William Frederic (Editor)
Treaties between the Empire of China and Foreign Powers, together with Regulations for the Conduct of Foreign Trade, Conventions, Agreements, Regulations, etc., etc. 4th ed., Shanghai, 1902.

Richardson, James D. (Editor)
A Compilation of the Messages and Papers of the Presidents, 1789-1897. 10 vols., Washington, 1896-99.

Rockhill, William Woodville (Editor)
Treaties and Conventions with or concerning China and Korea, 1894-1904, together with various State Papers and Documents affecting Foreign Interests. Washington, 1904.

Williams, E. T. (Editor)
Recent Chinese Legislation relating to Commercial, Railway, and Mining Enterprises. Shanghai, 1904.

Allen, Roland, *The Siege of the Peking Legations.* London, 1901.

Anderson, Æneas, *A Narrative of the British Embassy to China in the Years 1792, 1793, and 1794.* London, 1795.

Angier, A. Gorton, *The Far East Revisited.* London, 1908.

Annals of the American Academy of Political and Social Science, vol. XXXIX, Jan., 1912, whole no. 128, *China, Social and Economic Conditions.* Philadelphia, 1912.

Anonymous, *Last Year in China, to the Peace of Nanking . . . Letters .. by a Field Officer . . . with . . . Remarks on our . . . Policy in China.* Philadelphia, 1843.

—— ("By a Diplomatist"), *American Foreign Policy.* Boston, 1909.

—— *China, von einem Früheren Instructeur in der Chinesischen Arme.* Leipzig, 1892.

—— ("D. W. S."), *European Settlements in the Far East.* London, 1900.

—— ("Justom"), *England and China, two Episodes of Recent Anglo-Chinese History illustrating the British Policy in China.* London, 1877.

—— *Letter on the Case of the "Arrow," and the War with China.* London, 1857.

Asakawa, Dr. Kanichi, *The Russo-Japanese Conflict.* New York, 1904.

Auber, Peter, *China, an Outline of its Government, Laws and Policy, and of the British and Foreign Embassies to that Empire.* London, 1834.

Balfour, Fr. H., *Waifs and Strays from the Far East, being a Series of Disconnected Essays on Matters relating to China.* London, 1876.

Balmelle, Eugene, *Affaires d'Extrême-Orient de 1842 à 1902.* Carcassonne, 1906.

Beach, Harlan Page, *Dawn on the Hills of Tang, or, Missions in China.* New York, 1900.

Beresford, C. W. de la Poer, Lord, *The Break-Up of China, with an Account of its Present Commerce, Currency, Waterways, Armies, Railways, Politics and Future Prospects.* New York, 1899.

Bernard, W. D., *The Nemesis in China, comprising a History of the Late War in that Country.* London, 1847.

Beveridge, A. J., *The Russian Advance.* New York, 1904.

Bishop, Mrs. I. L. (Bird), *The Yangtze Valley and Beyond.* London, 1899.

Blakeney, William, *On the Coasts of Cathay and Cipango Forty Years Ago.* London, 1902.

Blakiston, T. W., *Five Months on the Yang-Tsze . . . with Notices of the Present Rebellion in China.* London, 1862.

Bland, J. O. P., *Recent Events and Present Policies in China.* Philadelphia, 1912.

——, and Backhouse, E., *China under the Empress-Dowager.* Philadelphia, 1910.

Boulger, D. C., *Short History of China.* London, 1900.

Bramm, Houckgeest A. E. van, *Authentic Account of the Embassy of the Dutch East India Company to China, 1794-95.* Trans. from French of L. E. Moreau de Saint-Mery. 2 vols., London, 1798.

Brand, Adam, *Journal of the Embassy from . . . Muscovy . . . into China . . . 1693-95.* Trans. from High-Dutch . . . by H. W. Ludolf. London, 1698.

Brand, M. A. S. von, *Dreiunddreissig Jahre in Ost-Asien, Errinerungen eines Deutschen Diplomaten.* 3 vols., Leipzig, 1901.

Brine, Lindsay, *The Taiping Rebellion; a Narrative of its Rise and Progress.* London, 1862.

Brinkley, Capt. Frank, *China, its History, Arts and Literature. In Oriental Series, Japan and China,* 12 vols., vols. 9-12. Boston, 1901.

Broomhall, Marshall, *Martyred Missionaries of the China Inland Mission, with a Record of the Perils and Sufferings of Some who escaped.* London, 1901.

——, *The Chinese Empire.* London, 1908.

Brown, Arthur J., *New Forces in Old China, an Unwelcome but Inevitable Awakening.* New York, 1904.

Brunnert, H. S., and Hagelstrom, V. V., *Present Day Political Organization of China.* Trans. from Russian by A. Beltschenk and E. E. Moran. Shanghai, 1912.

Cahen, Gaston, *Histoire des Rélations de la Russie avec la Chine sous Pierre le Grand, 1689-1730.* Paris, 1911.

Callery, J. M., and Yvan, Melchior, *History of the Insurrection in China.* Trans. from French by J. Oxenford. New York, 1853.

——, *Correspondance Diplomatique Chinoise relative aux Négociations du Traité de Whampoa.* Paris, 1879.

Cantile, James, and Jones, C. Sheridan, *Sun Yat Sen and the Awakening of China.* New York, 1912.

Carl, Katherine A., *With the Empress Dowager.* New York, 1905.

Casserly, Gordon, *The Land of the Boxers, or, China under the Allies.* London, 1903.

Chang, Chih-Tung, *China's Only Hope, an Appeal.* Trans. by S. Woodbridge. New York, 1900.

Chen, Huan-Chang, *The Economic Principles of Confucius and his School.* Columbia University Studies in History, Economics and Public Law, vols. xliv and xlv, nos. 112 and 113, 1911. New York, 1911.

Chen, Shao-Kwan, *The System of Taxation in China, 1614-1911.* Columbia University Studies in History, Economics and Public Law, vol. lix, no. 2, 1914. New York, 1914.

Ching, Wen, *The Chinese Crisis from within.* London, 1901.

Chirol, Valentine, *The Far Eastern Question.* London, 1876.

Chisholm, George G., *The Resources and Means of Communication of China.* London, 1898.

Clark University Addresses, G. H. Blakeslee, Editor, *China and the Far East.* New York, 1910.

——, *Recent Developments in China.* New York, 1913.

Colquhoun, Archibald R., *China in Transformation.* London, 1898.

——, *Problems in China and the British Policy.* London, 1900.

——, *Overland to China.* London, 1900.

Conant, Chas. A., *The United States in the Orient.* Boston, 1901.

Cordier, Henri, *La France en Chine au Dix-Huitième Siècle, Documents Inedits Publies sur les Manuscrits conservés au Dépôt des Affaires Etrangerès.* Paris, 1883.

——, *Histoire des Rélations de la Chine avec les Puissances Occidentales.* 3 vols., Paris, 1902.

——, *L'Expédition de Chine de 1857, '58: Histoire Diplomatique, Notes et Documents.* Paris, 1905.

——, *Le Consulat de France à Canton au XVIIIe Siècle.* Leyden, 1908.

——, *La Mission de M. de Chevalier d'Entrecasteaux à Canton en 1787, d'après les Archives du Ministère des Affaires Etrangerès.* Paris, 1911.

Cotes, Everard, *Signs and Portents in the Far East.* New York, 1907.

Courant, Maurice A. L. M., *L'Asie Central aux XVII et XVIII Siècles, Empire Kalmouk ou Empire Mandchou?* Lyons, 1912.

Curzon, George N., *Problems of the Far East.* London, 1898.

Davis, Sir John, *The Chinese.* New York, 1857.

Davies, Major Henry R., *Yunnan, the Link between India and the Yangtsze.* Cambridge, 1909.

Delano, A., *Narrative of Voyages.* Boston, 1857.

Denby, Charles, *China and her People.* 2 vols., Boston, 1905.

Dickenson, Goldsworthy Lowes, *Letters from John Chinaman.* London, 1903.

——, *Letters from a Chinese Official, being an Eastern View of Western Civilization.* New York, 1904.

Douglas, Sir Robert K., *Europe and the Far East.* Rev. ed., New York, 1913.

Eames, J. B., *The English in China, being an Account of the Intercourse and Relations between England and China from the Year 1600 to the Year 1843, and a Summary of Later Developments.* London, 1909.

Edwards, E. H., *Fire and Sword in Shansi; the Story of the Martyrdom of Foreigners and Chinese Christians.* New York, (——).

Eliot, Chas. W., *Some Roads towards Peace.* Washington, 1913.

Ellis, Henry, *Journal of the Proceedings of the Late Embassy to China (Amherst Mission).* 2 vols., London, 1818.

Fischer, E. S., *China's Weltmachstellung.* New York, 1900.

Foster, John W., *American Diplomacy in the Orient.* Boston, 1903.

——, *Diplomatic Memoirs.* 2 vols., Boston, 1909.

Gibson, Rowland R., *Forces Mining and Undermining China.* New York, 1914.

Giles, Herbert Allen, *Historic China and Other Sketches.* London, 1882.

——, *Chinese Literature.* New York, 1909.

——, *The Civilization of China.* London, 1911.

——, *China and the Chinese.* New York, 1912.

——, *China and the Manchus.* Cambridge, 1912.

Goodrich, Joseph King, *The Coming China.* Chicago, 1911.

Gowen, Herbert H., *An Outline History of China.* Part I. From the earliest times to the Manchu conquest A. D. 1644. Boston, 1913.

Gray, John Henry, *China, a History of the Laws, Manners and Customs of the People.* 2 vols., London, 1878.

Grosier, Jean Baptiste Gabriel, L'Abbe, *Description Générale de la Chine.* 2 vols., Paris, 1787. Engl. trans. London, 1788.

Gumpach, J. von, *The Burlingame Mission, a Political Disclosure.* Shanghai, 1872.

Gundry, R. S. (Editor), *Retrospect of Political and Commercial Affairs in China and Japan, 1873 to 1877.* Shanghai, 1877.

——, *China and Her Neighbors: France, in Indo-China, Russia and China, India and Thibet.* London, 1893.

——, *China, Present and Past, Foreign Intercourse, Progress and Resources.* London, 1895.

Gutzlaff, Charles, *History of China.* 2 vols., New York, 1837.

Halot, Alexandre, *L'Extrême-Orient.* Paris, 1905.

Hanotaux, M. Gabriel, *La Question d'Extrême-Orient.* Paris, 1900.

Hart, Albert Bushnell, *The Obvious Orient.* New York, 1911.

Hart, Sir Robert, *" These from the Land of Sinim,"* Essays on the Chinese Question. London, 1901.

Hatch, Ernest F. G., *Far Eastern Impressions.* London, 1907.

Herisson, Le Comte d', *Journal d'un Interprète en Chine.* 6th ed., Paris, 1886.

Hershey, Amos Shartle, *International Law and Diplomacy of the Russo-Japanese War.* New York, 1906.

Hesse-Wartegg, Ernst von, *Shantung und Deutsch-China, von Kiautschau ins Heilige Land von China und vom Jangtsekiang nach Peking in Jahre 1898.* Leipzig, 1898.

Hirth, Friedrich, *The Ancient History of China.* New York, 1911.

Holcombe, Chester, *China's Past and Future.* Reprint of *The Real Chinese Question.* London, (——).

Hooker, Mary, *Behind the Scenes in Peking; being Experiences during the Siege of the Legations.* London, 1910.

Hosie, Alexander, *Manchuria,* London, 1901.

Hsu, Chih, *Railway Problems in China.* Columbia University Studies in History, Economics and Public Law, vol. lxvi, no. 2, 1915. New York, 1915.

Huc, M., *L'Empire Chinois.* 4th ed., 2 vols., Paris, 1862.

——, *Souvenirs d'un Voyage dans la Tartarie et la Thibet, pendant les Années 1844, 1845 et 1846.* 5th ed., 2 vols., Paris, 1868.

Hulbert, Homer B., *The Passing of Korea.* New York, 1906.

Ides, E. Y., *From Moscow Overland to China.* London, 1698.

Jernigan, Thomas R., *China's Business Methods and Policy.* London, 1904.

——, *China in Law and Commerce.* New York, 1905.

Kemp, E. G., *The Face of Manchuria, Korea and Russian Turkestan.* London, 1910.

Kent, Percy H. B., *The Passing of the Manchus.* London, 1912.

Koo, Vi Kyuin Wellington, *The Alien in China.* Columbia University Studies in History, Economics and Public Law, vol. l, no. 2, 1911. New York, 1911.

Krausse, Alexis S., *Story of the Chinese Crisis.* London, 1900.

——, *China in Decay, the Story of a Disappearing Empire.* London, 1900.

——, *The Far East, its History and its Question.* 2d ed., London, 1903.

Lamairesse, E., *L'Empire Chinois; la Bouddhisme en Chine et en Thibet.* Paris, 1893.

Landor, A. Henry Savage, *China and the Allies.* 2 vols., New York, 1901.

Lavollee, C. H., *France et Chine: Traité de Whampoa (1844): Correspondance Diplomatique de M. de Lagrene: Expédition de 1860 contre la Chine.* Paris, 1900.

Lawton, Lancelot, *Empires of the Far East, a Study of Japan and of her Colonial Possessions, of China and Manchuria, and of the Political Questions of Eastern Asia and the Pacific.* 2 vols., London, 1912.

Leclerq, Jules, *Chez les Jaunes, Japon, Chine, Mandchourie.* Paris, 1910.

Little, Mrs. Archibald, *In the Land of the Blue Gown.* London, 1908.

Little, Archibald John, *Through the Yang-tse Gorges.* London, 1888.

Lin-La, *Ti-ping Tien-Kwoh: History of the Ti-ping Revolution.* 2 vols., London, 1866.

Leroy-Beaulieu, Pierre Paul, *The Awakening of the East: Siberia, Japan, China.* Trans. from French by R. Davey. New York, 1900.

McCarthy, Michael J. F., *The Coming Power, a Contempory History of the Far East, 1898-1905.* London, 1905.

McKenzie, Frederick Arthur, *The Unveiled East.* New York, 1907.

Martin, R. M., *British Relations with the Chinese Empire. Comparative Statement of the English and American Trade with India and Canton.* London, 1832.

Martin, William Alexander Parsons, *The Chinese, their Education, Philosophy and Letters.* New York, 1881.
——, *A Cycle of Cathay.* New York, 1896.
——, *The Siege in Peking; China against the World.* New York, 1900.
——, *The Awakening of China.* New York, 1907.
Mas, Sinibaldo de, *La Chine et les Puissances Chrétiennes.* 2 vols., Paris, 1861.
Maybon, Albert, *La Vie Secrète de la Cour de Chine.* Paris, (—).
——, *La Politique Chinoise. Etude sur les Doctrines des Partis en Chine.* Paris, 1908.
Maurer, J. H., *The Far East.* Reading, 1912.
Meadows, T. T., *The Chinese and their Rebellions . . . with . . . an Essay on Chinese Civilization.* London, 1856.
Méritens, Baron de, *A Sketch of our Relations with China during Three and a Half Centuries, 1517-1869.* Foochow, 1871.
Metin, Albert, *L'Extrême-Orient; Chine, Japon, Russie.* In Etudes sur la Politique Exterieure des Etats, vol. 4. Paris, 1905.
Michie, Alexander, *The Englishman in China during the Victorian Era, as Illustrated in the Career of Sir Rutherford Alcock.* 2 vols., Edinburgh, 1900.
Millard, Thomas F., *The New Far East.* New York, 1906.
——, *America and the Far Eastern Question.* New York, 1909.
Moore, John Bassett, *American Diplomacy, its Spirit and Achievements.* New York, 1905.
——, *A Digest of International Law.* 8 vols., Washington, 1906.
Morse, Hosea Ballou, *The International Relations of the Chinese Empire: The Period of Conflict, 1845-1860.* London, 1910.
——, *The Trade and Administration of China.* Rev. ed., London, 1913.
Moule, Arthur Evans, *New China and Old; Personal Recollections and Observations of Thirty Years.* 3d ed., London, 1902.
——, *Half a Century in China; Recollections and Observations.* London, 1911.
Nieuhof, Johan, *L'Ambassade de la Compagnie Orientale des Provinces Unis vers l'Empereur de la Chine . . . fait par P. de Goyer et Jac. de Keyser.* Trans. into French by J. de Carpentier, Leyden, 1665; into Engl. by J. Ogilby, 2d ed., London, 1673.
Norman, Henry, *The Peoples and Politics of the Far East.* New York, 1903.
——, *All the Russias.* New York, 1904.
Nye, Gideon, Jr., *Rationale of the China Question.* Macao, 1857.
——, *Memorable Year of the War in China.* Macao, 1858.
Oliphant, Laurence, *Narrative of the Earl of Elgin's Mission to China and Japan in the Years 1857, '58, '59.* New York, 1860.
Oliphant, Nigel, *Diary of the Siege of the Legations in Peking during the Summer of 1900.* London, 1901.

Osborn, Sherard, *The Past and Future of British Relations in China*. Edinburgh, 1860.

Parker, Edward Harper, *China's Intercourse with Europe*. Shanghai, 1890.

——, *China, her History, Diplomacy and Commerce*. New York, 1901.

——, *Studies in Chinese Religion*, London, 1910.

Paullin, Charles Oscar, *Diplomatic Negotiations of American Naval Officers*. Albert Shaw Lectures in Diplomatic History, 1911, Johns Hopkins University. Baltimore, 1912.

Pauthier, J. P. G., *Documents Officiels Chinois sur les Ambassades Etrangères envoyées près de l'Empereur de la Chine*. *Traduit du Chinois*. Paris, 1843.

——, *Histoire des Rélations Politiques de la Chine avec les Puissances Occidentales*. Paris, 1859.

Pott, F. L. Hawks, *The Outbreak in China, its Causes*. New York, 1900.

——, *Sketch of Chinese History*. Shanghai, 1903.

Potter, Henry C., *The East of To-day and To-morrow*. New York, 1902.

Ray, R. H., *Chinese Boxers; the History and Exposé of a Fiendish and Terrible Society*. New York, 1900.

Reid, Gilbert, *The Sources of the Anti-Foreign Disturbances in China; with a Supplementary Account of the Uprising of 1900*. Shanghai, 1903.

Reinsch, Paul Samuel, *World Politics at the End of the Nineteenth Century as Influenced by the Oriental Situation*. New York, 1900.

——, *Intellectual and Political Currents in the Far East*. New York, 1911.

Robbins, Mrs. Helen Henrietta (Macartney), *Our First Ambassador to China; an Account of the Life of George, Earl of Macartney, with Extracts from his Letters, and the Narrative of his Experiences as told by himself, 1736-1806*. London, 1908.

Roberts, Edmund, *Embassy to the Eastern Courts of Cochin-China, Siam and Muscat, in the U. S. Sloop-of-War Peacock, 1832-34*. New York, 1837.

Rockhill, William Woodville, *The Land of the Lamas: Notes of a Journey through China, Mongolia and Tibet*. New York, 1891.

Ross, Edward Alsworth, *The Changing Chinese; the Conflict of Oriental and Western Cultures in China*. New York, 1911.

Ross, John, *Manchus; or, the Reigning Dynasty of China, their Rise and Progress*. London, 1891.

——, *The Boxers in Manchuria*. Shanghai, 1901.

Russel, S. M., *Story of the Siege of Peking*. London, 1901.

Sargent, A. J., *Anglo-Chinese Commerce and Diplomacy*. Oxford, 1907.

Scidmore, Eliza Ruhamah, *China, the Long-Lived Empire*. New York, 1900.

Scott, J. W. Robertson, *People of China, their Country, History, Life, Ideas and Relations with the Foreigner.* London, 1900.

Sergeant, Philip Walsingham, *The Great Empress Dowager of China.* London, 1910.

Shanghai " Mercury," *Reprints of Chinese Politics.* Shanghai, 1906.

Shoemaker, Michael Myers, *The Great Siberian Railway.* New York, 1903.

Smith Arthur Henderson, *Chinese Characteristics,* Rev. ed., New York, 1894.

——, *Village Life in China, a Study in Sociology.* New York, 1899.

——, *China in Convulsion.* 2 vols., New York, 1901.

——, *China and America To-day.* New York, 1907.

——, *Uplift of China.* New York, 1908.

Speer, Robert E., *The Boxer Uprising.* In his "*Missions and Modern History.*" New York, 1904.

Staunton, George, *An Authentic Account of an Embassy from the King of Great Britain to the Emperor of China.* 2 vols., Dublin, 1798.

Takahashi, Sakuyei, *Cases on International Law during the Chino-Japanese War.* Cambridge, 1899.

Thomson, H. C., *China and the Powers, a Narrative of the Outbreak of 1900.* London, 1902.

Thomson, John Stuart, *The Chinese.* Indianapolis, 1909.

——, *China Revolutionized.* Indianapolis, 1913.

Timkowski, George, *Travels of the Russian Mission through Mongolia to China, and Residence in Peking in the Years 1820, 1821.* Trans. by H. E. Lloyd. 2 vols., London, 1827.

Tsu, Yai Yue, *The Spirit of Chinese Philanthropy.* Columbia University Studies in History, Economics and Public Law, vol. l, no. 1, 1911. New York, 1911.

Ular, Alexandre, *A Russo-Chinese Empire.* Engl. version of "*Un Empire Russo-Chinois.*" Westminster, 1904.

Viaud, L. M. J. (Pierre Loti), *The Last Days of Peking.* Eng. trans. of "*Les Derniers Jours de Pékin.*" Boston, 1902.

Walton, Joseph, *China and the Present Crisis.* London, 1900.

Weale, B. L. Putnam (Simpson), *Manchu and Muscovite.* London, 1904.

——, *The Re-Shaping of the Far East.* 2 vols., London, 1905.

——, *The Coming Struggle in Eastern Asia.* London, 1909.

——, *The Conflict of Color.* New York, 1910.

——, *Indiscreet Letters from Peking; being the Notes of an Eye-Witness, etc. (Boxer Rebellion).* New York, 1911.

Wei, Wen-Pin, *The Currency Problem in China.* Columbia University Studies in History, Economics and Public Law, vol. lix, no. 3, 1914. New York, 1914.

Weurlersse, G., *Chine Ancienne et Nouvelle, Impressions et Réflexions.* Paris, 1902.

Wildman, Rounsevelle, *China's Open Door, a Sketch of Chinese Life and History.* Boston, 1900.

Will, Allen Sinclair, *World-Crisis in China.* Baltimore, 1900.

Williams, Samuel Wells, *Our Relations with the Chinese Empire.* San Francisco, 1877.

——, *The "Middle Kingdom": a Survey of the Geography, Government, Literature, Social Life, Arts and History of the Chinese Empire and its Inhabitants.* Rev. ed., 2 vols., New York, 1907.

——, *The Journal of S. Wells Williams, Secretary and Interpreter of the American Embassy to China during the Expedition to Tientsin and Peking in the Years 1858 and 1859.* Shanghai, 1911.

Williams, Frederick Wells, *Anson Burlingame and the First Chinese Mission to Foreign Powers.* New York, 1912.

Wilson, Brig.-Gen. J. H., *China; Travels and Investigations in the "Middle Kingdom."* New York, 1894.

Yen, Hawkling L., *A Survey of Constitutional Development in China.* Columbia University Studies in History, Economics and Public Law, vol. xl, no. 1, 1911. New York, 1911.

Younghusband, Major F. C., *The Heart of a Continent, a Narrative of Travels in Manchuria, across the Gobi Desert, through the Himalayas, the Pamirs and Chitral, 1884-94.* New York, 1896.

Yule, Sir Henry, *Cathay and the Way Thither; being a Collection of Mediaeval Notices of China.* 2 vols., London, 1866.

INDEX

Abolition of queue, proposed by Wang Chao, 52
Adee, A. A., to Min. Conger, 79 n., 80 n.
Amoy, 21 n., 34 and n.
Anhwei, 119
Anting, 133
Annam, 34
Aoki, Viscount, reply to Kuang Hsu's letter, 143; objections to Li's credentials, 152; interview of Mr. Whitehead with, 188 n.
" Arrow " war, 23
Austria, concession at Tientsin, 165, 167 n.; accepts German proposal for punishment, 177; on proposals of Diplomatic Body, 194, 195

Balfour, Mr., on Russia's efforts for ice-free harbor, 30
Beau, Paul, 213
Belgium, concession at Tientsin, 167 and n.; on proposals of Diplomatic Body, 194, 195
Berlin, 29, 32 n., 38, 123, 126, 142, 155 n., 181, 194, 208
Berlin *Post*, 84, 85
" Big Sword " Society. See Boxer Rebellion.
Biagovestchensk, Russian massacre of Chinese at, 178
Boxer indemnity, in French proposals, 184 and n.; United States to France regarding, 185; discussion of by Diplomatic Body, 191 and n., 192; final agreement, 202 and n., 203, 209, 216-219
Boxer Rebellion, meaning of, 15, 16; overthrow of reform a vital cause of, 69, 70; other causes, 70-72; missionary question, 72-75; initial disturbances in Shantung, 76-82; in Peking, 83, 84; four parts to, 89; question of Legation guards, 92-100; edicts and decrees concerning Boxers, 101-112; dynastic succession, 114-116, situation in South China, at

Shanghai, 118, 119, in Yangtse region, 120-124; policy of United States during, 125-129; attack on Taku Forts, 129-132; Seymour expedition, 132, 134; siege of Tientsin, 134, 135; second Allied expedition, 135, 136; renewal of punitive expeditions, 155, 156, 160-164; version of in edict of September 25, 1900, 180; in preamble to Joint Note, 207, 208. See China
Brooks, murder of, 81
Bülow, Count von, on the German policy, 128 n.; *note verbale* in answer to Kuang Hsu's letter, 142, 143; on German proposal for punishment, 175, 182
Burlingame, Anson, mission of 1868, 23 and n.; criticism of, 24

Cambodia, 34
Campbell, Mr., assault on, 89
Canton, 18, 21 n., 35, 47, 70 n., 147
Catholics in China, 72 and n.
Cassini Convention, provisions of, 27, 28, 28 n.
Chaffee, Maj.-Gen., 168, 169 and n.
Chang Chih-tung, 119, 123, 158, 159 n.
Chang In-huan, decree denouncing, 62; efforts in his behalf, 63
Changli, 220
Chao Shu-chiao, 180, 199, 201, 215
Chaylard, G. du, 166, 167
Chefoo, 26, 78 n.
Chekiang, proclamation of Viceroys concerning, 123 and n.; Chuchow outbreak in, 156-159
Cheng (Tientsin *Taotai*), 169 n.
Chengtingfu, 155 and n.
Chen Kung-liang, 77
Chichow, 91
Chihli, 91, 92, 94, 112, 120, 121, 155 n., 162, 190, 210, 213, 222
Chi Hsiu, 116, 201, 215
China, meaning of Boxer Rebellion, 15, 16; early relations with Europe, 17-19; Opium war, 20, 21; policy after